Atomic Energy and Congress

Atomic Energy and Congress

by Morgan Thomas

in collaboration with Robert M. Northrop

Ann Arbor: The University of Michigan Press

London: Geoffrey Cumberlege, Oxford University Press

Publication of this work was made possible by a grant from the
Michigan Memorial–Phoenix Project of the University of Michigan

Library of Congress Catalog Card Number: 56–7685

Printed in the United States of America
by The Lord Baltimore Press, Inc.

Preface

Two principal kinds of research provided the basis for this book. There is, of course, an immense fund of documentary material on the political aspects of the development of atomic energy in the United States. Congressional debates and committee hearings, reports and prints, the publications of the Atomic Energy Commission, and numerous independent publications have all been examined by the political scientists who collaborated in the study. But it is evident to anyone who reads through such material that the documentary sources have left much unsaid. Most of the important decisions in the history of atomic energy were made behind closed doors. Even the revealing testimony in the Oppenheimer case in 1954 failed to clear up many obscurities.

The research team turned, therefore, to the people who had actually made the decisions. Working in pairs, the researchers interrogated the Commissioners and staff workers of the AEC, the members of the Joint Committee on Atomic Energy and staff, and many independent observers. The questions were the most searching and specific that the research men knew how to ask, and the answers were recorded on dictaphone tapes. The result is a unique collection of data from which much of the information in this book has been drawn.

The Institute of Public Administration at the University of Michigan was the parent organization for the group of re-

searchers who did this work. The author was in charge of the group, and his collaborator worked with it. The study has received the generous support of the University of Michigan's Memorial–Phoenix Project, a fund which was established in memory of the University's war dead to support research in the peaceful uses of atomic energy. The authors gladly acknowledge their gratitude to the Phoenix Project and to all the workers who collaborated in gathering the information upon which this report is based.

Ann Arbor   M. T.
August 4, 1955   R. M. N.

Acknowledgments

The publishers of works used in this book have willingly granted written permission for the quotations of their copyrighted material in the text.

All interviewees listed in Appendix D were cooperative in answering questions to the best of their ability, and helpful in attempting to reconstruct past events.

Philip Mullenbach, while a former employee of the AEC, kindly facilitated liaison with the Atomic Energy Commission.

The two former chairmen of the Atomic Energy Commission, David E. Lilienthal and Gordon Dean, and one former Commissioner, Henry D. Smyth, have read a draft of this book and generously offered suggestions to make it more accurate, although the authors alone must bear responsibility for opinions and interpretations.

Contents

I

Government Controls and the
Atomic Energy Program

Atomic energy was a governmental program from the very start. Until 1954 it remained entirely subject to Federal ownership and control, the most powerful governmental monopoly in history. During its relatively short life since the early World War II years, this atomic energy program has grown into a $12 billion colossus, made up of processing plants, production facilities, atomic reactors, laboratories, testing sites, and stockpiles, all operated by thousands of governmental and industrial personnel ranging from Ph.D.'s to plumbers, and coordinated since 1946 by five of the most important individuals in America, the members of the United States Atomic Energy Commission.

This study of the processes and people involved in directing and controlling the atom, then, is largely a study of government in action. It does not deal directly with H-bombs, atomic "piles," or U-235. It does not pretend to know the details of the gaseous diffusion process for producing fissionable materials. Such matters are left to the atomic scientists, with whom they belong. This study is interested in technical matters only insofar as they are related to the structures and processes of decision-making and control which have guided the development of this new force.

Atomic energy might well have had altogether disastrous consequences for democratic government in America. Yet we seem to have found the means not only to control the atom, but to do it in such a way that it can serve our own well-being and that of the rest of the world. It is an achievement which deserves more attention than it has had so far. For the atomic energy program, until recently a tight government monopoly, has been relatively free during most of its life from the controls that affect most government agencies and programs. If the atom has been dealt with more successfully than one might have expected, it is not because of the excellence of open democratic control processes. These simply have not functioned during the early years of atomic energy development.

The reason for this is the secrecy which has characterized the whole development of atomic energy since the time when it was no more than an idea in the minds of a few scientists. Not until the end of World War II did the public first learn of the top secret atom bomb project, which had been successfully concluded by the War Department's Manhattan Engineer District.[1] Even then, the secrecy continued into the peacetime period. Congress decided that the production of atomic weapons was the most vital part of our national defense, and hence security by strict concealment remained an important factor in the atomic energy program.

The problem of striking a balance between the requirements of security and the desirability of normal open democratic controls remains a difficult one even today. No attempt will be made here to evaluate the line Congress has drawn between a complete "blackout" and full public control. This study attempts rather to describe the governmental machinery which was established to develop and control the atom within a protective circle of unusually dense secrecy. It concentrates upon those groups and individuals "on the inside" who have been primarily responsible for the guidance of the atomic energy program in the best interests of an often ignorant public "on the outside."

An analysis of atomic energy in the government need not stop here, however. The establishment of the Atomic Energy Commission in 1946 and its history since that date offer to political scientists a remarkable case study; seldom has it been possible to see so clearly and within such a short period of time what happens when a major new agency is projected into the administrative organization of the government and into an essentially political environment. In this sense, the AEC cannot be considered by itself, but only in its relationships with other groups and agencies, public and private, which affect its operations and limit its authority.

The reception of a new agency into the whole structure of government seems to offer a particularly useful opportunity for one to test one's conceptions of the governmental processes. In the early stages of organizational life, relationships are fluid and behavior patterns have not yet become fixed and habitual. The members of the agency are forced to think consciously of their relationships with the other units in the governmental environment, to formulate new concepts of their own positions and functions during the difficult period of adjustment. Hence the governmental forces at work are easy to identify. The later history of an agency becomes more understandable if one has examined the original interplay of forces through which the agency assumed its role in the governmental complex. Hence the AEC's comparatively short history makes it a workable case study of the governmental process.

Thus, the story of atomic energy and Congress has a twofold purpose: to give a clear analysis of decision-making, and to relate this analysis to certain broader theories of government in the United States.

To tell this story requires an understanding of the statutory framework within which atomic policy grew. The institutional pattern in the controlling circle was created by the Atomic Energy Act of 1946.[2] This basic statute was the result of months of legislative study during late 1945 and the first half of 1946.[3] A number of significant organizational issues faced the framers of this Act during their deliberations. The opposing choices open to them in the more important areas pertinent to this study may be summarized as follows:

1) A commission-form of control agency vs. a single administrator.

2) Extreme independence for the controlling agency vs. departmental status directly subservient to the President.

3) A civilian control agency vs. a predominantly military agency.

4) Primary control by laymen vs. primary control by specialists (atomic scientists, engineers, and technicians).

5) A Congressional committee system roughly comparable to the ordinary pattern vs. special committee arrangements to provide an extra measure of surveillance and control.

The following description of the statutory provisions is presented in terms of these possible choices and of the final decisions actually made by Congress.

■

The central element in the governmental machinery set up to deal with the atom is the Atomic Energy Commission. This new federal agency was given primary responsibility for atomic energy development. At midnight on December 31, 1946, the Commission received control of the vast project from the Manhattan Engineer District, and its work formally began.

In placing this unique program in the hands of a five-man commission, rather than a single administrator, Congress indicated its realization that many tough policy problems would arise after this formal transfer of authority. A commission, it is generally conceded, is better suited to the processes of policy formulation. This job requires less in the way of fast managerial decisions, and more in the way of deliberation upon alternate or opposing paths, some of which might be lightly dismissed or ignored in the necessarily limited perspective of any one individual.

The new AEC, it was seen, would have more than a full measure of policy problems to solve. A number of big decisions had become part of the project during Manhattan District days. The MED, for example, had managed the facilities indirectly by contracting with industrial firms and universities to carry on the actual operations. Would this contractor system be an appropriate or advisable way to operate the program during peacetime? According to later reports, the Manhattan District organization was centralized, with Oak Ridge the chief control point. Was this a good system for the new civilian agency, or should it decentralize the organization and delegate broad authority to several major operational centers? [4]

In addition to this reassessment of MED operating procedure, the new agency faced new problems. Informed observers were aware of alarming weaknesses in the program, weaknesses that would require basic decisions by the new administrators. The facilities and personnel soon to be surrendered by the Manhattan District were suffering from a postwar letdown. Many of the scientists and technicians wanted to get back again to academic or other duties, and the exodus from Los Alamos in particular was cause for concern. This was all the more serious because the state of the program itself was unsatisfactory. Certain of the installations were facing unforeseen mechanical problems, such as the pile deterioration at Hanford which seemed likely to cut off plutonium production. To make matters worse, the weapons stockpile was remarkably small. There was no diversification of atomic weapons, and the feasibility of peacetime use had not

even been thoroughly examined. The raw materials supply was
extremely limited. There was no permanent weapons-testing
station. The program, then, seemed dangerously near a stand-
still, having almost completely run down from its peak of hectic
wartime activity.[5]

It was the new agency's task to revitalize this stumbling program, and the difficulties, some technological, were great. One
of the touchiest problems lay in the fact that the program had to
be pushed forward behind a thick curtain of secrecy. Could the
AEC bend over backwards to guard the monopoly of the bomb,
and still renew a lagging program with the utmost speed? This
need to combine security by achievement with security by concealment plagued the Commission through the early years of its
work.

Such were some of the crucial issues that awaited the new
agency. Congress determined that they could best be met by
five full-time Commissioners, appointed by the President subject to Senate confirmation.[6] But the appointments were intended to be nonpolitical; partisanship was felt to have no place
at all in an area so vital to national defense and security.

This legislative decision did not resolve completely, however,
the organizational challenge posed by the new agency. It was
not to be denied that there were compelling reasons for vesting
final authority in a multiple executive, but the atomic energy
project itself comprised a large industrial organization, requiring
effective administrative coordination. A single manager was
needed to direct the administrative task of getting forward with
such matters as research, both through contractual arrangements and through the Commission's own facilities. A single
manager was needed to work out the arrangements for obtaining raw materials, to supervise the production of source materials and fissionable materials, to superintend the programs of
military applications, and to control the utilization of atomic

energy materials, whether on the basis of licenses or on the basis of certain distribution arrangements for research and medical therapy use.

In short, the AEC was to operate a vast undertaking, and strong managerial controls, centering upon one man, seemed necessary. Therefore, Congress created not only a multiple executive for policy matters, but also a post of General Manager.[7] The Special Senate Committee on Atomic Energy reported:

> This form of organization is based on administrative experience developed in both government and industry. Such experience points to the need for a high level policy group which can discharge its functions without the additional burden of passing on current operations. Day to day administration is best directed by a single manager. While the scope and importance of his duties are such as to require his appointment directly by the President, the manager is to work under the general supervision and direction of the Commission, "to discharge such of the administrative and executive functions of the Commission as the Commission may direct." [8]

The Act, of course, could not attempt to specify the more detailed organization of the new agency below the level of the General Manager. It did provide for four statutory program divisions under the General Manager: research, engineering, military application, and production. Two additional program divisions were created by the Commission: raw materials, and biology and medicine. The six directors of these divisions reported to the General Manager, and were relied upon for "long-range program planning and staff judgment on the technical and scientific aspects of the program." [9] General management offices were established, including those for such functions as security and intelligence, organization and personnel, and finance.

The substance of the AEC's program was carried out at the start under the direction of five highly decentralized field offices, organized largely by function. Directors of these Operations Offices (as they were later called), located in New York, Oak Ridge, Chicago, Santa Fe, and Hanford, reported directly to the General Manager, making a total of twenty-three persons under his immediate supervision. This decentralized system was later modified, with directors of Operations Offices (numbering ten in 1955) reporting to certain of the division directors in Washington, and most of these reporting, not directly to the General Manager, but to assistant general managers.[10]

Under the system in effect through 1955, the AEC Operations Offices supervised subordinate Area Offices. The chief task of this field hierarchy was not to carry on operations, but rather to oversee and supervise the AEC's contractors, mostly business firms and universities engaged by contract to carry on such operations as production, processing, town management, and research and development. This contractor system, carried over from the MED, involved some of the most prominent of the nation's industrial and academic institutions. Production facilities were developed and run by such companies as duPont, General Electric, and Union Carbide and Carbon. The University of California contracted to operate the Los Alamos Laboratory, and the University of Chicago the Argonne National Laboratory. A group of universities combined to form a special new corporation to manage the Brookhaven National Laboratory.

As the project grew, other contractors entered the picture to run the new installations. Having turned Hanford over to General Electric, duPont returned as contractor-operator of the Savannah River Works. The Goodyear Tire and Rubber Company contracted to operate the production facilities at Portsmouth, Ohio. The increase in the number of major research and development installations (nearly twenty by 1955) brought additional colleges and universities, and some new industrial firms, into the circle of AEC contractors.[11]

These AEC contracts can properly be termed administrative contracts because they designate roughly the area of work but leave to the AEC the supervisory authority to plan, direct, order, and stop the actual work being done. This contractor system, based on cost-plus-fixed-fee terms and an administrative relationship, has been particularly well adapted to the uncertainties and shifts of policy in the atomic energy program.[12]

Some conception of the scope of the atomic energy program and its physical plant is required for a proper understanding of the AEC and its history.[13] At the start in 1946, the program was generally limited to military ends, but the facilities had already reached vast proportions. To produce fissionable materials (U-235 and plutonium) and to develop and build atomic weapons, the MED had created three primary installations, supported by research and development work carried on elsewhere in university and government laboratories. At these three widely separated sites, the heart of the atomic energy program was located.

Production centered at two of the three major installations: Oak Ridge, Tennessee, and Hanford, Washington. Several production methods for U-235 were tried at Oak Ridge, until gaseous diffusion was shown to be the most efficient. The first gaseous diffusion plant there, called K-25, was originally and may still be the largest continuous process plant in the world under one roof; information on the new diffusion facilities is unavailable. Important research and development facilities were also at Oak Ridge.

At Hanford, the Manhattan District built the first giant atomic reactors for the production of plutonium, together with the necessary chemical separation plants and supporting conveniences. The remote site in Washington was chosen partly to make use of a huge volume of water from the adjacent Columbia River to cool the reactors.

All work on the weapons themselves was originally centered at the Los Alamos Scientific Laboratory, on a high mesa with a mountain backdrop near Santa Fe, New Mexico. Here the scientists and technicians carried out the work that led to the first A-bombs of 1945. At the start, the weapons were fabricated at Los Alamos, but weapon manufacture was later transferred, and the laboratory concentrated on a program of long-range weapons research and development. The original testing site was also in New Mexico, near Alamagordo. Here the first atomic bomb was successfully detonated.

All three of these basic installations were remote and isolated, for reasons of security. Consequently, it was necessary to construct at each site a new community to house the many scientists, technicians, and other workers who operated the facilities. These "atomic cities," still government-owned in 1955, included not merely housing, but a full complement of community facilities and services—from schools and churches to gas stations and barber shops. The AEC determined that private concerns should operate the communities, under cost-plus-fixed-fee contracts with the government.

The scope of the atomic energy project has moved far beyond the 1946 limits just described. Enlargements and improvements have been made at the original installations, but these only begin to tell the story of expansion. By the end of the first postwar decade, three huge new production centers were partially or wholly in operation, located on the Savannah River in South Carolina, at Paducah, Kentucky, and near Portsmouth, Ohio. These and the original but greatly enlarged production plants required expanded raw materials programs, which led to stepped-up AEC drilling and other encouragement of private exploration, and to increased and improved refining of uranium ores.

On the military side, the 1950 decision to pursue thermonuclear work added a major new aspect to the weapons program. In addition, the passage of time brought the development of an ever more diversified array of fission weapons. The Commission also opened a new weapons laboratory at Livermore, California, and developed a new test site in Nevada and huge proving grounds in the Pacific.

Reactor development for military or peacetime power, in its earliest stages in 1945, grew through the subsequent decade to encompass a wide variety of programs. Aided by the development of a large-scale reactor materials testing station in Idaho, work was pushed forward on reactors for propulsion of submarines, surface vessels, aircraft, and locomotives, and the first atomic submarine was operating successfully in early 1955. The AEC's program for central-station civilian power reactors was formalized in 1954. Five promising types of reactors were to be developed over a period of five years, and private industry was encouraged under the 1954 Act to assume as much as possible of the burden of achieving competitive atomic electric power. In addition, the AEC directed efforts toward developing a military "package" nuclear power plant, the components of which could be easily transported by air to remote military bases.

This brief survey of basic programs by no means exhausts the activities of the AEC. It fails to mention such important programs as physical research (chemistry, physics, and metallurgy), biology and medicine, and civil defense, and such supporting activities as security, declassification, information-sharing, and labor relations. Yet it should suffice to give an impression of an enormously complex and diversified program and a huge physical plant.

Another altogether different problem which faced the Congressmen who wrote the Atomic Energy Act concerned the relationship between the Chief Executive and the program. How much should be left to the supervisory discretion of the President?

As between the extreme independence of some regulatory agencies and a subordinate departmental status, Congress chose a middle ground. The Commission itself, as noted, was to be relatively independent. But the Act did make provision for the regular exercise of Presidential influence over certain aspects of the program.

With respect to the appointing power, Congress decided that the Commissioners and General Manager should be Presidential appointees, subject to Senate confirmation. The degree of Presidential control, however, was somewhat circumscribed by the provision that the President could not remove the Commissioners except for specific causes enumerated in the Act, indicating a desire to give the AEC a certain amount of autonomy. Outside the AEC itself, the Act provided for Presidential appointment of all nine members of a General Advisory Committee.[14]

The framers of the Atomic Energy Act saw that certain high policy problems might best be left to unfettered Presidential discretion. They therefore wrote into the statute provisions requiring the President to assume responsibility for certain of these decisions. Three may be noted briefly.

First, the President was to determine at least once each year the quantities of fissionable materials to be produced by the AEC.

Second, the AEC production of atomic weapons was to be carried on only to the extent allowed by Presidential consent, obtained at least once each year.

Third, the President was empowered to direct the Commission, from time to time, to deliver fissionable materials or weapons to the armed forces for such use as he might deem necessary. He could also authorize the armed forces themselves to produce or acquire weapons utilizing atomic energy.[15]

The President, then, received a substantial measure of specific authority over production, custody, and transfer of fissionable materials and atomic weapons. But although his responsibilities were thus spelled out, they were not implemented with commensurate facilities to aid him in the performance of his duties. Regular and sustained Presidential consideration of top-level problems came only in later years when the National Security Council became active and was provided with an adequate secretariat.

One of the important issues in drafting the basic statute was between civilian and military control. In Congress, this issue was joined between the McMahon Bill, which became law and established civilian control, and the May-Johnson Bill, which contemplated a much greater role for the military in the administration of the new program.[16] The Special Senate Committee on Atomic Energy, which endorsed the McMahon Bill, gave its opinion as follows:

> The decision to limit membership eligibility to civilians was adopted by the Committee in keeping with established traditions of our government. It accords with principles cherished and maintained throughout American history. Departure from these principles has occasioned judicial, executive, and legislative disapproval. This is not to say that the Committee fails to recognize legitimate and important areas of atomic energy development and control, touching on the responsibilities of the military department. Indeed, throughout the Bill, wherever these areas are involved, provision is made for full military participation, and independent activities of the military department, espe-

cially in research and development, are not infringed but expressly encouraged.[17]

In other words, the AEC could not fulfill its paramount responsibility for the military aspects of the atomic energy program without coordination with the military agencies. The Special Senate Committee recommended the establishment of a Military Liaison Committee to be appointed by the defense departments. As the Act was finally written, both the new Atomic Energy Commission and the new Military Liaison Committee were placed under a clear obligation to keep one another fully informed of developments. Moreover, the Military Liaison Committee was empowered by the Act to appeal to higher authorities in the defense establishment and ultimately to the President, should it find itself in disagreement with AEC policy.[18]

In short, this liaison committee, composed of military representatives, was to be intimately involved as an advisory group in the administrative structure. The Special Senate Committee reported:

> This provision has been adopted to give the armed forces a proper voice in such matters as development, manufacture, storage, and use of bombs; allocations of fissionable materials for military research; control of information relating to the manufacture and use of atomic weapons.[19]

The military voice was brought into the AEC also by the provision that "the Director of the Division of Military Application shall be a member of the Armed Forces." [20] By means of these various provisions, coordination between the military and the Atomic Energy Commission was made possible without sacrificing ultimate civilian control.

It was clear to Congress in 1946 that many of the problems

which would confront the new agency would involve matters of the utmost scientific complexity. The subject matter of nuclear physics in particular was intimately bound up with the problem of the realistic use of men and materials to achieve the most favorable results from the peaceful and military applications of atomic power. The issue of lay versus specialist responsibilities was, therefore, a critical one. The decision to establish lay control did not, of course, mean that the Atomic Energy Commission would not require the highest level of scientific fitness for many of its administrative personnel. Instead it meant that the policy decisions to be made by the new agency in carrying forward its program must ultimately rest upon the authority of individuals with a general rather than a special orientation. The Special Senate Committee put the matter this way:

> Many witnesses emphasized the grave responsibilities for national security and welfare devolving upon the Commissioners, the need for continuous study of changing technical developments, and the many innovations in administrative techniques that will be involved. While the Commissioners need not be scientists or technical experts, they must combine clear judgment with imagination and courage, and they must, like the members of the judiciary, be so divorced from private and competing concerns as to give complete, disinterested, and undivided attention to their tasks.[21]

Thus there were cogent reasons for putting the ultimate authority for atomic policy in the hands of laymen. Technical advice, of course, was always available from the many scientists employed by the Commission, but it seemed advisable to provide also for skilled appraisals by scientists not attached to the Commission. Such men, it was felt, might have a more objective viewpoint. Furthermore, Congress wished to make continuously available to the AEC the judgment of the most eminent and highly qualified scientists in the nation, whether or not they happened to be employed by the Commission.

For these reasons, it seemed advisable to create a nine-member General Advisory Committee, whose members were to be appointed by the President from among the chief scientists of the country. They were to serve terms of six years, to choose their own chairman, to meet at least four times a year, and to receive per diem compensation, plus all necessary expenses.[22]

In the question of Congressional control, the decisions made by the framers of the 1946 Act had a profound influence on the later history of the relationships between the AEC and Congress. These decisions grew out of still another choice between alternatives. Congress could provide for a quite ordinary relationship in the future by giving the atomic energy program to one of the existing Congressional committees in each chamber. The committee would thus add the atom to its other responsibilities as simply one more among several programs to be dealt with. On the other hand, Congress could provide a special arrangement for the atomic energy program and thereby strengthen its own control over the AEC.

Many Congressmen felt that the nature of the atomic energy program made it necessary to assure a strong Congressional hand in the processes of appraisal and planning. Whenever considerations of security enforce secrecy in the operation of a government project, the legislature becomes doubly important. The normal democratic processes of public discussion, political debate, and pressure group activity are unable to function in an area which is hidden by secrecy, and Congress must rely solely upon its own investigative authority to turn up practices or policies which may be contrary to the public welfare. In the case of the atomic energy program, Congress saw that it must take the initiative itself, in order to be always certain that the program remained strong and effective.

Congress as a whole is a large and unwieldy body. For this reason, the real force of Congressional influence usually lies in its committees. Again, this was particularly true in the case of atomic affairs because of the need for secrecy; the whole Congress could scarcely undertake to deal with the classified aspects of the program, if these were to remain classified. Hence it was seen that especially great responsibility would lie with the committees of Congress which dealt with the program. These are the considerations which lay behind the decision to deviate from the traditional committee system.

The deviation was least noticeable and least troublesome in the case of the appropriations process. The Committees on Appropriations, which are hard pressed to keep up with the purely budgetary aspects of their work, are incapable of maintaining a sustained review of any agency's program and performance. In both houses, the Subcommittees on Independent Offices of the Committees on Appropriations were appointed the additional task of reviewing the AEC's budget requests. Congress obviously felt that these subcommittees would be able to bring their customary influence to bear on the atom. Some complications were evident, of course—the technical complexities of the program, the secrecy that clouded certain aspects of the atomic energy budget. But these only slightly modified the normal appropriations process. Most Congressmen felt that they could look forward with good reason to exercising their customary degree of control over administration through the appropriations process.

Hence it became evident that if Congress were to obtain more than its customary control over this new administrative agency, it must do so by changing its traditional legislative committee structure. Each house had an Armed Services Committee which could have attempted to deal with the AEC. However, this would have de-emphasized the important peacetime applications of atomic energy, submerging them in the military problems which rightly preoccupy the Armed Services Committees. The only answer seemed to be the creation of new legislative committees which would be parallel to the Executive's new civilian agency.

Even more important was the obvious fact that the job of continuous review and control in such a large field would be too big for any existing committee to undertake; all the committees were busy with other matters. Over and over, during debate on the Act, the legislators reiterated their conviction that halfway measures would not suffice, and that Congress must place the tightest possible legislative rein on the new agency. At the hearings of the Special Senate Committee on Atomic Energy, Democratic Senator Edwin C. Johnson expressed perhaps the most extreme view by proposing that the atomic energy program be administered temporarily by a Congressional Commission of five Senators and five Representatives.[23] His proposal emphasized the widespread feeling that Congress should control the AEC with a tighter hand than it had controlled any other agency, and that this could not be done under existing arrangements.

The outcome was the new Joint Committee on Atomic Energy, made up of nine members from each chamber.[24] Congress gave the body unusual responsibilities for overseeing the AEC. It was to be a permanent committee, required to "make continuing studies of the activities of the Atomic Energy Commission and of problems relating to the development, use and control of atomic energy." Its power under these provisions was enhanced by the additional power given in the Act to employ as extensive a professional, technical, and clerical staff as it thought was necessary or advisable. Equally important, a key phrase in the Act provided that the Commission must "keep the Joint Committee fully and currently informed with respect to the

Commission's activities." By this language, Congress left no doubt that the Joint Committee was to share all the secrets of the project. By making it a statutory requirement that the AEC volunteer information on its policies and operations to the Committee, Congress provided the Joint Committee with a unique capacity for influential surveillance.

One other feature of the Act considerably increased the Joint Committee's responsibility and power. Convinced that the Act would require many future amendments, as experience revealed problems which could not be anticipated, Congress gave the Joint Committee the full legislative powers of a regular standing committee. All bills or other matters pertaining to atomic energy were to be referred to the Joint Committee by both chambers. In addition, the Committee was given the full complement of investigative techniques possessed by the standing committees. It was obvious that this committee would derive from its close surveillance of the AEC a unique knowledge of atomic affairs, and that it alone would be competent to deal with proposed legislation. In no other case has a joint committee of this kind been given legislative powers.[25]

In one important way, the Joint Committee was denied a power which legislative committees normally possess. This may be called the power of authorization. As a rule, when new government facilities are proposed, they must first be specifically authorized by legislation which has been approved by the appropriate committees and passed by Congress; only then can the appropriations be made. Sometimes the total budget for an agency or program must be authorized annually, instead of the individual construction projects. In the Atomic Energy Act of 1946, the authorization was made for all future sums "as may be necessary and appropriate to carry out the provisions and purposes of this Act." [26] This, in effect, made the authorization power a part of the appropriations power. As a legislative committee, the Joint Committee was denied one of the weapons normally used by such committees in their conflicts with the Appropriations Committees. Committee prerogatives derived from the basic distinction between the authorization process and the appropriation process were therefore modified in an important manner with respect to the atomic energy program.

The Committee's lack of the authorization power provided a cause for rivalry and disagreement between the Appropriations Committees and the Joint Committee. Such an exceptional substantive committee might be expected to feel, with its intimate knowledge of the program, that its views should be given great weight in connection with AEC appropriations. Since the Appropriations Committees traditionally work rather independently, it was not difficult to see that the passage of AEC appropriation acts might be the occasion for contests between Joint Committee members and their colleagues in the appropriations groups.

On the whole, however, the 1946 Act revealed that the Joint Committee was a potentially powerful group. Its leverage, both with the AEC and with such outside groups as other Congressional committees, did not seem even then to be seriously threatened by the absence of annual authorization procedures. The lack of this single formal power appeared heavily overbalanced by the extensive reviewing and substantive authority given the Committee, and by the prestige which naturally descended upon a new committee created solely to deal with the glamorous atom. All told, one must agree that, after they had decided to assure Congress an unusual degree of control over the atomic energy program, the drafters of the Act were careful to see that their decision was adequately implemented.

The chief spheres of influence in the atomic energy program, that is, the units of governmental authority, were all established by the Atomic Energy Act of 1946. They were complex, but

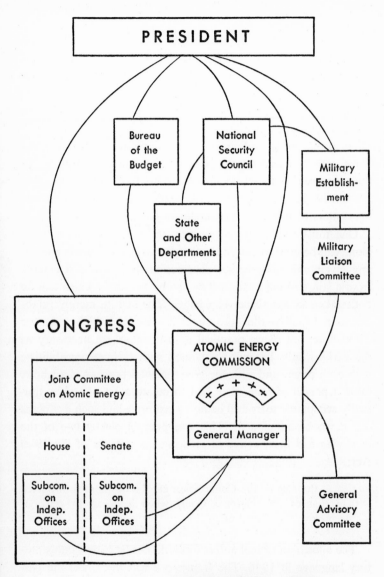

**GOVERNMENTAL UNITS
IN THE ATOMIC ENERGY FIELD**

not nearly so complex as they might have been or as they undoubtedly would have been if the atomic energy program had not been largely concealed by the cloak of security. To a large extent, normal outside controls could not function, and the result was that the governmental machinery, both executive and legislative, which was established to deal with the atom, formed a self-contained complement of functions and offices. Within these general organizational limits, the various spheres of influence were able to act upon one another freely. But there were few outside influences, and on the inside the number of interacting centers of influence was relatively limited.

One must not assume, however, that the statutory pattern alone can be used to determine the precise degree of influence of any given unit. The actual distribution of power will emerge from a study of the relationships among the units, which will be undertaken in the succeeding pages. The statute merely established in broad outline the channels through which influence could flow, but many practical adjustments were necessary as the various units became acquainted with their responsibilities, with each other, and with the governmental process as a whole. Over a period of time, they had to create a set of stable, mutually acceptable roles and behavior patterns, and such a process can never be anticipated. This was pointed out by two of the men who had been active in securing the passage of the 1946 Act:

> . . . the role of the Commission can be no more firmly fixed than that of the Supreme Court when it began the task of interpreting the Constitution.[27]

The allocation of real authority could not be frozen into statutory language in 1946. The framework was there, but the patterns of power within this framework would inevitably change over the years.

II

The New Teams at Work

On October 28, 1946, President Harry S. Truman named the original members of the Atomic Energy Commission while Congress was in recess. David E. Lilienthal, former chairman of the board of the Tennessee Valley Authority, was designated as chairman. He came to the AEC with the knowledge gained by jointly directing, with Secretary of State Acheson, the preparation of the so-called Acheson-Lilienthal report on international control of atomic energy. Three of the other Commissioners, Sumner T. Pike, Lewis L. Strauss, and William W. Waymack, had had no direct connection with government control of atomic energy, although the fifth member, Robert F. Bacher, was a physicist and "had been rather intimately associated with work of the Los Alamos project." [1]

The Commission began its selection of staff personnel in November, 1946, and took up the matter of a General Manager. After due consideration, Carroll L. Wilson was suggested to the President and nominated by him on December 30, 1946.[2] Mr. Wilson had been a secretary of the military services' Research and Development Board and had participated in the preparation of the Acheson-Lilienthal report on international control of the atom.

The AEC top team was then complete, and ready to work. Personnel recruitment for the lower echelons presented a great immediate task, because many jobs continued to be filled by Manhattan Engineer District personnel who desired to leave government service or to return to a military organization. Many makeshift arrangements of this kind could not be extended much longer. In addition, the team began to look into the tremendous programmatic problems arising from the general postwar letdown. But before much progress could be made toward working out solutions to these problems, the organization found that its time was occupied with protracted confirmation hearings on the Commissioners and the General Manager.[3] This was the AEC's first real contact with the Joint Committee on Atomic Energy, whose Senate Section was responsible for passing on these Presidential appointments.

Shortly after Congress convened under the new Republican control in January, 1947, the Joint Committee on Atomic Energy held its organization meeting.[4] Its newly appointed membership included a number of important legislators. Senators Vandenberg, Hickenlooper, Knowland, Millikin, and Bricker made up the GOP majority from the upper chamber, with Senators McMahon, Russell, Connally, and Edwin Johnson representing the Democrats. From the House came Republican Representatives Cole, Elston, Hinshaw, Van Zandt, and Patterson, and Democratic Representatives Thomason, Durham, Holifield, and Price. At its first meeting, the Committee chose Senator Hickenlooper chairman and Representative Cole vice-chairman, and then plunged into the confirmation hearings. The Senate Section, of course, had primary responsibility for passing on the nominations and making a recommendation to the upper chamber, but the Senators invited the Representatives on the Committee to sit in if they wished.

With the beginning of the confirmation hearings, on January 27, there commenced a series of attacks on Mr. Lilienthal which developed into a full-scale controversy lasting into April. Several factors played a role in the controversy:

1) Opposition to Lilienthal personally, especially from Senator McKellar. Clashes between the two went back to Lilienthal's TVA days.

2) Opposition to Lilienthal as a New Dealer and "bureaucrat." Senator Taft and many other important GOP members opposed him on this ground. Mr. Lilienthal was accused of backing the socialistic TVA, of being "soft" on Reds, of being a "big-government" advocate, and so on.

3) Opposition to Lilienthal in the hope of discrediting the Democratic administration and capitalizing on GOP control of Congress to gain the Presidency in 1948. Some Senators went out of their way to attack any Truman nominee who seemed to be vulnerable.

4) Opposition to Lilienthal as an advocate of civilian control. This is hard to assess but is generally conceded to have been a factor in the background.

5) Opposition of those not so strongly anti-Lilienthal (or who maintained they were not) but who felt that no controversial person should head the AEC.

Of primary concern was the Joint Committee's position during the hearings, which were mostly taken up with a diatribe by Senator McKellar against Mr. Lilienthal. The Senator, though not a Joint Committee member, attended the hearings at the invitation of the Senate Section to any fellow Senators. He began an unrelenting assault on the character and philosophy of David Lilienthal, which was an ordeal for nearly all concerned, nominees and Congressmen alike. It completely overshadowed the questioning of the nominees (mostly on the question of AEC cooperation with the Joint Committee and the military).

When the vote came on the nominations, eight of the nine Senate members of the Joint Committee voted to confirm Mr.

Lilienthal. With only Senator Bricker in opposition, the Committee's 8 to 1 recommendation went to the floor of the Senate, where the controversy resumed.[5]

In passing, it should be noted that the Joint Committee voted unanimous approval of Commissioners Bacher, Strauss, and Waymack, whose confirmation was never in question. The vote on Pike and Wilson, however, was only 6 to 2 in favor of confirmation, Senators Bricker and Johnson opposing with Senator Connally abstaining. The fate of these latter appointees rested entirely on the outcome of the Lilienthal fight. If he had been rejected, there seems little doubt that Pike and Wilson would have been too.[6]

From the hearings and the vote, it could be concluded only that the Joint Committee's Senate Section had decided to back the nominees. The precise degree of the members' support became a little clearer during the extensive and heated floor debate that followed. Two GOP Committeemen, Senators Hickenlooper and Knowland, joined Senator McMahon to lead the fight in favor of confirmation. Beginning the long debate, Senator Hickenlooper argued:

> . . . the sum total of the record before the Senate Section of the Joint Committee on Atomic Energy fails to disclose that Lilienthal is either a Communist, a "fellow traveler," or that he at any time encouraged or supported communistic activities.

The Senator went on:

> . . . evidence further establishes in my mind that Lilienthal is a man of high intelligence, great administrative ability, and vigorous devotion to successful operation of any enterprise with which he is associated.[7]

Senator Hickenlooper was not, however, completely convinced of Lilienthal's fitness; in answer to a suggestion that

Lilienthal was not responsive to the wishes of the legislature, he said:

> When I said yesterday, in effect, that [Lilienthal] may be a man who is restless at certain legislative restraints or legislative procedure, I was speaking, perhaps forensically, or admitting forensically, for the sake of the argument, taking the assumption that he might be. I am not in a position to say that he is not. There are those who accuse him of being restless and, as I have said, he may be, I do not know. I have not any evidence that he wishes to override legislative authority. If he does accentuate that feeling, if he is strongly of the opinion that he wants to disregard all legislative restraints upon a public body, I would say he probably would be ruthless, but I am not convinced he is that kind of man.

A few days later, after listening to attacks on Lilienthal from several other Senators, Republican Senator Knowland of the Joint Committee had this to say:

> . . . if there had been any question in my mind as to the loyalty of any of these [nominees] to the government of the United States or to the constitution of our country, I would not have supported them in committee or on the floor of the Senate. I reiterate that there is not one bit of evidence that supports directly or indirectly any such theory. These men are not Communists. . . . They are patriotic American citizens.

In regard to Mr. Lilienthal's qualifications, Senator Knowland asserted:

> I believe that David Lilienthal is well qualified for the position of Chairman of the Atomic Energy Commission.
>
> There has been the question raised . . . as to whether Mr. Lilienthal is the most qualified man for the position. I do not know that any man could honestly answer that question in either the affirmative or negative. . . .

I have no hesitation in saying however that Mr. Lilienthal has qualities which would place him in the top category of the candidates for the position in the field that the President had available to choose from.

In spite of this support from two powerful Republican Senators, in addition to the Democratic backing, the tide seemed to be turning against the Lilienthal nomination. At what turned out to be the very end of the debate, Republican Senator Vandenberg took the floor to deliver a lengthy address in favor of confirmation. He said first that seven weeks of committee hearings had dispelled the adverse prejudice he had had at the start. He went on:

I have been driven to the belief that logic, equity, fair play, and a just regard for the public welfare combine to recommend Mr. Lilienthal's confirmation in the light of today's realities.

This is not to say that the Senator wholeheartedly backed Mr. Lilienthal. He stressed the fact that the appointment was for eighteen months. To charges that Lilienthal was devoted to public ownership and high-handed administrative practices, he argued:

We, the Congress, have declared by law that the control of atomic energy must be the tightest government monopoly ever set up in the United States—pending the day when the destructive use of atomic energy shall be outlawed for keeps. . . . We solemnly and unavoidably decreed that government ownership and management, no matter how much we dislike it in other aspects of our national economy and life, is an indispensable public necessity for the sake of national security in respect to the control of atomic energy. . . . Therefore one of the most available men to run it is the successful manager of the greatest existing comparable example of public ownership and management. Whether we like it or him or TVA, this sequence leads logically to David Lilienthal's door. His liability under other circumstances thus becomes an asset for the time being.

Senator Vandenberg's support of the nominee seems to have turned the tide back in favor of Lilienthal, who was confirmed, 50 to 31. Nineteen Republicans joined with 31 Democrats in voting to confirm Mr. Lilienthal, while 5 Democrats and 26 Republicans voted against him.

Evidence is lacking to show the position of the Republican House members of the Joint Committee. In spite of the fact that only the Senate is empowered to approve Presidential nominations, there was some discussion of Mr. Lilienthal in the lower chamber, including vehement opposition from Representatives Busbey and Cox. Representative Holifield was the only Joint Committee member to rise in support of Lilienthal's nomination.

It is difficult to assess the precise effect of this strong opposition to Mr. Lilienthal upon the relations between the Commission and the Joint Committee. Since his nomination was supported by a majority of both the Republican and Democratic members of the Joint Committee, it is probably safe to say that, at least in the beginning, Lilienthal did not have to work with the odds hopelessly against him, in spite of the fact that the Joint Committee was dominated by Republicans. On the other hand, Senator McKellar's performance at the hearings and the debate on the Senate floor had made it quite clear that Lilienthal and the Lilienthal viewpoint were bitterly opposed by many influential legislators. Lilienthal was, to say the least, a controversial figure. Observers both within and without the Commission noted that the situation was delicate, and undoubtedly this intensified an attitude of careful and critical watchfulness during the succeeding days, especially among the Republican Committee members who could not accept Lilienthal as fully as did, for example, Senator McMahon.

■

At the confirmation hearings, Mr. Lilienthal was questioned about his views toward the Joint Committee. He was outspoken in welcoming it, and referred to the 1941 *Harvard Law Review* article, of which he was co-author, which favored a similar arrangement. In this article, Mr. Lilienthal had advocated a new procedure by which Congress could better evaluate the program of a government enterprise. He suggested an annual review of the agency's operation by a joint Congressional committee, including at least some of the members of the Appropriations Committees. This would afford the agency an opportunity to present fully its achievements and its problems, and to discuss its plans for the future. In this way, Congress could always have sufficient information to perform its functions as the "board of directors of the enterprises concerned." On the other hand, the agencies themselves "would profit from the assurance that their record and needs would be appraised only after a consideration of the entire program entrusted to them." [8]

Before the Joint Committee, Lilienthal developed these ideas and applied them to the immediate situation. He said he would be disappointed if the committee function became perfunctory, since it was a real handicap for an administrator if his opportunities for consultation with Congress were limited to crisis situations, to the brief annual requests for appropriations, or to cases where some legislative change might be desired. On the contrary, said Lilienthal, the conception behind the Joint Committee provision "is of a continuing relation with a Congressional group, in which one can get the benefit of the judgment of legislators, discuss policies not when they become crises but in the process of their development, and anticipate the needs for legislation." [9]

Mr. Lilienthal indicated that it would be the Commission's intent to make the fullest possible use of its special Congressional contact. He said he hoped the Joint Committee members, despite the pressure of other duties, would give to this job a great deal of time and effort.

Mr. Lilienthal seems to have hoped that the Joint Committee would participate as a consultant in the solution of the policy problems facing the AEC—the larger issues connected with the program, such as the place of atomic weapons in the defense structure and the extent to which peacetime uses of atomic energy should be given attention. Probably Lilienthal's hope arose not only from his general point of view regarding relations between Congress and the executive agency, but also from a cause more directly related to the atomic energy program itself. This may be described in general terms as a deep-rooted desire among those who had directed the program during the war to divest themselves of at least some of the responsibility for the direction and scope of the postwar program.

Much has been written regarding the sense of moral guilt from which many scientists are said to have suffered at war's end. Certainly it is true that the men who had worked and struggled to create the atomic energy program during the war were eager to escape the terrible burden of responsibility which until 1946 had been theirs alone. Undoubtedly this desire to shed some of the responsibility communicated itself to Lilienthal and the other Commissioners, and it also seems likely that they would have been glad to have the Committee assume some share of the burden.[10]

As it turned out, the Joint Committee in these early years did not often participate in discussions of policy. Nor did the Committee show a desire to accept any broad responsibility for the Commission's program. Under Senator Hickenlooper, the Joint Committee evidently felt that it was not in a position to enter the policy-making area. Senator Hickenlooper encouraged the Committee to restrict its activities to the approval or disapproval of policies already formulated by the Commission, with, of course, a watchful eye on the development of the agency as a whole.

The 1948 hearings on labor policy offer a case in point.[11] On that occasion the Joint Committee brought together the AEC and labor representatives to discuss the dangers inherent in allowing plant work stoppages and to attempt a solution of labor difficulties which had been plaguing the Commission for some time. An executive session was first held late in 1947. In 1948 two closed sessions were followed by open hearings in March. From Senator Hickenlooper's opening remarks, it was clear that the Joint Committee was open-minded and prepared to listen receptively to the views and suggestions of the Atomic Energy Commissioners. Mr. Lilienthal matched their candor by expressing his own gratification in the Committee's willingness to seek only facts and tentative suggestions.

It soon became evident, however, that the Joint Committee was looking for some concrete policy proposal from the AEC. Representative Lyndon Johnson said, "I hope that they will counsel with us on some new procedure that can meet this novel situation." [12] And Senator Hickenlooper, toward the close of the hearings, voiced his dissatisfaction with the Commission's approach to the problem:

> I am frankly a little in doubt as to what kind of a résumé we will have because we have succeeded in getting many nebulous suggestions without much concrete data. I do not know what the rest of the hearings will turn up, but afterwards we would like to have the opportunity, if it seems indicated, to go over any possible suggestions that may come up with you for your further advice.[13]

The Committee clearly wanted the AEC to work out and to be responsible for the necessary policy, which the Committee could approve or disapprove, as it saw fit.

The Lilienthal Commission also felt that the Joint Committee could and should act as an instrument of public control. Meetings of the Joint Committee could provide a forum to stimulate discussion of all aspects of the atomic energy program which could be discussed openly without endangering national security. Partly, it seems, this attitude of Mr. Lilienthal's had its roots in his TVA years, when he came to value the exhaustive public debate over the controversial TVA program, and to feel that public reaction was a significant feature of democratic control. His continuing concern over the problem of achieving the greatest possible public interest, knowledge, and debate about atomic energy was often expressed during the early years.[14] He clearly felt that the Joint Committee could play a key role. In a 1948 address devoted in part to the Joint Committee, he said:

> The setting up of this permanent high level joint committee . . . is an example of the political inventiveness which has characterized American history. . . . Increasingly as times goes on the people of this country will come to look to this committee as a principal means whereby the broad policy decisions that atomic energy will require may be studied, weighed, and recommendations reported to the Congress as a whole, and to the people.[15]

Again the Joint Committee did not share the Lilienthal viewpoint. The Committee did not feel impelled to act as a focal point for public and Congressional discussion of the atomic program. It communicated very little with Congress as a whole in the early years, and made no attempt to educate the public. In fact, the members relied almost exclusively on executive hearings. During 1947 only the confirmation hearings were open; in 1948, the Joint Committee's only public sessions, five in number, dealt with labor problems at atomic energy installations. Only one Committee report went to Congress, and it was of a rather tentative character.[16] All in all, the Joint Committee felt that the program should be considered only by those who were privy to the program secrets.

In this limited role the Joint Committee centered its critical attention primarily on a few specific aspects of the work of the AEC, placing such stress on these matters that a great deal of friction gradually developed between Committee and Commissioners. These areas were (1) secrecy and security, (2) decentralization and delegation of authority, and (3) the relationship of the military with the AEC. Each contributed to the growing friction, suspicion, and lack of sympathy, and each must now be considered in turn.

Security and Secrecy

Part of the limited role of the Joint Committee during the first two years was a narrow preoccupation with security and secrecy among some of its members. Any broad interest they might have had in the program was sacrificed to an extreme sensitivity to security considerations.

This interest in security by concealment among certain Joint Committee members was undoubtedly genuine, although at the same time it was intensified and even exacerbated by the predilections of the staff of the Committee. The Executive Director, Fred B. Rhodes, Jr., and the one other influential member of the staff, David S. Teeple, had both previously been security officers in the Manhattan District and hence were particularly aware of security problems. These men recognized that security administration in the Manhattan District had been necessarily somewhat haphazard, due to the haste enforced by the wartime emergency, and they felt that considerable improvement in security was extremely desirable under the AEC.

The preoccupation with security caused Mr. Lilienthal and three of the other Commissioners to conclude that the Committee was unwilling to deal with the genuinely important issues.

Hence it became clear as time went on that, while on the one hand the question of security itself was a distinct area of friction between the Commission and the Joint Committee, on the other hand the Commission was almost inevitably beginning to go its own way on the major issues which did not involve matters of security, leaving the Committee to occupy itself with its favorite topic.

At first the issues concerning security were almost imperceptible, but gradually they became more and more prominent. Finally, in mid-1949, a combination of circumstances brought them suddenly into such prominence that no one could look the other way; it was then that Senator Hickenlooper charged David Lilienthal with "incredible mismanagement" of the nation's atomic energy program.

Early in 1947 the Joint Committee became involved with the President in a dispute over the question of FBI investigation of appointees to the Commission. At the time of the confirmation hearings, Senator Hickenlooper wrote to President Truman and asked him to make available to the Senate Section of the Committee any information which might be in the possession of the government's investigative agencies, including the FBI.[17] The President, in reply, cited a long-established policy that executive investigative reports are the confidential property of the Executive branch, and that Congressional and public access to them is unwise. He added, however, that the records had been checked, and that no derogatory information about the appointees had been disclosed.

Apparently there was no way, then, to require an FBI investigation of the Commissioners and the General Manager. The Joint Committee as a whole had statutory power to do so, Senator Hickenlooper reported to his colleagues on the floor, but the FBI felt, and he agreed, that the Senate Section had no such power.

These facts were a cause of concern to Joint Committee members, and Senator Knowland introduced a bill making an FBI investigation mandatory for nominees to the Commission and to the General Manager's position, with the report to be made available to the Senate Section of the Joint Committee on Atomic Energy.[18]

The bill remained in committee until April, 1948, shortly before the original unextended terms were to run out. It was brought to the floor after the President submitted the names of all five Commissioners to be reappointed to regular staggered terms. Various Democratic Senators (including Senator McMahon) raised strong objection to it as an interference with the President's appointive power. It was finally amended to provide for such investigation only if the Senate Section of the Joint Committee specifically called for it. In this form, Congress passed the bill. President Truman vetoed it, however, and the veto was sustained.

In this particular controversy the Commission took no part. The incident does serve to illustrate, however, the stress placed by Joint Committee members on the question of security.

A second issue, also relating to the security problem, was raised at the confirmation debate by Senator Bricker, the only Joint Committee member to vote against Lilienthal's confirmation. On the floor, Senator Bricker read from a memorandum prepared by Fred Rhodes, director of the Joint Committee staff:

> A careful review was made of certain of the security files on a few of the key employees in the Washington headquarters of the Atomic Energy Commission. A total of 23 files was reviewed, and out of this number, derogatory information of a significant nature was developed in 5 cases.[19]

Senator Bricker then read summaries of the allegedly derogatory information on the five and made the point that Lilienthal had shown poor judgment in retaining such people on the Commission staff.[20]

This was only the first episode in a long behind-the-scenes controversy on the whole problem of AEC personnel clearances for access to restricted data, concerning both Commission and contractor employees, as well as other persons permitted such access for one reason or another. The details of the AEC's personnel security program, as established and modified during 1947 and 1948, need not be of concern here.[21] It is enough to say that the Joint Committee took an interest in two aspects of the problem.

First, Committee members were disturbed by a number of cases where persons were allowed access to restricted data in spite of the discovery of "substantial" derogatory information against them. Senator Hickenlooper reviewed the Committee's interest in this problem at a 1949 hearing:

> . . . as early as July, 1947 . . . the joint committee held a meeting with the Commission and certain of its representatives at which time the matter of the seriousness of a vigorous administration of personnel security was discussed at length. Certain cases were mentioned and the joint committee was informed that these cases and any other similar cases would be vigorously pursued and that speedy determinations would be made in the public interest.
>
> This field, among others, became one of continued interest to the joint committee and was the subject of continuing review. On the day after Thanksgiving in 1947, during that traditional holiday period when most people are inclined to be restful, this matter was considered of such importance that an executive meeting of the joint committee was held lasting all day. The meeting was attended by 10 members of the joint committee; all of the Commissioners, with the exception of Chairman Lilienthal, who had an engagement out of town of some long standing; the General Manager of the Commission and his assistant; the Associate General Counsel and the Director of Security and three of his

assistants. At that meeting it was again pointed out by the joint committee that a substantial number of cases involving serious doubt and substantial derogatory information, some of which had been referred to in the July meeting, were still pending and undetermined.[22]

Second, the Joint Committee was disturbed by the Commission's policy of granting emergency clearance to persons whose services were urgently needed. In such cases, access to restricted data was allowed on the basis of an FBI file check; full investigation followed during the employee's first two or three months on the job.

For authority to follow this procedure, the Commission relied upon Section 10 of the Atomic Energy Act, which provided that:

> Except as authorized by the Commission in case of emergency, no individual shall be employed by the Commission until the Federal Bureau of Investigation shall have made an investigation and report to the Commission on the character, associations, and loyalty of such individual.[23]

In following this practice of granting emergency clearances— 818 were granted in 1947 and 2,013 in 1948 [24]—the Commission was trying to balance the need to push the program forward without delay against the risk that a few individuals of questionable loyalty might be allowed access to classified information. The Commission felt, obviously, that the advantages of speed far outweighed the risk.

Members of the Joint Committee took a different view. Senator Hickenlooper said during the 1949 investigation that he had "remonstrated with the Commission in rather extensive correspondence with Chairman Lilienthal, dating back to 1947" when these "extraordinary emergency clearances in such numbers began to come to my attention." [25]

During the years 1947–1949, a good deal of behind-the-scenes controversy arose over the international aspects of atomic energy. About the middle of 1947, Senators Hickenlooper and Vandenberg discovered the details of the agreements reached by Prime Minister Churchill and President Roosevelt at their wartime meetings in Quebec and Hyde Park.[26] The two Senators, shocked (as was presumably the AEC) to find that the United States had agreed not to use the A-bomb without the consent of the British, immediately protested to the President and the Secretaries of State and Defense. At a meeting on November 16, 1947, attended by the two Senators, Secretary of Defense Forrestal, and Undersecretary of State Lovett, other details came to light, including agreements on the sharing of information and cooperation in atomic development. Discussions with the British and Canadians in January, 1948, led to the removal of the restriction on the use of the bomb and clarification of the program for exchanging information on the technical aspects of atomic energy development.

The subject came up again the same year, however, and this time the same two Senators found a situation created by the AEC itself which seemed to call for action as prompt and decisive as that taken upon discovery of the Quebec and Hyde Park agreements. Commissioner Strauss informed Senators Hickenlooper and Vandenberg that Dr. Cyril Smith, an AEC scientist, had gone to Britain with authority to discuss various matters with the British.[27] One of these matters was the "metallurgy of plutonium." Feeling this to be beyond the Commission's authority under the new American-British-Canadian agreement and under the Act, the two Senators met in Secretary of Defense Forrestal's office with D. F. Carpenter, Chairman of the Military Liaison Committee, Dr. Vannevar Bush, Chairman of the Joint Research and Development Board, and Forrestal.

The result of this discussion is not clear. Evidently Forrestal shared Senator Hickenlooper's view that possession of such information as that dealing with the basic metallurgy of plutonium by Britain could be a major danger to the United States, and he got in touch with Commissioner Pike, acting chairman while Lilienthal was out of town. Dr. Smith was reached, and he reported that he had not yet engaged in any discussion of plutonium metallurgy. His authority to do so was, of course, canceled.

Later it was asserted that Pike was slow to take action, although an interviewee stated that this charge arose because Pike's telegram used Greenwich mean time which was five hours later than the dispatch from Washington. Nevertheless the incident was used to cast doubt on Pike's fitness and gave ammunition to those opposing him.

No question of the physical security measures taken by the Commission became the subject of public discussion in the Joint Committee during the first two years, but there is little doubt that the Committee did give considerable attention to this aspect of the program. As early as December 4, 1947, the Committee held an executive session to discuss a staff security report on various AEC installations. A second hearing was held on January 20, 1948.[28]

The impression gained from interviews was that many members of the AEC staff felt that the Joint Committee spent too much time on this subject in this early period. Fred Rhodes and David Teeple, the most influential members of the Joint Committee staff, were said to be particularly concerned with such matters as the claim that a shell fired from a mortar located beyond the fences at Oak Ridge could have reached the production areas.

This seems to have been a field in which friction between the AEC and the Committee developed rapidly, not because of any glaring inadequacies on the part of the Commission, but rather because the Commission was impatient with the emphasis the Committee placed upon what it felt to be a minor aspect of the program and because the Committee felt that the Commission's attitude left a good deal to be desired.

One of the sharpest disagreements about security occurred over the Commission's fellowship program, which provided grants to graduate students for research in biology, medicine, and the physical sciences.

Senator Hickenlooper took an active interest in the early stages of the program. In a letter dated July 30, 1948, he requested a statement of views from the AEC on the nature of the investigation, if any, which should be made into the "character, loyalty, and associations" of recipients prior to the awarding of the fellowships. In Mr. Lilienthal's words (in a letter dated October 11, 1948), the AEC "gave long and careful consideration" to the advisability of requesting the same FBI security clearance of fellows engaged in nonsecret work as the law required for those having access to secret data.[29] The Commission's reply to the Hickenlooper letter set out some of the reasons behind the decision not to require security clearance of fellows who did not have access to restricted data.[30]

Senator Hickenlooper replied, in a letter dated January 12, 1949, that the Joint Committee staff had informed him that a few fellowship applicants for nonsecret work had been investigated at the start, and that "substantial derogatory information" had been revealed against certain ones who were subsequently authorized to receive grants. The Senator stressed his own opinion that expenditure of public funds to educate a Communist was indefensible. He concluded with a promise that the matter would be brought before the Joint Committee as soon as possible.[31]

Disagreement between Committee and agency on specific security matters reflected a real division on the importance of security measures generally. To Senator Hickenlooper and other Joint Committee members, secrecy and tight security were virtually more important than anything else. In their view, it fell to the Joint Committee to guard security because the AEC's own program was too lax. Their chief concern was to retain the monopoly of knowledge which the United States had in bomb technology by building and maintaining an impregnable wall around the secret and all the men who knew it.

The AEC, contrariwise, was more impressed with the need to push ahead with the development of fissionable materials and the programs for military preparedness and basic research. Security problems were secondary to the Commission's main interest. Consequently, the Joint Committee's emphasis on questions of security, to the exclusion of at least some of the AEC's programmatic aims, seemed to the Commission an unnecessary interference with men who were doing their best with an almost impossibly complex job. The Commission felt that it had to be less than infallible in its security program in order to get on with the production and weapons programs and to attract the people who were needed to do the jobs. Furthermore, in administering the security clearance program, the Commission staff tended to place as much emphasis on procedures to protect the rights and privileges of individuals as on procedures to guarantee an organization free of security risks. The Joint Committee, on the other hand, in its anxiety to ensure a thorough security program, was inclined to place its trust in professional security officers who had shown a particular ability to detect signs of disloyalty or character deviation.

It was a matter of which aim should be given priority: to get on as quickly as possible to new achievements, or to conceal what had already been achieved. With such a clear divergence between the Commission and the Joint Committee, friction was bound to increase. The explosion came when Senator Hickenlooper made his charges against Lilienthal and the AEC, and the investigations of 1949 began.

Decentralization-Delegation

Other matters, too, contributed to the distant Committee-Commission relationship in these years. One was the delegation of authority by the Commission to the General Manager.

The AEC, of course, was operating under a philosophy according to which the Commissioners worked at a high-policy level while the General Manager handled most of the day-to-day administrative matters.[32] Mr. Lilienthal explained this theory repeatedly:

> We have avoided the practice of dividing the functions or vesting any day to day administrative responsibility in the Commission as a commission. This was contemplated in the law, and I believe very wisely, that the general manager is in effect the president of the company. The statute creating the position of general manager, who is appointed by the President and confirmed by the Senate, we believe, justifies this form of organization. . . . [W]e feel it is very important that there should be five men disassociated from day to day administration to give what they may have and to try to find answers to some of the questions which are so complex and new in American society.[33]

The Commissioners were not, according to this theory, to engage in daily decision-making; nor were they supposed to testify before Congressional committees on questions of the AEC's functioning. Instead, the General Manager, the program directors, and the operations officers were delegated the task of testifying.

Basically, members of Congressional committees would rather talk to an agency head than to a staff member. In this case, the members of the Joint Committee found that Commissioners were not even able to answer some of the detailed questions put to them concerning operational matters. Several interviewees who were present at these meetings have made this assertion. In addition, Carroll Wilson, the General Manager, inspired little confidence among the Joint Committee members. It became necessary for Mr. Lilienthal not only to defend the theory of broad delegation, but also to shield the General Manager himself.

A number of former AEC staff members have cited one particular executive session as an indication of the difficulties caused by these factors. Mr. Lilienthal and other Commissioners, the story runs, were present but silent, letting Wilson reply to the Committee members. A Senate member of the Joint Committee became irritated by Wilson's testimony, and turned to Lilienthal. "Just what do *you* do?" he asked of Lilienthal. Mr. Lilienthal's reply, an explanation of the functions of the Commission and General Manager, was not convincing to the Senator, according to the observers.

At any rate, dissatisfaction with Mr. Lilienthal's idea of the best way for the AEC to operate seems to have increased gradually in the first two years. Joint Committee public hearings do not reveal it, but since they were few in number and dealt with special topics, one cannot conclude that dissatisfaction on this score was not present. The evidence from former staff members indicates clearly that it was.

Military Versus Civilian Control

A third area of sensitivity was the role of the military in the atomic energy project. The military interests and needs, it will be recalled, were to be coordinated with the various research, production, and weapons programs of the AEC through a Military Liaison Committee, which was to be kept fully informed of the Commission's activities. Those who opposed the MLC felt that the wise decision in favor of civilian control was partly negated by the creation of this "military watch-dog." Those supporting the provision for a liaison committee suggested rather that the MLC would do a great service by ensuring communication and cooperation between the AEC and the military establishment—and after all, the Commission's biggest job was to safeguard the nation by a strong weapons program, which could be properly carried out, it seemed, only by close coordination with the Department of Defense.

It must be admitted, at the outset, that this arrangement did not entirely satisfy those who had been fighting all along for complete military control. These people tended to be resentful of the AEC simply because the agency represented the victory of civilian control. It made no difference how attentive the Commission might be to military requirements, nor how well it might cooperate with the MLC. The Commission was resented simply because it was running the program, and the Department of Defense was not.

There are indications that as early as the 1947 confirmation debate, these military interests were bringing pressure to bear against the nominees to the Commission.[34] Dissatisfaction with civilian control continued to manifest itself through legislative proposals seeking in various ways to increase military participation in the atomic energy program. During 1947 and 1948, seven bills were introduced in Congress to this end.[35] Later, in mid-1949, Republican Senator Cain responded to the mounting criticism of AEC policies and administrative practices by sponsoring a measure which would have replaced the Commission with a board of eight military men and one scientist.[36]

In 1948 the military establishment made a direct effort to re-establish military custody of atomic weapons. Secretary of Defense James A. Forrestal took a formal request for custody to the White House, but President Truman's decision was to leave custody with the Commission.[37]

Some of the Joint Committee members were sympathetic with the military viewpoint and particularly sensitive to military criticism of the AEC.[38] Although the Joint Committee did not support these extreme measures, did not want to do away altogether with civilian control or even to weaken it seriously, the bitter military opposition to the AEC *was* serious precisely because of this sensitivity among the Committee members.

Most of the Committee members fell somewhere between the extreme positions; they wanted civilian control, but they also welcomed the Military Liaison Committee and insisted that its relationship with the AEC should be close and harmonious. Their point of view became apparent as early as the confirmation hearings. The question came up of the desirability of permitting MLC representatives to be present at AEC meetings.[39] After Mr. Lilienthal had assured the Joint Committee that the Commission had been in touch with the Liaison Committee, and that no hindrance would be placed in the way of channeling information to the MLC, Senator Millikin asked if this meant that MLC people had sat in on Commission meetings. He seemed concerned when Mr. Lilienthal said they had not, and that the Commission did not contemplate such an arrangement. Senators Knowland and Vandenberg joined in, the latter asserting that it would not be satisfactory if there were even a single closed door to the Military Liaison Committee, but adding that he did not mean that the AEC should meet only when such liaison personnel were present.

Mr. Lilienthal was not at all pleased with the idea of MLC attendance at Commission meetings. Although he would not agree to the wisdom of the idea, Joint Committee pressure forced him to express at least a degree of acquiescence, and he suggested that the matter could be worked out, and stressed that there "need be no situation where, upon request of the Liaison Committee . . . there will be nonaccess. . . ." [40]

Joint Committee concern to guarantee a close AEC-military relationship was expressed again in connection with the question of cooperation between the AEC and General Groves, wartime head of the Manhattan District. At the confirmation hearings, Mr. Lilienthal admitted that the AEC had been in touch with the MLC since taking over the project, but not with General Groves.[41] This was made into a major issue during floor debate on the confirmation. While some Joint Committee members were critical at the hearings of this lack of consultation with the General, several came to the AEC's defense during debate. Senator Knowland pointed out that when the Lilienthal statement was made, on January 27, less than four weeks had passed since the AEC took over. Senator McMahon remarked that for most of this brief period General Groves had been taking a rest in Florida anyhow.

Whatever the dates, it is now clear that there was some limited contact between the General and the AEC, before and perhaps after the Commission assumed control at the end of 1946. It is equally clear that the contact developed a sharp difference of opinion between Mr. Lilienthal and the General. An illustration of the variance of viewpoint is seen in Groves's comments about letters he wrote to Lilienthal suggesting that consideration be given to dismissing certain employees who were originally cleared in spite of derogatory information. General Groves explained:

. . . these letters were only written because previous verbal discussions which were very limited had proven unavailing and because Mr. Lilienthal had made it very plain that he wanted no advice of any kind from me. He wanted nothing whatsoever to do with me. He thought that I was the lowest kind of human being, and he was not going to get anything from me.[42]

This friction did not, of course, go unnoticed. Some indication that it was widely believed to exist may be seen in the fact that the Secretary of War later felt it necessary to urge the General to issue a disclaimer. In July the press reported the resulting statement from him, to the effect that he had never made any effort to place the Atomic Energy Commission in an unfavorable light in the eyes of the American people.[43]

In such circumstances, an effective relationship between the military and the AEC was scarcely possible. Yet the Joint Committee continued to insist that Mr. Lilienthal should consult with General Groves.

Another condition in this AEC-military relationship which displeased the Joint Committee was the unfruitful relationship between the Military Liaison Committee as a whole and the AEC. The Joint Committee, in the confirmation hearings, had expressed fears that this relationship might not function well. These fears proved as well founded as the fears that General Groves and the Commission were not working together.

The difficulty, however, was not the failure of the AEC to communicate with the Liaison Committee.[44] Interviewees from the AEC side are unanimous in their feeling that the MLC failed to live up to expectations. Various reasons may be given for this failure. It has been said that the MLC members represented their own services too narrowly, and that they were relatively low-ranking officers and had not the prestige in the military establishment to make their knowledge of atomic energy matters felt. Personalities have allegedly played a role in adding to the difficulty of effective work by the MLC, specifically in regard to certain unfortunate choices of MLC members.

Whatever the explanation, the fact remains that the MLC did not act as an effective coordinator, nor did it bring about smooth intercommunication between the AEC and the military. There simply were no satisfactory working relationships between the

Commission and the defense establishment. Chairman Lilienthal could go directly to the heads of the military service departments and the Department of Defense, but without staff assistance in the field of atomic weapons the military chiefs could not talk to him effectively.

In short, there was a partial vacuum on the military side of this relationship. Without effective liaison, the military obviously could not and did not base their requirements for atomic weapons on a realistic knowledge of the production levels and capacities of the atomic energy production program. It was as if the two groups were separated by a wall, with weapons requirements coming periodically from the Joint Chiefs of Staff to the Commission through a one-way chute.[45]

The loss was everyone's, of course. Undoubtedly the poor cooperation between the AEC and General Groves and the MLC was reflected in the attitudes of members of the Joint Committee, especially those with military sympathies. At the same time, the AEC suffered from insufficient consultation on large policy questions and program direction and was unable to benefit fully from the experience of those, including General Groves, who had run the Manhattan District during the war. And the Chiefs of Staff were not properly informed about the nation's primary defense effort.

As noted earlier, the General Advisory Committee was vested in the Atomic Energy Act with authority to "advise the Commission on scientific and technical matters relating to materials, production, and research and development. . . ." At the beginning of 1947, the General Advisory Committee consisted of nine prominent scientists and engineers, including James B. Conant, then President of Harvard; Lee DuBridge, President of California Institute of Technology; Enrico Fermi of the University of Chicago; I. I. Rabi of Columbia; Hartley Rowe, Vice-President of United Fruit Company; Glenn Seaborg of the University of California; Cyril Smith of the University of Chicago; and Hood Worthington of duPont. By all odds the key figure in the GAC, however, was the ninth member, Dr. J. Robert Oppenheimer, who was chosen chairman at the first meeting in 1947 and was re-elected to the post each year until his term expired in mid-1952.[46]

During Dr. Oppenheimer's chairmanship, the General Advisory Committee met some thirty times and transmitted about the same number of reports to the Commission. Perhaps the most important factor determining its role was the fact that it was really the only top-level body which had an intimate knowledge of the program and the installations. Dr. Oppenheimer stressed this point:

> . . . in the early days we knew more collectively about the past of the atomic energy undertaking and its present state, technically and to some extent organizationally or some parts of it, than the Commission did.
>
> The Commission was new; its staff needed to be recruited. We knew about Los Alamos; we knew about Sandia, we knew about the Argonne Laboratory. . . .[47]

This knowledge did not immediately diminish. Excellent channels of communication continued to exist whereby the GAC might keep track of the work at the various installations. Of great importance was the fact that the Committee's secretary, Mr. John Manley, was Associate Director of Los Alamos. Furthermore, many GAC members were consultants to the various installations. Dr. Rabi was a founder of Brookhaven Nation Laboratory and kept close watch on its development. Dr. Fermi was a consultant at Los Alamos. Others had connections with Oak Ridge and the Argonne Laboratory.

As a result, according to Dr. Oppenheimer, "it was very natural for us not merely to respond to questions that the Commission put, but to suggest to the Commission programs that it ought to undertake; to suggest to the Commission things that needed doing of a technical sort."

The Commission, for its part, relied on the GAC very heavily for all kinds of advice, not only on matters contemplated in the phrase "technical and scientific." For example, Dr. Oppenheimer asserted that "very frequently" the GAC was asked questions relating to organization, security procedures, and the custody of atomic weapons. Although the GAC avoided some of these questions, or limited its answers to technical considerations, it did not believe that its statutory frame of reference was being violated, and had great concern to give the AEC "every possible encouragement and support." Mr. Lilienthal subsequently testified that he "did have great respect for the views of the GAC" on technical matters. Mr. Lilienthal continued:

> I took very much to heart their statement that their conclusions were planted in technical considerations. I had such respect for the wisdom of men like Conant and Oppenheimer and Fermi and other men that I certainly paid close attention to what they said on matters that were not technical.[48]

From all the evidence, then, it appears indisputable that the AEC relied heavily on the judgment of the General Advisory Committee during the Lilienthal years. The prestige which atomic scientists enjoyed at the end of the war made this an inevitable relationship. Furthermore, the Commission found in the GAC a group with a common outlook and a great technical mastery of the program—a group which it was easy to confer with and rely on for program discussions.

At the same time, the scientist-members of the GAC had developed an interest in public affairs as a result of their realization that they had created a force which was destined to have a tremendous impact on all public life.[49] They wanted to participate in policy formulation along with the AEC Commissioners; they wanted to project themselves into the larger issues and become in fact a *general* advisory committee.

Moreover, the choice of Dr. Oppenheimer as chairman of the GAC served to heighten this aspect of the role played by the Committee.[50] He had the tremendous prestige of "the man who made the atom bomb." He himself has admitted that he "combined a little more experience, a little more power, a little more of influence than anyone else" among all the scientists who took part in the H-bomb discussions.[51] His intense interest in political affairs and his great persuasiveness have been repeatedly pointed out by those who worked with him.[52] He became a driving wedge for the GAC itself. Some have asserted that Dr. Oppenheimer completely controlled the AEC [53] and earlier had under his thumb even General Groves.[54]

In any case, it appears certain that the GAC was extremely influential in all types of policy formulation in this period. It also appears certain that Dr. Oppenheimer intensified this influence. As a result the AEC found an outside body which could help it bear some of the responsibility for the new civilian program, and consequently felt less need for using the Joint Committee in this capacity. The effect of this upon the Joint Committee was to make the members feel that the distance between them and the AEC was widened by the extremely close advisers the AEC had found in this special advisory committee in the Executive branch of the government.

One additional factor remains to be mentioned in the early AEC-Joint Committee relationship. The influence of the Joint Committee, already displaced to some extent by the General Advisory Committee, was further weakened by the appearance of partisan splits within the Committee. It is to be expected, of course, that Congressional committees made up of both Democratic and Republican members will have differences of viewpoint on controversial matters. But atomic energy seemed at the close of the war to have such importance that bipartisan cooperation was clearly necessary. The Joint Committee's record shows comparatively little evidence of narrow partisanship; and the record also indicates, as might be predicted, that the influence of the Joint Committee is greater when it can stand united, and falters when its membership is split.

The confirmation hearings showed what seemed to be a surprising unanimity among the Senate members on Mr. Lilienthal. Yet it was clear that most of the Republican Joint Committeemen had reservations, and some were outright in their opposition both to the membership of the Commission and to the concept of the civilian Commission itself. An instance of this continuing and ever growing distrust among the GOP members, and an example of Democratic defense of the Commission, occurred in 1948 when Chairman Hickenlooper appointed a subcommittee to investigate complaints about the AEC's condemnation of land for a permanent Argonne National Laboratory in Du Page County, Illinois. The chairman of the subcommittee was Representative Elston, probably the strongest Joint Committee proponent of military control of atomic energy. The second GOP member was Senator Bricker, who opposed Mr. Lilienthal vigorously. Representative Price made up the Democratic minority.

After considering the situation, the subcommittee reported, splitting 2 to 1.[55] Representative Elston and Senator Bricker doubted the necessity of acquiring this particular site, and roundly condemned the Commission and the grant of power in the Act which enabled it to make such condemnations. They recommended an amendment of the Act to provide for Congressional supervision of such future operations by the AEC.

Representative Price, the Democrat, disagreed. He felt that the site was carefully and wisely chosen, and that it was acquired in a fair manner. He had no criticism of the agency to make whatsoever.

In 1948, an issue came up which split the full Committee on party lines. President Truman had reappointed the original Commissioners to staggered terms. An extension bill was written by the Republican leadership as a substitute measure.[56] This extension bill provided for additional terms of two years for the original Commissioners and thus would have had all their terms expire after the inauguration of the next President, whom the Republican majority on the Joint Committee hoped would be a Republican. In its report on the measure, the Joint Committee split 11 to 5, the Republican majority (plus one Democrat) favoring it on the ground that the AEC had not yet had time to make a record on which to judge the reappointments, and five Democrats urging that the interest of the atomic energy project and the nation would not be served by such a politically motivated measure.[57] The minority asserted that the basic soundness of the Commission's purposes and policies had been amply demonstrated already. In the floor debate that followed, before Congress finally passed the bill, the split in the Committee was re-emphasized.[58]

This controversy was only one manifestation of partisan maneuvering at the time. The fact is that a Democratic Administration occupied the White House, while a new Republican 80th Congress held forth on Capitol Hill. The GOP had been encouraged by the 1946 election successes, and many Republicans felt certain that all signs pointed to the election in 1948 of the first Republican President in nearly two decades. Through 1947 and 1948 there grew the opposition to Mr. Truman along with the widespread belief that he would surely not remain as President after 1948.

In this political environment, the Republican leadership of the Joint Committee naturally shared most of the sentiments of their fellow party-members, and although the grave nature of their responsibility served to dampen the most extreme partisan enthusiasms, they could scarcely avoid applying some of the thoughts which occupied them as Republicans to the matters that came before them as members of a joint committee. The same political factors which had operated in the confirmation controversy continued to influence them. They would, of course, be extremely watchful and quick to criticize when the object of their surveillance was such a New Deal, left-wing Democrat as they thought Mr. Lilienthal to be, and they would pounce swiftly on any seeming abuse of power or carelessness in matters of security.[59] The partisan issue of "Communists-in-government" did not really become prominent until after the Hiss case in August, 1948, but already it was the Republicans who persisted in making security a political issue.

In a sense, the Commission and the Joint Committee were traveling in different orbits. Generally speaking, they dealt with the same subject, but their aims were not the same, nor were their ideas of procedure and technique. Each group grew to feel that the other was somehow alien and unsympathetic. In such an atmosphere, political motivations are bound to flourish.

The disagreements between the AEC and the Joint Committee have been emphasized, not because they pervaded every aspect of the relations between the two groups, but because, as subjects publicly discussed, they illustrate the "growing pains" of the two newly created bodies. In part at least, each partner to this relationship had formed certain expectations regarding the other which, when unfulfilled, contributed to the friction. The AEC expected the Joint Committee to play a role which the Joint Committee had no capacity to play. It will be recalled that the Commission generally felt that the Joint Committee should act (1) as a public forum and (2) as a consultant in the solution of policy problems facing the AEC. The Joint Committee's decision to communicate very little with Congress or the public was a keen disappointment to Mr. Lilienthal, and so was the failure of the Committee to assume a share of the responsibility for the atomic energy program. He was annoyed because the Committee—and especially the Committee staff—was preoccupied with details, particularly the details of individual security cases. Even in the purely military aspects of the atomic energy program, Lilienthal felt the Joint Committee was not giving as much policy guidance as it should, in spite of the fact that several members of the Committee were also members of the House and Senate Armed Services Committees and hence ought to have been in a position to offer valuable suggestions on those points in the atomic energy program which impinged directly on the nation's immediate defense requirements.

Writing in 1951, former Commissioner William W. Waymack expressed a similar viewpoint.[60] At first the Joint Committee functioned too narrowly, he asserted, and was inhibited by "an obsession with security narrowly defined." In his view, the Committee members, like most people at the time, did not possess enough knowledge to understand the major problems of atomic policy and did not have enough time to inform themselves rapidly and systematically. In any case, according to Mr. Waymack, unsuccessful efforts were made by the AEC to organize joint meetings with the Committee, in order to give the Committee members the information they would need to understand the whole program. These efforts were continuous, he wrote, but Committee interest was lacking and the joint sessions became infrequent; when they did occur, they were limited to specific matters, "usually controversies and fears of the moment."

The Joint Committee's decision to assume a narrow role, acting purely as a review board and stressing certain limited aspects of the program, can be attributed to several factors. It was apparently believed that the Committee would be faced with a situation like that of other standing committees. Its members assumed that a substantial amount of legislation would be handled, and that Committee dealings with the agency's program would have to be limited to a review of decisions already made—a "post-audit" which would be facilitated by a free flow of information to the Committee but which would not develop to such a degree that the Committee was taking the initiative and responsibility for the program.

During the first years, it must be remembered, the Joint Committee had neither the staff nor the background to identify itself with a program of atomic energy development. The members were relatively unfamiliar with the agency, its facilities and its work, in spite of the fact that they did receive reports from the AEC, hold briefing sessions, and make trips to the various installations. During debate in the Senate in 1948, Senator Hickenlooper made the point that the Joint Committee did not really begin to operate with effectiveness until mid-1947.[61] The confirmation hearings and debate occupied several months in the early part of the year, and it was only after their termination that the Joint Committee could begin to get acquainted with the program and attempt to organize a smoothly working committee staff. There was something of a handicap, too, in the fact that the experience and interest of the most influential staff members was such as to lead them to emphasize the security aspects of the program. Although Senator McMahon and several other Committeemen pointed out that the Joint Committee had received a great body of information from the AEC, it is probably

true that most of the membership had not had time to absorb
much of it, nor to gain much of a "feel" for the program.[62]

■

From these various predicaments—the AEC's disappointment
with the Joint Committee, the Joint Committee's disagreement
with many of the AEC's views, and the political and personal
friction—one basic problem emerged: how could the Commission deal with its responsibility for conducting the atomic energy
program in spite of the handicaps? Generally speaking, the Commissioners tried to solve the problem in four ways.

First, Chairman Lilienthal and his four colleagues tended to
rely on their own judgment and assumed a considerable degree
of independence in matters of policy, and they developed a
resistance to Joint Committee pressure to change that policy.
This independence stemmed from the fact that the majority
group of the Joint Committee turned out in practice to have a
set of priorities which did not agree with those of the Commission. Mr. Lilienthal thought that to adopt the Joint Committee
viewpoint regarding secrecy and security would have been to
some extent to sacrifice the program. In the case of the personnel
security program, for example, the AEC defended its viewpoint
vigorously and refused to defer to the Joint Committee's judgment.

Furthermore, since the Commission was unable to obtain
policy guidance of a broad kind from the Joint Committee, it
tended to rely on policies which were independently formed.
The AEC thus accepted what it felt were the requirements of
program development and sacrificed any hope of encouraging a
closer, more harmonious relationship with the majority group of
the Joint Committee.

Second, the Commission tended to be somewhat careless

about giving full information to the Joint Committee. This is supported by the statements of a number of interviewees who suggested that during this period the Commission was not giving the Committee the whole story and was, in fact, actually withholding certain information.

The Committee's fear that it was not receiving complete information was increased by the attitude of suspicion created among some of its members by the charges made during the confirmation hearings. Disagreements over security matters and such glimpses into the Commission's operations as that provided by the Cyril Smith incident served to aggravate this fear. The fact that the Committee learned about the Commission's policies and activities by means outside the regular flow of information from the AEC to the Committee convinced many members that the AEC was not reporting completely.

Third, Chairman Lilienthal felt impelled to attempt to gain public support as a potential counteracting force to the mounting dissatisfaction in the majority group of the Joint Committee. During 1947 and 1948, Mr. Lilienthal took advantage of every opportunity to speak publicly and to meet with groups in all parts of the country to discuss the Commission's activities and objectives.[63] Doubtless this laid a foundation of popular support for the Commission which was of value during the critical days of the Hickenlooper investigation.

Fourth, and probably most significant, the AEC came to place increased reliance on the General Advisory Committee. As has already been pointed out, this reliance was in some measure due to its scientist-members' experience and enthusiasm for the program and their enormous prestige in the eyes of the Commission, the Congress, and the nation as a whole. In addition, the AEC's reliance on the GAC was strengthened by the unfruitful relationship between the Commission and the Joint

Committee. Finding the Committee unsympathetic and unwilling to share responsibility, the Commission naturally turned even more readily to the GAC, whose members were deeply interested in the program and willing to participate fully in its development.

III

Crisis and Transition

During the latter half of 1948, Congress was in session only a few weeks.[1] It was election time, with the Republicans eager to retain their control of the legislature and to capture the Presidency for the first time in two decades. Their hopes, of course, were in vain, for Harry S. Truman returned to the White House, and a Democratic majority reorganized the new 81st Congress in January, 1949.

The Senate membership of the Joint Committee on Atomic Energy remained the same in 1949 with one exception: Republican Senator Bricker (the one Joint Committee opponent of David Lilienthal at the 1947 confirmation) was replaced by Democratic Senator Millard E. Tydings. On the House side, Representatives Patterson and Lyndon Johnson were replaced by Representatives Henry M. Jackson and Paul J. Kilday.

On January 28, the Joint Committee held its first meeting of the year, electing Senator McMahon chairman and Representative Durham vice-chairman. A week later, Senator McMahon announced the appointment of a new executive director, William L. Borden, to head the Joint Committee staff.

After these changes, there was some basis for believing that the growing lack of confidence in the AEC, principally on the part of the former Republican leadership of the Joint Committee, would never come to public attention. Senator Hicken-

looper had relinquished the all-important chairmanship to Senator McMahon, who was the strongest Congressional advocate of
the Commission and Mr. Lilienthal. Senator Bricker had lost
his membership on the Committee. The two extremely security-
conscious staff members of the preceding years departed also.

As it developed, however, controversy over the administration
of the atomic energy project reached its highest point in 1949.
A combination of circumstances during the early part of the
year shattered all prospects for harmonious AEC-Joint Committee relations. By the last week in May, the Commission was
on the front pages of the nation's press. On the first day of
June, before a battery of cameras and newsmen in the Senate
caucus room, the Joint Committee opened the first full-scale
Congressional inquiry of the year, the so-called Hickenlooper
investigation into the United States atomic energy project.[2]

Looking back, one can see that the eruption of the Hickenlooper investigation was in part due to chance. The inquiry was
precipitated by several incidents which occurred within a short
time of one another. If they had occurred over a longer period
of time, they might have been treated individually in a much less
spectacular way.

Nearly all the specific issues fell in the category of security;
hence, in one sense, the roots of the investigation go back to the
beginning of 1947. But public and Congressional sensitivity to
matters of security was heightened by the general deterioration
of international affairs during the latter half of 1948. Such
events as the Berlin blockade, the breakdown of attempts at
international control of atomic energy, and the Hiss case gave
increasing evidence that the nation's security could by no means
be taken for granted.

Congress had not been in session a month when Senator Mc-
Mahon called a meeting of the Joint Committee to consider
with AEC representatives the Commission's Fifth Semiannual

Report and other project developments.[3] Senators Tydings and Connally objected strongly to various aspects of the report, in its references to progress in atomic weapons and its information—with photographs—concerning AEC equipment and installations.[4] Representative Hinshaw complained along the same lines, although it was established that most of the photographs had previously been released by the Manhattan District and published in various periodicals. Representative Elston also inquired about relaxation of security regulations at Oak Ridge.

In March, this issue came up again, in conjunction with another. Dr. Frank Graham was named by the Governor of North Carolina to the United States Senate. The appointment gave rise to much opposition in Congress, and Senator Bricker on the floor of the Senate took the occasion to demand an investigation of Dr. Graham's clearance by the AEC on January 12.[5] The Commission had overruled its Director of Security and its Personnel Security Review Board headed by Owen J. Roberts, and had allowed Dr. Graham access to restricted data as President of the Oak Ridge Institute of Nuclear Studies. Later the Roberts Board was dissolved, and Admiral Gingrich resigned as Security Director. Senator Bricker implied that this was because of disagreement with Mr. Lilienthal.

During the floor debate on this issue, Senator McMahon defended the Commission. He also defended it when Senator McCarthy reopened the argument over the data and photographs contained in the Fifth Semiannual Report.[6]

It was not until May, however, that a real public issue developed. This concerned the Commission's fellowship policy. On the evening of May 10, radio commentator Fulton Lewis, Jr., devoted part of his broadcast to revealing that the AEC had granted a predoctoral fellowship to an avowed Communist, Hans Freistadt. Two days later, Representative Cole read the text of the broadcast into the Congressional Record, while Senator Clyde Hoey informed the Senate of the matter.[7] Senator Hoey had received a letter from a student at the University of North Carolina complaining about this grant of funds to Freistadt, whose Communist activities were becoming a source of irritation to some of his fellow-students on the campus at Chapel Hill. Public interest in the Freistadt case was immediate, and grew rapidly. Senator McMahon announced that the Joint Committee would look into the matter, and an open hearing was set for May 16.

On May 18 another incident hit the headlines, although the Joint Committee had known of it since April 27. This was the loss of four grams of uranium-235 from the Argonne National Laboratory.[8] The incident was all the more disturbing in that the Commission learned of the missing U-235 in April, two months after the loss was first discovered on February 8. Notification of the FBI occurred on March 28, 1949. Together, the Freistadt fellowship and the loss of uranium generated a growing volume of public criticism in the days that followed.

In addition, two other matters of concern came privately to the attention of the Joint Committee. On April 28, the Commission sent a shipment of iron isotopes to the Norwegian defense establishment, for unclassified research of a scientific nature. It had apparently been a subject of Washington gossip for some time that the Commission was divided on the foreign distribution of isotopes, but that was the first shipment to a foreign military establishment, and it seemed to Senator Hickenlooper, as he said later, a clear violation of the Act.

Finally, the AEC's internal report on a startling overrun in the construction costs of a production facility at Hanford came to the attention of the Joint Committee. The report was highly critical of both the AEC and the contractor at Hanford, General Electric.

Another factor which influenced the Hickenlooper investigation was the reaction of the AEC to criticism of its fellowship policy. It is probably safe to say that this, more than any other single issue, brought on the Congressional loss of confidence in Mr. Lilienthal. In this controversy, Lilienthal met the initial criticism with a sweeping defense of AEC's policy. He took his stand at the open hearings on fellowships conducted by the Joint Committee on May 16 and succeeding days.[9]

The National Research Council was directing the choice of persons to receive AEC fellowships. It was the Council's view, of course, that FBI investigation of fellows to be engaged in nonsecret work would be unwise. Mr. Lilienthal supported this viewpoint, and warned against the potentially dangerous infringement of academic freedom implicit in such investigations.

When Representative Elston asked him what the AEC's policy would be if the Council recommended a Communist, Mr. Lilienthal answered that there were two alternatives. One would be to accept the recommendation, the other to "accept the resignation" of the National Research Council. By far the lesser evil would be to go along with the experienced judgment of the Council, in Mr. Lilienthal's opinion.[10]

In taking this position, Mr. Lilienthal doubtless expected the full support of the National Research Council. What he got was somewhat less. Dr. A. N. Richards, head of the National Academy of Sciences, and Dr. D. W. Bronk, Chairman of the Council, also testified.[11] They agreed with several Committee members that steps had to be taken to prevent recurrence of such a case as Freistadt's. Both assured the Joint Committee that neither the Academy nor the National Research Council would be offended if the AEC subjected persons who had been recommended by the Council to additional tests for subversive views. Dr. Richards suggested that fellowship recipients should be required to sign a loyalty oath.

Mr. Lilienthal thus only added fuel to the fire. His opposition to any interference (whether by loyalty oath or investigation) with the National Research Council's choice of fellows and his forthright admission that, if the Council recommended a Communist, he would accept the Council's judgment, were incomprehensible to many Congressmen, who felt that even the faintest possibility of using government funds to educate a Communist was unthinkable.

■

The controversy surrounding the AEC had grown to considerable proportions by the third week in May. Although there had been talk for some days of a general investigation into the administration of the project, Senator Hickenlooper finally brought it on with his charge, on May 22, of "incredible mismanagement." [12] The observer can only speculate on the various factors entering into the decision to issue such a strong condemnation of Mr. Lilienthal's administration. At the time, the press pointed out repeatedly that the Senator was to be up for re-election in 1950, and that a movement was developing in Iowa to oppose him in the primaries. This doubtless was of some significance, but another more compelling consideration suggests itself. Whatever may be said of the intemperateness of Senator Hickenlooper's charges, it is not surprising that he felt it necessary to react in some way. He, after all, had been chairman of the Joint Committee during its first two years. He, more than any other member of Congress, was in a position to know and evaluate the Commission's work. When one disclosure after another seemed to cast doubt on the soundness of the Commission's policies, the Senator could hardly have remained silent. To have done so would have cast doubts on the manner in which he had fulfilled his *own* responsibility as head of the Congressional group charged with continuing surveillance of the atomic energy project.

As a further factor, interviewees have pointed out that Senator Vandenberg at this time expressed dissatisfaction with Mr. Lilienthal on the subject of security. Senator Hickenlooper, it is said, attached great weight to the opinions of the Senator from Michigan, and felt that these expressions of disagreement by Senator Vandenberg made it all the more appropriate for the former Joint Committee chairman to state publicly his own disagreements and misgivings regarding the Commission and the program.

David Lilienthal replied to Senator Hickenlooper's charge of "incredible mismanagement" by demanding, in a letter to Senator McMahon, a full-scale investigation of the AEC.[13] He suggested a broad survey of the atomic energy program, including a comparison of the project at that time with its condition when the Commission took over. Such comparison was desirable, he felt, with respect to production and improvement of weapons, production of fissionable materials, basic and applied research, physical security, and investigation and clearance of personnel.

The Joint Committee ordered the investigation, and Senator McMahon, to facilitate the probe, turned the Committee staff over to Senator Hickenlooper, who was to act as chief inquisitor. On May 26, at a preliminary session, Mr. Lilienthal restated his hope that the investigation would be a full one, not "only one dealing with particular episodes, and the occurrences and instances of operation, such as the missing uranium oxide and the fellowship issue, but where, on the fundamental questions, we are after two years of the operation of the Atomic Energy Commission under the McMahon Act." [14]

Senator Hickenlooper replied to this, admitting that he had no specific questions to ask because he had not received prompt notice of the meeting, but elaborating on his conceptions of the problems involved:

The issues are in administrative policies, not so much in the matter of quantum production.

The issues, as I have them in mind, are in the general trend and tenor of the progress of administration and policies which not only in the past but now, and, from an indication, in the future, will mitigate one way or another on the future progress and development of this great new and unique operation in which the American people are so vitally interested. . . .

From the standpoint of actual production, the Atomic Energy program has gone forward due to the zeal and the loyalty of the scientific and technical personnel in charge of the various projects. The point of my objection is not to the activities of these people but to the administrative policies which the Commission under Mr. Lilienthal's guidance and influence has followed and continues to follow. These I believe to be harmful and not in the best interests of the continuing development of the basic programs outlined by Congress.[15]

The Senator began his presentation of evidence on June 1, and continued it throughout the month. His first assertion was that there had been a startling lack of continuity in a number of key administrative positions in the AEC. Mr. Lilienthal presented figures indicating that the Commission's separation rate was only slightly above that for the federal government as a whole.[16]

Senator Hickenlooper then turned to more controversial matters of security.[17] His first criticism was of the large number of emergency clearances granted by the Commission, according to information furnished to the Senator since 1947. In reply, Mr. Lilienthal explained that a full FBI investigation was too time-consuming and that, after an emergency clearance, it could be conducted while the employee was on the job. He later furnished the information that in only nine out of 4,095 emergency clearances was employment later terminated because investigation indicated the possibility of questionable associations. Throughout his argument ran the AEC's emphasis on security by achievement, while Senator Hickenlooper pointed out the virtues of security by concealment and insisted that the AEC's policy of granting large numbers of emergency clearances was undesirable.

Senator Hickenlooper went on to a consideration of the AEC's general personnel security procedures. He undertook to deal with specific cases, without identifying the persons by name, in which employment was allowed or continued in spite of the disclosure of derogatory information. In discussing "Case A," however, the Senator identified the person as the one who prepared the AEC's top-secret reports to the Committee. Mr. Lilienthal objected strongly that this was the same as giving the employee's name, and protested the exposure of "Case A" to unfair attack without allowing him a chance to defend himself. At this point, Senator McMahon suggested an executive session to decide upon future procedure in such cases. The discussion that followed was inconclusive, and the personnel security cases thereupon disappeared from the public record, to be considered later in secret session.

Blocked in his attempt to establish AEC laxity in respect to employment of "questionable" persons, Senator Hickenlooper brought up the shipment of isotopes to the Norwegian defense establishment. This he described as a "departure from the announced policy and I believe a clear violation of the purposes and program as laid down by the President, as well as by the Commission. . . ."

Mr. Lilienthal replied that, in fact, no violation had occurred. The Act provided that, "There shall be no exchange of information with other nations with respect to the use of atomic energy for industrial purposes" [Section 10(A)1]. He maintained, however, that (1) radioactive isotopes are not atomic energy, and (2) that isotopes are not in themselves "information."

On issues such as this, it became apparent that the General Advisory Committee was always wholeheartedly in support of Chairman Lilienthal's position. However, indications of a split in the Commission itself were revealed. One member, Admiral Strauss, had dissented on a number of these same issues when the Commission had considered them. His dissents now served to weaken Mr. Lilienthal's position which otherwise would have been strong because of the solidarity of support in the Executive branch.

Shifting from matters of security, Senator Hickenlooper next called attention to the overrun on the production facility at Hanford. The estimate on this installation jumped from $6,255,000 in December, 1947, to $25,219,000 in January, 1949. The Senator's criticism was this:

> I believe this is true . . . that the Commission itself did not know of this great over-run, and the unusual almost quadrupling of this contract until one of the Commissioners on a routine inspection trip early this year . . . in the course of a routine investigation discovered this matter.
>
> In other words, the point is, and I think it is amply proven in this report, that because of a lack of organizational set up in the Atomic Energy Commission, these matters of this tremendous over-run from $6,000,000 to $25,000,000 were not brought to the attention of the Commission, and that the Commission's methods of checking caused an error there in which overages of this kind can and in fact in this instance did occur.

Mr. Lilienthal, explaining the overrun, stressed that the scope of the work was considerably enlarged between the two estimates and that it was urgently necessary to complete this facility in order to take immediate advantage of the Eniwetok tests. He also defended the Commission's practice of allowing its contractors wide discretion. A General Electric spokesman then described his company's excellent over-all record, but admitted some laxity in reporting the overrun as it developed.

Senator Hickenlooper next launched into a discussion of another matter which was not promptly reported to the Commissioners, the FBI, or the Joint Committee. This was the uranium loss at the Argonne National Laboratory.[18] Most of the hearing was occupied by the testimony of Dr. W. H. Zinn, head of the Laboratory, and Dr. Ernest W. Thiele, special consultant to the Joint Committee. These gentlemen testified that four grams of U-235 were still missing, but that there was little likelihood of foul play.[19]

During the next ten days Senator Hickenlooper moved rapidly over a number of matters. He questioned the AEC on an over-run in connection with the new Hanford junior high school, and on several other minor matters at Hanford. He alleged extravagance and faulty construction in housing at Los Alamos. He noted, in respect to Oak Ridge, a number of complaints about veteran employment, and high fixed fees paid to the community and transportation contractors, and the high cost of concrete garbage can bases furnished to the dwellings there.

Having touched on these and other aspects of the program, Senator Hickenlooper announced on the last day of June that he could proceed no further until the Joint Committee took action in connection with the personnel security cases being dealt with in executive session. Senator McMahon thereupon gave the AEC an opportunity to make what Mr. Lilienthal called an "affirmative" presentation rather than a defense—a general accounting of the Commission's stewardship.[20]

The Commission's account of its stewardship put the principal stress on "security by achievement." Mr. Lilienthal first outlined the accomplishments of the AEC in terms of production, weapons, research, and the like. Dr. R. F. Bacher, a former Commissioner, testified in more detail as to the serious condition of the project in 1947, and the advances of the first two years in overcoming such problems as lack of topflight scientific personnel and pile deterioration at Hanford. Following Dr.

Bacher were a number of witnesses from the AEC and its various advisory committees.[21]

After ten days of testimony, the AEC rested its case, and the Joint Committee retired to executive session. Senator McMahon later revealed that he had written to all the Committee members, prior to the conclusion of the AEC's presentation, asking whether any other witnesses should be called or documents requested. He received no replies.

Six executive sessions were held on the personnel security cases. At five of these, a quorum was not present. Senator McMahon's letters to the Committeemen were to no avail, and so on August 25 he announced that the investigation was closed.

The Senator pointed out, however, that the Joint Committee was not leaving a job half done, for it had already laboriously explored personnel security problems. He noted that the group had

> . . . devoted upwards of ten meetings to problems growing out of personnel security. Of 34 cases brought specifically to the Committee's attention, 14 or more have been discussed in considerable detail, and much additional meeting time has been spent considering the standards that should be applied in evaluating the Commission's personnel security decisions. Even further, summaries of all the 34 specific cases have been made available to individual Committee members for some time.
>
> I feel that the Committee, as regards personnel security cases, has already done its job and done it thoroughly.[22]

Not until October 13 did the majority of the Joint Committee publish its report, with the minority issuing separate views subsequently.[23] In the intervening period, the President announced that the Soviet Union had achieved its first atomic explosion.[24] This event, coming some years earlier than American scientists had predicted, had wide repercussions, some of which will be considered more fully later. But among its immediate effects was the note of urgency in the Joint Committee reports on the Hickenlooper investigation, which put greater stress on driving ahead with the atomic energy program than might otherwise have been the case.

The report of the majority first examined the paramount objective of the Act—"assuring the common defense and security" —and noted that this calls for the striking of a "sane and judicious" balance between two indispensable but competing elements: security by achievement and security by concealment. The majority took up the former first, discussing in detail the Commission's achievements with respect to weapons, production, reactor development, research, and community operations. This was followed by consideration of security by concealment —personnel security, physical security, control of information, and related topics.

In its conclusion, the report questioned Senator Hickenlooper's charges, and pointed out the evidence:

1) That responsibility for the direction of the atomic energy program was vested in five men, not just Chairman Lilienthal (against whom the original charges were made);

2) That no complaints had come from either the President or the MLC;

3) That the overwhelming number of decisions reached by the five-man Commission had been unanimous;

4) That the GAC vigorously supported the Commission;

5) That the Joint Committee had been furnished with information regarding most of the topics discussed since 1947 without taking any critical action; and

6) That the accusations of "incredible mismanagement," "misplaced emphasis," "maladministration," "waste," and "equivocation" gave the impression that

. . . we lack a substantial bomb stock pile, that little progress has been made in weapon design, that production of fissionable materials is slow, and that our research efforts are faltering. But when the indictment was made specific at the investigation, such matters were left outside the area of criticism. In fact, the results achieved during the past 2½ years were conceded to be good. Here is one phase of the paradox.

The other phase becomes clear by considering that the committee has before it an indictment which, on the one hand, says the results are good but which, on the other hand, insists the management is bad. . . . Every axiom of experience leads toward the conclusion that both management and results have been good or that both have been poor.

Accordingly, since the indictment itself concedes that results are commendable, this same indictment tends to rebut its own allegations of mismanagement.

The majority then summarized. From the evidence submitted at the hearings, a satisfactory balance had in fact been struck between security by achievement and security by concealment, said the report. Nor had there been any violation of the McMahon Act. The majority specifically approved the AEC's decisions to retain control of its communities and to perpetuate the contractor system, although it did point out certain shortcomings in both areas and in progress on reactor development. This criticism was immediately softened:

> . . . entries on the debit side of the Commission's ledger involve account books covering an industry which extends through 41 States in our own country alone and 1,270 locations ranging through half the world. This industry occupies more land than all the area of Rhode Island; it utilizes more than 1,000 contractors and subcontractors, plus other thousands of suppliers; it directly conditions the lives of 200,000 people, including employees and their dependents; and it spends a billion dollars yearly. In proportion to the scope of the account books, debit entries are well scattered through pages of accomplishment.

Later in the month appeared the minority views. Senator Vandenberg did not associate himself with any of the reports. Representative Hinshaw submitted a separate opinion in which he said he could not disagree with the majority but regretted its glossing over of certain deficiencies. The other six Republicans —Senators Hickenlooper, Millikin, and Knowland, Representatives Cole, Elston, and Van Zandt—disagreed with the report of the majority. They first criticized the AEC's approach to the supreme task of carrying out programs "that will strengthen our reserve of atomic materials and aid the objective of capturing and having available for effective use the largest practicable degree of the power of those atomic materials for weapon and other purposes." The Commission's approach to this task, they asserted, had been leisurely and indecisive. This clearly was not the point of Senator Hickenlooper's charges, nor the point over which the minority had previously been exercised; the influence of the Soviet atomic explosion is obvious. The minority went on to criticize security practices, and to allege inadequate supervision of area managers and contractors.

Representative Hinshaw specifically said that the majority report is an "interesting and informative essay . . . smartly designed to both give due credit to the Atomic Energy Commission for its many accomplishments and at the same time to indicate to the careful reader that there is plenty of room for criticism of its failures and shortcomings. However, the criticism is well hidden in the haystack of language." As a result, Representative Hinshaw did not "disagree" with the majority report, but regretted the circumstances which compelled the majority "to rise to defend the Commission and its Chairman politically."

Representative Hinshaw clearly put his finger on the partisan motivations behind the language of the majority report. The same was equally true of the minority report. Taken together, they represent the partisan division among the members of the Joint Committee which had existed all along.

■

It is always difficult to assess the significance of an isolated series of events in the life of any organization, and it is doubly so in the case of the Hickenlooper inquiry into the AEC. The announcement, on September 23, that Soviet Russia had successfully detonated an atomic explosion introduced an element of urgency and confusion into what had been, until then, a fairly clear-cut case of basic disagreement. The announcement had a profound effect on those who had been the staunch advocates of "security by concealment." It destroyed forever the hope, which many had held, that the "big secret" could be kept indefinitely by the United States. Probably the Hickenlooper inquiry by itself would have enabled some members of the Joint Committee to get the narrow preoccupation with security out of their systems —at least the interview data suggest this likelihood—but the Soviet explosion provided a considerably more potent purgative than any Congressional investigation possibly could.

Another obstacle to discovering the impact of the Joint Committee's inquiry on AEC policies lies in the fact that pressure for policy alteration came not exclusively from the Joint Committee, but from the Appropriations Committees, other Congressmen, the press and radio, and the general public. The controversy over the AEC, as we know, was a public controversy, discussed throughout the nation. One of the most hotly disputed issues— the fellowship program—was finally decided not by the Joint Committee, which held the first hearings on the matter, but by a rider attached to appropriations legislation by the Senate Appropriations Subcommittee members under the leadership of Senator O'Mahoney.[25] The Senate subcommittee was holding hearings on AEC funds in May, 1949, when the fellowship issue and the uranium-235 loss came into the limelight. For a time it seemed that there would be a jurisdictional squabble between the Joint Committee and the Senate subcommittee, for the latter was as disturbed by the AEC policies, especially regarding fellowships, as was the Joint Committee, and the two groups were hearing the same witnesses on the same subjects.

Furthermore, the Joint Committee was not even responsible for bringing to light the Freistadt fellowship issue. A radio broadcast by Fulton Lewis, Jr., and a letter to Senator Clyde Hoey of North Carolina, read by him on the floor of the upper chamber, set off the controversy.

For these reasons, it cannot be said that the Joint Committee, through its formal inquiry, was responsible for all the repercussions of the controversy over atomic energy which occurred during May, June, and July of 1949. One final difficulty is this: While it is true that Joint Committee pressure affected AEC policies and procedures, one must be careful not to interpret the pressure which gave impetus to an already existing trend as the pressure which initiated the trend.

But in spite of these difficulties, some conclusions can be clearly drawn from the Hickenlooper investigation.

What of Senator Hickenlooper's charge of "incredible mismanagement," brought against David Lilienthal? There is no doubt that the Senator failed to prove his case. It became clear that his specific charges against the administration of the project were largely peripheral. Most of them were answered successfully by the Commission. It is true that on a few occasions Senator Hickenlooper pointed out aspects of the AEC's operations which were open to criticism, but in doing so he failed almost completely to consider the atomic energy program as a whole. He made no specific charges of misemphasis or significant breakdown in the program. His charge of "incredible mismanagement" had been startling and evocative; his documentation of it consisted chiefly of pot shots at the fringes of the project.

The failure of the inquiry to live up to the expectations which had been shared by many people can be seen clearly in the treatment given to it by the press.[26] In late May and early June, every front page told of the accusations and exposures in connection with the atomic energy project. The investigation itself got off to an auspicious start in the Senate caucus room, scene of many highly publicized investigations before and since. The setting reminded one of the 1948 Howard Hughes investigation, which had been completed a few months before in the same room before the same battery of cameras and newsmen.

In less than ten days, responsible newspapers were suggesting that the hearings had failed to reveal as much as was expected, and that Senator Hickenlooper was not proving his charges. As the days went by the amount of coverage given the investigation dropped, and the newspapers and commentators in increasing numbers reported that Senator Hickenlooper was taking up a great deal of the AEC's time without establishing any substantial evidence of maladministration.

The minority report itself offers evidence of the fact that "incredible mismanagement" simply was not proved. After condemning the Commission for lack of aggressiveness, of all things, the minority found only minor instances of lax security and imperfect contractor supervision to point out. These hardly amounted to basic shortcomings which would support such serious charges as the Senator's.

Although the investigation failed to justify Senator Hickenlooper's attack on Mr. Lilienthal, its effect on the Commission was nevertheless great. In the first place, it was clearly a difficult ordeal for the Commission. From the first of June until well into July, the AEC's energies were divided between running the project and defending the record. This meant a number of things.

There were long hours of testifying at the hearings themselves. Needless to say, the Commission could not send one or two subordinates to present the AEC position on the matters under discussion. The Commissioners themselves appeared, almost invariably no less than four of the five, and they were usually backed by a dozen or so AEC and contractor officials. Mr. Lilienthal, of course, was the primary object of attack, and he took the major role among the Commissioners. On occasion, however, other Commissioners carried the burden. Mr. Pike, for example, represented the AEC when the Joint Committee's attention was focused on the decision of the AEC to construct a natural gas pipeline to Oak Ridge despite formally stated Congressional opposition.

The necessity of appearing at the hearings with a substantial contingent of the high-level staff became even more disrupting to the AEC's normal operations on the occasions when notice of questions to be taken up by Senator Hickenlooper did not reach the Commission or became confused in the process of communication. Mr. Lilienthal at one point specifically requested that he be given accurate notification of the proposed subjects of discussion so that he would not again bring valuable personnel with him to testify on matters familiar to them, only to have their time wasted during discussion of completely different matters.[27] The Commission also faced the opposite problem of being unprepared for matters which Senator Hickenlooper did bring up. In addition, defense of its record meant for the AEC not merely appearances before the Joint Committee, but also long hours of evening and Sunday work in preparing its case and in fulfilling the Joint Committee's requests for information, facts, and figures.

The efforts which the inquiry required of the AEC, then, were substantial simply in terms of man-hours expended. Moreover, they were efforts made under extreme pressure. The attack on Mr. Lilienthal and his administration went on unremittingly inside and outside Congress. Perhaps the most persistent critic was Fulton Lewis, Jr., the radio commentator, but his was only one of many voices raised against Mr. Lilienthal.[28] The military interest, too, was reawakened, and those who still deplored civilian control took this occasion to speak out against the Commission. As a focus for these elements, Senator Harry Cain introduced his proposal to abolish the AEC and restore military control.[29]

It may be assumed that the Commission realized that the passage of such a measure was extremely unlikely in the absence of proof of a fundamental inadequacy in the AEC. What was much more likely of passage was a measure sponsored by the Joint Committee itself providing for the specific authorization of AEC projects. Authorizing legislation had been under consideration by the Joint Committee staff for some months, and the need for it seemed particularly great after the AEC's decision to go ahead with the natural gas pipeline in spite of Joint Committee opposition. During the Hickenlooper investigation, the pipeline incident and the Hanford overrun excited considerable discussion of the proposal. Representative Kilday came out publicly in favor of it, and Senator McMahon and Representative Durham introduced bills [30] on July 7 which would have required Congressional authorization for (1) the programs set forth in the annual AEC budget and (2) the total amount of money and contract authorization annually requested (including deficiency budget requests).

These two bills naturally were referred back to the Joint Committee on Atomic Energy. Senator McMahon revealed about a week later that, as a result of discussions with the AEC, the Joint Committee had decided not to take immediate action on the measure. The Senator stated, however, that he did expect to get the proposal to the floor before consideration of the next Independent Offices Appropriation bill.[31]

The AEC, then, was being hammered from all sides, and threatened by Congress with legislation which would formalize the procedures necessary to launch new projects, greatly increasing the Joint Committee's leverage with the Commission. In addition to the impact which all this pressure must have had, Mr. Lilienthal sustained a specific defeat on the fellowship policy, on which he had taken a strong stand, and he was condemned in many quarters for his attitude toward security generally.

The long-range effects of this general pressure, for which the Joint Committee was more or less a representative, were several. It is probably true that the inquiry was in part responsible for an effort by the AEC to reform and improve its security practices, but there is also evidence that the effort had begun before the formal inquiry was opened.[32]

Again, the so-called Hanford overrun came in for detailed consideration at the inquiry, and the loose system of contractor controls, exemplified by the communication breakdown in the Hanford overrun, was criticized in both majority and minority reports. Interview data indicate, however, that Joint Committee hammering on this point did not constitute a turning point in Commission policy, but that prior evidence had convinced the AEC of the need for altered contractor supervision practices, with a shift toward better supervision already in progress in the spring of 1949.[33]

It should be pointed out that the decentralized operation was already being slowly abandoned by the Atomic Energy Commission for various reasons. One of these was undoubtedly the fact that the AEC was unable to satisfy the Joint Committee that it was sufficiently in control of its operations. Another reason was that it was unable to satisfy the Appropriations Committee on the same question. A third reason was that the inner workings of the AEC itself were leading to this transformation. The program directors were becoming more control-minded and were pulling the reins tighter over the field officers; they were at times by-passing the General Manager in order to get to the Commission itself. In other words, a gradual centralization was taking place throughout the whole administrative structure of the AEC, only part of which can be attributed to the influence of the Joint Committee.

An indirect result of the inquiry and the Committee-AEC friction, and a far more significant result than any specific policy alteration, was the departure of David Lilienthal. It is true that Mr. Lilienthal successfully defended his record on the whole, and that the Democratic majority of the Joint Committee defended him in reporting on the investigation. Nevertheless, the controversy at the time of the inquiry resulted in a widespread loss of confidence in Mr. Lilienthal. In spite of his vindication on most counts, many people who were closely involved felt that his usefulness as chairman of the AEC was at an end. Clearly the hearings indicated that Republican support had been completely dissipated [34] and that even Democratic support was more partisan than sincere.

The consensus among those interviewed is that the defeats and the loss of confidence just before and during the Hickenlooper investigation, in addition to the growing tension between Mr. Lilienthal and the Joint Committee, made it certain that he would leave the project soon thereafter. It was reported in the press before Senator Hickenlooper's charges were issued that Mr. Lilienthal was planning to resign then.[35] He of course did not do so, but chose to stay and fight to clear his name of the alleged maladministration. In spite of this successful endeavor, interview data suggest that the die was cast, and the investigation made it certain that he would terminate his government service.

■

At this point, a particular incident in the relations of the AEC and the Joint Committee must be recounted in order to reveal the extreme point of AEC independence. Called the "natural gas pipeline controversy," it occurred at the time of the Hickenlooper inquiry, but it was not part of the "incredible mismanagement" theme of the rest of the investigation. Rather it was an example of the AEC's lack of sensitivity to the wishes of the Joint Committee, which in this case acted as the spokesmen for strong economic interests.

The facts of the case are briefly as follows. Plans for bringing natural gas to Oak Ridge had been in the making since 1948, with construction about to begin in May, 1949.[36] They were based on fear that it was risky to rely on coal as the single fuel source. At this point, Chairman McMahon received protests, and he appointed a subcommittee to investigate. This subcommittee submitted a report on the day after Senator Hickenlooper made his "incredible mismanagement" charges. In the report, the members took issue with the Commission's reasoning on the need for an additional fuel supply, and complained that the action was taken without consultation with the National Security Resources Board. The subcommittee recommended that the Joint Committee be given power to deal with similar cases in the future.

This subcommittee report was submitted to the full Committee, which adopted it unanimously. The Joint Committee then sent the report to the AEC, together with a statement of unanimous endorsement. In addition, Senator McMahon telephoned the Commission, and suggested that any further action on the pipeline should be delayed. Mr. Shugg, the Deputy General Manager, passed this message to Commissioners Lilienthal and Pike. A few days later, on June 2, the newspapers carried a story released by the pipeline company, stating that they were pushing ahead with construction of the line.

In view of these facts, Senator Hickenlooper and other Committee members were very eager, at the investigation, to learn what action, if any, the AEC had taken as a result of such a clearly expressed Joint Committee viewpoint. Commissioner Pike, as the chief AEC spokesman, tried to convince Committee members, first, that they, the Committeemen, had underestimated the case for building the pipeline, and second, that the AEC had given due consideration to the strong manifestation of Joint Committee opinion.

He said that the AEC had held a meeting, decided the original decision was sound, and had begun to draft a letter asking for a meeting with the full Committee. Because the impending Hickenlooper investigation seemed to offer such an opportunity, or because of sheer oversight, the letter was not sent. Commissioner Pike was vague on this point. He was interrogated sharply by Senator Hickenlooper and Representatives Cole, Elston, and Van Zandt, in such exchanges as this:

> *Representative Van Zandt.* You received the suggestion and apparently did nothing about it.
> *Commissioner Pike.* I took it up with the Commission, I think, the next time we met; whether it was the next morning or not, I am not sure. We had several days go by without doing it at a Commission meeting at all. I would have to check the record.
> . . .
> *Representative Van Zandt.* Well, apparently the Commission disregards entirely the suggestions of this committee, and—
> *Commissioner Pike.* I do not think it has been our policy. . . .
> *Representative Van Zandt.* Apparently; no action was taken. You must understand that we, the members of the committee, represent various sections of the country, and we have the economy

of this country at heart just the same as you people should have, and our suggestions are apparently tabled; period.[37]

Other Committee members joined the discussion from time to time. Representative Holifield, for example, felt that there was a case either way on building the line, but he agreed with Senator McMahon's suggestion that the Joint Committee ought to have power to authorize all substantial AEC projects in the future.

There seems to be no later instance of such categorical AEC insistence on its own viewpoint against a clearly enunciated Joint Committee opposition. The ordeal of months of grueling investigation created an attitude of caution in the Commission. Former decisions, policies, and practices were examined and reexamined. The importance of a clear record, without evidence of errors of judgment in policy formulation or execution, was dramatized to the Commission as never before. The impression of the inquiry was not a fleeting one, but remained as an indication of the seriousness and the potency of an investigation as a Joint Committee weapon. The inquiry was felt throughout the AEC as a lesson to the organization that a recurrence of this ordeal was to be avoided.

As for the Joint Committee members, the psychological effect of the inquiry was no less a factor in their later behavior. The Republican minority had developed a strong opposition to the Lilienthal leadership of the AEC, which of course was the moving factor in the inquiry. While the investigation itself did not change this opposition into warm support, interview data indicate that it did have a considerably chastening effect on the minority Joint Committee members. There was evidently some realization that the preoccupation with detail which had characterized the approach of this part of the Committee was in fact a complete neglect of the Commission's achievements or shortcomings in the really important aspects of the program.

Moreover, the minority members felt that they could reduce their stress on these minor matters after the inquiry. The issues had been brought out and public attention was focused on them, whereas formerly they were not known to the public nor to the Congress as a whole. With every indication that the pressure from various sources was resulting in tighter security and better control and supervision at the Commission level, the minority members could relax their vigilance to some extent and join with the majority in broader consideration of the program.

The inquiry, then, gave rise to a tendency in the direction of closer AEC-Joint Committee harmony. It made for a more cautious AEC policy, which would inspire more confidence among members of the Committee, and it enabled the critical Committee members to rid themselves of some of their narrow preoccupations so that they could acquire a sympathetic approach to the agency and the program in the future.

■

Though important, the Hickenlooper inquiry was soon overshadowed by the events which followed the Soviet Union's atomic explosion. While news of the Soviet A-bomb had far-reaching effects on the Congressional and public approach to the problems of atomic secrecy, its most spectacular repercussion was the controversy over the hydrogen bomb. The general public knew little of this intense struggle which went on behind the scenes throughout the fall and part of the winter of 1949–1950. The secrecy was broken by a celebrated television broadcast made by Senator Edwin Johnson of the Joint Committee on November 1.[38] The Senator referred to the top-level consideration then being given to a new "super-weapon," many times more powerful than the atomic bombs of Hiroshima and Nagasaki. Such a weapon, he said, was believed feasible by the scientists, if they were given the funds for facilities and the

authority to proceed. Senator Johnson's remarks were reported
by the newspapers, and by mid-December Washington was filled
with rumors of top-secret policy conferences on the awesome
hydrogen bomb. Following this came President Truman's January 31 announcement that careful consideration of the alternatives had led him to order the Atomic Energy Commission to
proceed with development of the H-bomb.[39]

It may never be possible to give a complete, accurate account
of the opinions and discussions which preceded the H-bomb
decision. Many relevant conversations were never recorded;
those that were, remained classified, together with the few documents and memoranda on the subject. However, the broad outlines of the controversy have been publicly revealed since 1950,
and this information, supplemented by interview data, gives us a
general view of the forces which were acting upon one another
in the conferences over the "super-bomb."

The theory of using fusion rather than fission to produce the
explosive release of vast quantities of energy was not new in
1949. As early as April, 1942, principally in conversations between Dr. Edward Teller and Dr. Enrico Fermi, the possibility
of such a fusion reaction was established. After the intense wartime efforts had materialized in the A-bomb, there was discussion within the newly organized Atomic Energy Commission of
going ahead rapidly in the thermonuclear field toward a workable H-bomb. Although a handful of scientists continued a
limited research program, the AEC determined not to support a
full-scale H-bomb effort—a decision which interview sources
say was not revealed to the Joint Committee at that time.[40]

Chairman Cole of the Joint Committee has described the factors which led to this decision:

At the end of World War II, there was a general slowdown
in our entire military program, including atomic weapon develop-

ment. This relaxation was due in large measure to a general belief that a lasting peace had been accomplished, that we would enjoy atomic monopoly for some years, and that there would be international control of atomic weapons.

Consequently, no major consideration was given to the question of undertaking active development of an H-bomb, although a small, research program on thermonuclear energy was continued.[41]

Before the issue was reopened in September, 1949, according to the same sources, the Joint Committee had occasionally discussed the hydrogen bomb with the Commission. There was, however, no sustained pressure for a reversal of the original negative decision, in spite of the sentiment in favor of the H-bomb in the Committee. Immediately after the President's revelation of the Soviet atomic explosion, however, the Joint Committee asked its staff to canvass the possibilities for United States countermoves. The resulting staff paper suggested that the achievement of a workable H-bomb would again afford this nation a substantial advantage in military might, but the AEC responded, as it had to previous Joint Committee comment, that it was doing all that could be done in thermonuclear work.

According to interviewees, the debate opened in earnest when Commissioner Strauss submitted a memorandum to the other Commissioners on October 5, 1949.[42] In this document Admiral Strauss expressed his conviction that a "quantum jump" was necessary for the United States to regain its clear weapons supremacy. He advised convening the General Advisory Committee to consider, not *whether* to proceed as fast as possible with the H-bomb, but *how* to proceed.

The Commission did in fact request an opinion from the General Advisory Committee. The GAC at that time was made up of eight prominent scientists and engineers, in addition to Dr. Oppenheimer, the chairman.[43] Eight of the nine attended the

October meetings to consider and answer two related questions submitted by the Commission: first, whether, in the light of the Soviet atomic explosion, the AEC's program was adequate (and if not, in what way it should be altered), and second, whether a "crash" program for development of the H-bomb, known as the "super," should be part of a new program.

The GAC report, according to Dr. Oppenheimer, made a number of specific recommendations in answer to question one. Regarding question two, however, the Committee was unanimous in opposing a "crash" program to create a fusion bomb. Most of the report dealt with technical aspects of the problem, but two separate annexes were attached to explain the political and moral considerations which the members felt compelled them to their negative recommendation.

Early in November, the AEC gathered together the available evidence, including the GAC recommendations, and prepared a memorandum to be sent to the White House. It stated that any decision in favor of a "crash" thermonuclear program was so important that it should be made by no one but the President himself. The document gave background material of a technical nature, and reviewed considerations bearing on national security and the prevention of war. All five members of the AEC agreed to this, the main part of the memorandum.

The document also summarized the various opinions of the Commissioners. Although there was no formal vote on the issue, the opinions fell into two broad categories at this time. Chairman Lilienthal and Commissioners Pike and Smyth recommended against pushing development of the H-bomb on the basis of information then available. Commissioner Strauss said he strongly favored an immediate "crash" thermonuclear program, and Commissioner Dean expressed agreement, but with some slight qualifications.

Although the recommendations fell broadly into these two groups, the matter was so complex that the Commissioners sent additional, independent, advisory opinions to the President. No one of these statements was identical with any of the others; they all differed in their emphasis and, to some degree, in their conclusions. However, it is accurate to say that three of the members thought it best not to proceed, while the remaining two favored going ahead.

In the following weeks, it became clear that the State Department felt that no international advantage could be gained by postponing the H-bomb program (although the AEC did not receive a formal statement of this). It also turned out that the Department of Defense could specify certain military advantages in possessing such a bomb. On the basis of this additional information, Commissioner Smyth (and probably Commissioner Pike as well) moved into accord with the position favoring the thermonuclear program. At the time of the original memorandum, however, only the minority of Strauss and Dean assumed this position.

The two dissenting Commissioners took their case to the Joint Committee, where strong support developed.[44] This took concrete form in five letters which Senator McMahon sent to the President, urging the utmost speed in pushing ahead with the fusion bomb, and he spoke to Mr. Truman personally on several occasions. Interview sources reveal that the McMahon viewpoint had such support among Joint Committee members that the Committee, early in 1950, was considering submission of a formal resolution to the President, favoring development of the H-bomb.

All these various strands and more came together on the last day of January, 1950, when the final decision resulted from two remarkable meetings in Washington. The President had designated three men as a National Security Council subcommittee to make a recommendation to him. These three were Dean Acheson, then Secretary of State, Louis Johnson, then Secretary of Defense, and David E. Lilienthal. This subcommittee, interview data indicate, had made plans for a prolonged consideration of the issue over a period of six weeks or so. On January 30, however, Secretary of Defense Johnson got word from England of the arrest of Klaus Fuchs, the atomic scientist who had worked with the most secret data at the Los Alamos Laboratory from August, 1944, until June, 1946. The degree of Fuchs's aid to the Soviet Union was, of course, not precisely calculable, but it was obvious that the Russians had not achieved the A-bomb entirely on their own, and the uncertainty as to just how much Fuchs had given to them made it even more urgent that the United States take immediate steps to counteract the Soviet gains. As a result, the three-man subcommittee met, and the decision was made all in one hectic day, January 31, 1950.

The outlines of the two meetings are now a matter of public record. First, the three men conferred in the offices of the National Security Council, with top-level military and AEC personnel present. Secretaries Acheson and Johnson disagreed on many things, but they agreed on the advisability of immediate and full-scale efforts toward development of the super-bomb.

Mr. Lilienthal presented the opposing viewpoint. A number of arguments were put forward during the discussions. One was a technical problem; there was still considerable doubt concerning the technical feasibility of the thermonuclear weapon. A huge expenditure of time and money might give no results at all, or results which were dangerously inadequate.

Mr. Lilienthal also emphasized the point that any military values which the new weapon might provide could be attained far more easily, and with much less expense, by a new fission program which was then under way at Los Alamos. It was felt in some quarters that resources would be far more efficiently employed in expanding this program than in building the tremendously difficult H-bomb. It also seemed that a "crash" H-bomb program might actually weaken our position in fission weapons, and hinder possible future efforts at improving and diversifying them.

In an article written later, Chairman Lilienthal indicated that his principal objections went further.[45] Besides hindering the fission work, a "crash" program on the H-bomb would only perpetuate and strengthen our unjustified confidence in big bombs. He felt no such effort should be undertaken until we had carefully reassessed our military and diplomatic needs, and had developed a comprehensive program for maximum national security. In this program, fission and possibly fusion weapons would find their place, but their importance would no longer be magnified out of all proportion.

It is impossible to attribute priority to any one of the arguments against the H-bomb which were articulated by Mr. Lilienthal and others. Some interview sources have asserted that Mr. Lilienthal and many scientists objected most seriously on moral grounds. They felt, according to these interviewees, that such an inconceivably devastating weapon should not be built until every possible means of reaching a disarmament agreement with Soviet Russia had been exhausted. Probably this moral consideration was an element in the thoughts of some, although Mr. Lilienthal has stated that other reasons were dominant in his own mind.

At the first meeting with Acheson and Johnson, Chairman Lilienthal proposed a plan of action. In essence, the Lilienthal argument favored improving the A-bomb and creating new and flexible atomic weapons, while at the same time reviving efforts to achieve international control of all atomic weapons. Mr. Lilienthal's immediate suggestion was that the President "direct the

Secretary of State and the Secretary of Defense to undertake a re-examination of our objectives on our strategic plans" in the light of the probable atomic capacities of the USSR.

Mr. Lilienthal was outvoted, however, 2 to 1. The subcommittee drafted a statement which embodied essentially the Johnson proposals, and this was taken to the White House. In a ten-minute meeting, President Truman accepted the decision of the subcommittee majority and later that afternoon issued the announcement of his decision to order immediate work on development of the hydrogen bomb.

The H-bomb decision was clearly the end of the Lilienthal period in the sense that it showed how his point of view and methods were being, and were to be still more, displaced. It was a further indication that the AEC would have to listen to other voices than those of the scientists represented by their spokesmen on the GAC.

Moreover, the Joint Committee had clearly taken on new life under Chairman McMahon. It injected itself into the discussions of the H-bomb and took a prominent lead—even to the point of lobbying among the higher echelons of the Executive branch.

David E. Lilienthal submitted his resignation on November 23, 1949.[46] In his letter to the President, he did not specify his reasons for leaving, although he did express his wish to return to private life and "to engage in public discussion and public affairs with a greater latitude than is either feasible or suitable for one who carries specific public responsibilities." President Truman, in an exceedingly cordial reply, thanked the retiring chairman for "twenty years of public service in tough pioneering jobs, always under tremendous pressure and often under destructive criticism."

Although he had originally intended his resignation to take effect on December 31, Mr. Lilienthal stayed on after that date to continue the discussions of the H-bomb question. This settled, he left the Commission on February 15, 1950.

In effect, Mr. Lilienthal's departure signified an end to the influence of the group which had been loyal to him and to his point of view, and this in turn signified a pronounced change in the Atomic Energy Commission and the nature of its role in the national drama.

IV

The New Roles Unfold

The period following February 15, 1950, has been called "the Dean period," taking its name from Gordon Dean, who was AEC chairman until the summer of 1953. For five months after David Lilienthal left the Commission, however, the AEC was technically without a chairman, although Commissioner Pike acted in that capacity during the interim. On July 11, President Truman named Commissioner Dean to the chairmanship.

The events of the five-month-interim period foreshadow the coming of a new relationship between the Commission and the Joint Committee. Generally speaking, they denote the final passing into the background of the Oppenheimer-Lilienthal-Pike-Wilson regime, and the establishment of an era of harmony quite different from the final months of the Lilienthal period.

Several incidents of the Pike interim indicate the Joint Committee's loss of confidence in the Lilienthal viewpoint and the personnel associated with that viewpoint. The first occurred in April, 1950. At that time Senator McMahon and Representative Durham introduced in their respective chambers a bill [1] which, in its original form, would have raised the General Manager's salary, changed the term of that officer, then indeterminate, to three years, and terminated Carroll Wilson's tenure at the end of June, 1950. [2] The measure was referred back to the Joint Committee on Atomic Energy, as are all proposals dealing with atomic energy. In providing for an amended procedure after the end of June, the bill plainly required prompt action. Nevertheless, it remained in committee past that date and through the month of August.

While this proposed amendment remained pending, President Truman nominated the four incumbent Commissioners—Smyth, Murray, Dean, and Pike—to one-, two-, three-, and five-year terms, respectively.[3] (The current terms of all the Commissioners were to end at midnight on June 30, 1950.) On June 26, all were confirmed but Mr. Pike, whose nomination had not been reported out by the Joint Committee.

Three days later the Joint Committee's Senate Section met in open session to consider Mr. Pike's appointment.[4] Four House Committee members attended, although they had no responsibility for confirmations. The Senators engaged in a very general discussion of Mr. Pike's qualifications, without raising any specific charges. Later the Committee reconvened in executive session.

When the vote came on Mr. Pike, the Joint Committee's Senate members went on record 5 to 4 against the appointment. Senators Hickenlooper, Millikin, Knowland, Bricker, and Johnson opposed, and Senators McMahon, Russell, Connally, and Tydings supported the confirmation.

Commissioner Pike's tenure on the AEC expired at the end of June, and he therefore left the Commission, pending action on his reappointment. On July 10 the question came before the Senate.[5] Senator McMahon opened the debate by admitting that he still was not clear as to the reasons for the opposition to Mr. Pike. Senator Hickenlooper replied, first by stating that *his* judgment was based broadly on three and one-half years of observation of the Commission, and second by elaborating specific issues which he felt tipped the balance against Mr. Pike. Later Senator Johnson joined the debate, as did Senators Millikin and Knowland. Several Senators (including McMahon, O'Mahoney, and Douglas, among others) rose to speak in support of the nomination.

The case against Commissioner Pike, as it emerged on the Senate floor, was based on the following considerations:

1) His endorsement of the policy of granting large numbers of emergency clearances to AEC personnel.

2) His support of the policy of distributing radioactive isotopes to foreign countries.

3) His defense of the Commission's decision to go ahead with the natural gas pipeline at Oak Ridge.

4) His alleged laxity regarding the authorization given to Dr. Cyril Smith in 1948 to share information on the metallurgy of plutonium with the British (and his position in favor of sharing information with Great Britain generally).

5) His resistance to raising prices of ores which would have accelerated discovery and exploitation of domestic sources of uranium (urged, of course, by the two Senators from Colorado, both Joint Committee members).

6) His alleged lack of "diligence" in pursuing the development of the H-bomb.

7) His delay in filling the position of the AEC Director of Security, despite Joint Committee concern over such delay.

8) His support of policies of extreme decentralization which had led to the Commission's ignorance of certain expenditures and operations.

On all these matters the AEC had in the past disagreed with members of the Joint Committee, although it could by no means be said that all the evidence was known or that the Committeemen had been proved correct in their views. Mr. Pike was plainly considered an adherent of the Lilienthal policies, and he had therefore become discredited in the eyes of the Republican

Joint Committee members especially. Senator Millikin made this point during the debate:

> Mr. Pike has identified himself with those on the Commission—and I am not speaking of present members, but of those who have been on the Commission in the past—who condoned loose security practices. . . .
>
> On that Commission Mr. Pike was identified with those who showed loose practices in the selection of persons to the fellowship program which included a confessed Communist. Mr. Pike was identified with the policies which caused the Commission in several important areas to be completely ignorant of what was going on as to the expenditure of many millions of dollars.

The strong opposition to Sumner Pike among the Joint Committee members, then, was another aspect of their desire to get rid of the remaining vestiges of the Lilienthal regime. This opposition was strong enough to force the President to reassure the Senate that Mr. Pike would not be the new chairman (there were rumors that he would be) before that body voted in favor of confirmation, 55 to 24. Perhaps he had never seriously considered Mr. Pike for the chairmanship. If he had, the Senate debate on confirmation made it obvious that Pike was a controversial figure, as David Lilienthal had been, and Mr. Truman could scarcely have forgotten the storm of dissension which accompanied the Lilienthal confirmation in 1947. In any case, the President turned to Gordon Dean and appointed him the new chairman on July 11, the day after the Pike confirmation. This appointment was received with warm approval by the Joint Committee.[6] Thus began the three-year chairmanship of Gordon Dean, whose previous experience had been as a lawyer in business, government, and education.

Mr. Dean had been chairman less than a month when a third incident dramatized again the fact that a new era had begun.

On August 8, Carroll Wilson resigned from the General Man-
agership, stating that he "lacked confidence" in the new chairman and that he felt the interest of the American people could
not be served by his staying in office without such confidence.[7]

In his statement, Mr. Wilson also spoke of the way in which
the Commission was assuming "the direct role of management of
the program." He expressed the fear that this would lead to a
"cumbersome, slow-moving, administrative machine, incapable
of giving the country the kind of direction needed to maintain
and increase our leadership in the atomic field." Although Mr.
Dean declined to comment, the Joint Committee issued a statement expressing unanimously its confidence in the chairman.

With the departure of Carroll Wilson, the last important hold-
over from the Lilienthal period disappeared from the center of
influence.[8] One remembers that Lilienthal, Pike, and Wilson
were the only ones who received less than unanimous approval
from the Joint Committee at the very beginning, in early 1947.

As if to complete the work begun by the Hickenlooper inquiry, the Joint Committee late in August, 1950, reported out
the bill which originally had been designed to end Mr. Wilson's
tenure as General Manager.[9] In its amended form, this bill was
enacted, changing Section 2(a) to provide for appointment of
the General Manager by the Commission, rather than by the
President. The General Manager, under the amended provision
enacted into law, serves at the pleasure of the Commission, is
removable by the Commission, and receives compensation at a
rate fixed by the Commission but not to exceed $20,000 per
year. In this way the Joint Committee increased the authority of
the Commission vis-à-vis the General Manager, and took another step away from the policy of extreme decentralization
which had been followed under the Lilienthal chairmanship.

■

The "Lilienthal period" was clearly over. Lilienthal and Wilson were gone; Commissioner Pike remained but had been pushed into the background. (He resigned at the end of 1951, long before his term was to expire.) Commissioner Smyth, who with Lilienthal and Pike had been unwilling to go ahead with the H-bomb program based on the facts presented in November, 1949, also remained, but he was not strongly opposed to the new program, and the fact that he had come to the Commission in 1949 meant that he was not associated with the Lilienthal regime in the minds of the Congressmen. Dr. Oppenheimer stayed on as head of the General Advisory Committee until mid-1952, but interviewees have said that his viewpoint, which originally had been so influential among the scientists and Commissioners, became less important after the H-bomb controversy was settled contrary to the recommendations of the GAC.[10] Furthermore, as a closer working relationship developed between the Commission and the Joint Committee, reliance on the GAC considerably declined.

All available evidence seems to indicate the existence of a close and harmonious working relationship between the AEC and the Joint Committee during Gordon Dean's chairmanship. There were no more Hickenlooper investigations. No sharply contested issues arose between the AEC and the Committee. No bitter statements were issued to the press, such as the one of Senator Edwin Johnson (under criticism for his celebrated November 1, 1949, television broadcast), in which he accused Mr. Lilienthal of a "nefarious plot" to share "so-called super-bomb" secrets with the British.[11] No evidence can be found of behind-the-scenes friction or suspicion.

The new chairman's background was such that he escaped almost entirely the initial controversy which surrounded Mr. Lilienthal. Although Mr. Dean could be associated with the Democratic Party, there was nothing to stand in the way of bipartisan support from Committee members. Moreover, he was not identified with the Lilienthal regime; most or all of the Joint Committee had confidence in him. Since he had arrived on the Commission in May, 1949, he had shared no part of the responsibility for the fellowship debacle, nor for the other incidents which turned many of the Committee members against David Lilienthal. Further, and of great importance, Mr. Dean joined with Admiral Strauss to favor the full-scale thermonuclear program which most of the Joint Committee wanted at the end of 1949.

One other point must be mentioned, although its importance is difficult to evaluate. This is the fact that Mr. Dean already had a close personal tie with Senator McMahon, for the two men were law partners in Washington from 1940 to 1943, and had also worked together in the Department of Justice for a time.[12]

On the whole, then, there were a number of reasons for close AEC-Joint Committee cooperation in the Dean period. The political stage was set for harmony.

Mr. Dean (and the same applies to Dr. Smyth) received his first impressions of the AEC during the Hickenlooper investigation. It seems likely that such an ordeal at the very outset would have some impact on an administrator's outlook, and Mr. Dean said as much when he was interviewed. He indicated that a strong impression was made on him by the enormous expenditure of time and energy by the AEC staff as a result of the investigation, and the disrupting influence which this had on the work of the project. Partly as a consequence of this, Mr. Dean developed the view that good Congressional relations were no less than essential for successful operation of the AEC.

This viewpoint was developed in remarks delivered by Chairman Dean to the Commission and the Washington staff on August 9, 1950.[13] The occasion was the resignation of Carroll

Wilson, the manner of which Mr. Dean deplored. He went on to say this:

> I have had a conviction ever since joining the Commission fourteen months ago that if we have suffered from any one thing it has been controversy. We have been bedeviled by it from the outset.

Continuing, Mr. Dean stated that, while controversy is good if there is a real issue to fight for, too much of it is bad. In his view, the AEC was partly to blame: it had insisted on the rightness of its positions, had been reluctant to admit error, and had maintained a chip-on-the-shoulder attitude. He warned against the danger of "becoming punch-drunk from minor league fights, only to lose out in championship battles."

What was his prescription? Not to become subservient, not to "succumb to every pressure," but to "do some selling—not by asserting our perfection, but by demonstrating our skill and our sincerity."

■

Mr. Dean was well equipped to do such a job of selling. He brought to the Commission a knack for inspiring confidence and good will, for getting along with Congress and other outside groups. From all sources on Capitol Hill and within the Commission, interview data underline the fact that Gordon Dean was a master of Congressional relations. This ability of his appeared in many different ways. It included minor courtesies, such as his practice of dealing directly with Congressmen rather than through subordinates, as Mr. Lilienthal had done. It also included a manner of dealing with the Joint Committee in the realm of basic policy. Mr. Dean apparently knew when and how to consult with the Committee. All important matters, interviewees have stated, were made the subject of consultation long before final decision. (The same applied to lesser matters which might have had some particular significance for one or more of the Joint Committee members.) Lesser issues were resolved by the AEC, but all such decisions were communicated to the Committee. Gordon Dean was used to working with a board of directors, and this doubtless made it easier for him to operate in such close touch with an outside body, conferring, obtaining approval, and accepting guidance where the former leadership would probably have acted more independently and with less attention to satisfying the wish of the Congressmen to keep their hand in policy formation.

Mr. Dean undertook policies *within* the Commission which found favor with the Congressmen. Interviewees have described him almost unanimously as an efficient, hardheaded business man, a welcome contrast to the idealistic Lilienthal. Carroll Wilson, of course, had accused the Commission of interfering with the management of the program. But the Joint Committee, in voting confidence in the Commission, approved the new conception of the Commission's role. Mr. Dean expressed the shift of emphasis when he said:

> We, as Commissioners, can't know all the details of this program, and we should not attempt to know all the details, but I will say this: I think the Commissioners should know as much as they humanly can about this program, and if they don't I think they are derelict in their duties. This does not mean that you are going to have management by Commissioners. This, admittedly, would be quite unfortunate. But it does mean that the Commissioners should know enough about the program so that when the larger policy questions do come before them they will have the requisite knowledge to understand the effect of the policies they work out.[14]

The Joint Committee was pleased by many of the changes occurring in the AEC and atomic energy policy. The new organizational philosophy, the new personnel, and the new business practices received favorable and unanimous support from the Joint Committee. The specific changes of policy in regard to personnel security gave the Committee members confidence in the judgment of the Commissioners.

At the same time, the Joint Committee members had been learning a good deal about the intricacies of the atomic energy project. With new confidence in the direction and policies of the AEC, these Committeemen were free to make use of this more extensive knowledge in analyzing more broadly the Commission's programs and over-all goals.

Such re-evaluation became necessary when it was learned that Soviet Russia had the secret of the atomic bomb. The orientation of Senator Hickenlooper and others who had shared his viewpoint changed markedly following 1949 from security by concealment to even more stress on security by achievement. Senator Hickenlooper became in time an outstanding advocate of the AEC. He joined Senator McMahon and the other Joint Committee members in a new role, championing the AEC's program, insisting on the utmost speed in its development, and defending the program from outside threats, principally from the attacks of the Appropriations Committees.

In this way, a common goal tended to unite all members of the Joint Committee and the AEC. That goal was an expanded, strengthened atomic energy program to meet the threat of Russian atomic achievements, and the urgency increased in the summer of 1950 when the fighting began in Korea. Evidence of the Joint Committee's emphasis on rapid program development is abundant. In the Committee's second report to Congress, the Committee surveyed its activities in respect to the various AEC programs and, in nearly every case, portrayed its role as that of a prodder, urging speed in the conclusion of raw materials agreements, exerting pressure for a step-up in plutonium production, pressing for vigorous reactor development, insisting on the most strenuous efforts in the thermonuclear weapons field, and so forth. Concluding, the Joint Committee commended the Commission for substantial progress, but its final word was this:

> On the other hand, as this report indicates, there are areas in our atomic program which need to be shored up, and there are opportunities for faster advancement which need to be vigorously exploited. If the Committee has a single general comment to offer, it is this: Greater boldness and more scientific and technical daring should be brought to bear upon the program.[15]

A 1952 report by the Joint Committee on raw materials expresses a similar conviction that the AEC, though making progress, should press forward even more boldly.[16] In this case, the Joint Committee urged increased development of domestic sources of uranium (including exploration and techniques of processing) and increased importation of foreign ores. The report criticized the AEC—and the Defense Department to some extent, as well—for clinging to the view that raw materials are rigidly limited. In the Committee view, the military should fix weapons requirements solely on the basis of need. At one time requirements were based on the assumption that raw materials rigidly limit production. With requirements so fixed, the AEC did not step up its procurement program because requirements could be met without expanded effort. It was a circular process, which the Joint Committee report took credit for breaking.

The Joint Committee had been characterized as a "pushing" force in the expansion of the atomic energy program. This was particularly true in several areas of the program—weapons, sources of fissionable materials, and reactor development. In order to see the attitude and the influence of the Joint Committee in the actual context of these years, it will be necessary to

explain briefly the major expansion programs which were undertaken.

The Dean period is marked by repeated, large-scale ex-
pansions in the facilities and programs of the Atomic Energy
Commission, with budgets of a correspondingly larger size.[17]
The expansion programs began in the fall of 1949, when President Truman announced that he had released AEC reserves in
order to advance the beginning of a quarter billion dollar expansion program by several months. This was done shortly after the
Russian atomic explosion became known.

Less than a year later, the President announced plans to implement the H-bomb decision by means of additional plant expansion. A supplemental budget request for $260 million had
already been submitted to Congress at the time of this announcement (August 2, 1950), and it was revealed that the duPont
Company had been engaged to build and operate the new production facilities at a large site yet to be determined. The site
finally chosen consisted of 200,000 acres near Augusta, Georgia,
and is known as the Savannah River installation. This facility
finally cost a total of one and one-half billion dollars.

Four months later, at the beginning of December, the Chinese
had entered the Korean conflict, and United Nations forces were
in full retreat. President Truman submitted a request for supplemental defense appropriations totalling $17.8 billion. Of this
amount, $1.05 billion was budgeted for the AEC. About half
was to be spent in acquiring ore and in increasing storage facilities and the production of weapons; the other half—about
$500 million—was for a new production facility near Paducah,
Kentucky.

Interview data show that the Joint Committee was as active
in urging this expansion program, including the Paducah installation, as it had been earlier in advocating the "crash" program for the H-bomb. But the Joint Committee's most promi-

nent activity came still later. By mid-1951, the members of the Committee felt that, although substantial gains had been made in all phases of the atomic energy program, even more attention should be devoted to atomic and thermonuclear weapons of all kinds, strategic as well as tactical. As a result, Chairman McMahon called a Committee hearing in September, 1951, at which the heads of the armed services and the civilian secretaries of Army, Navy, Air, and Defense appeared to testify.[18] The purpose of the hearing was to obtain testimony on a resolution which had been introduced in the Senate and the House by Senator McMahon and Representative Durham; it read in part:

> *Resolved* . . . That it is the sense of the Congress than an allocation of 3 cents in each military dollar for our best and cheapest weapon is unreasonably and imprudently small; that the Army, Navy, and Air Force must each be rapidly equipped with atomic weapons in far greater numbers and variety, looking toward more security for the United States at lower annual defense budgets. . . .[19]

As a result of this hearing the Joint Committee unanimously adopted the following resolution:

> *Resolved,* That the Joint Committee on Atomic Energy hereby requests the Atomic Energy Commission and the Department of Defense (after appropriate consultation with other agencies) to jointly transmit to the Joint Committee by January 3, 1952, a definite and concrete report on maximizing the role which atomic energy can and should play in the defense of the United States, including estimates of the amounts of money required, the specific extent and type of new facilities estimated to be required, the priorities in materials and manpower involved, the probable impact upon other defense projects and the national economy as a whole, and the joint views of the Atomic Energy Commission and the Department of Defense as to the precise program which should be carried out in the atomic energy field.[20]

On January 21, 1952, the Joint Committee received plans from the military whereby the proportion of the nation's defense dollar spent on atomic weapons might be increased.[21] This was approved by the National Security Council on January 22. The Joint Committee kept prodding the AEC to submit a supplemental budget request, which finally was received on May 29, 1952 (the time lag indicating an attempt on the part of the Executive branch to cut costs to a minimum). The biggest single outcome of this program was the huge production facility at Portsmouth, Ohio, still under construction in 1955.

Another incident which must be examined in order to assess the new role of the Joint Committee concerns the establishment of a second weapons laboratory, to supplement Los Alamos. The laboratory was established on July 9, 1952, at Livermore, California, on the site of a former Naval facility.[22] On that date, the AEC signed a contract with the University of California to operate the installation. Dr. Ernest Lawrence, head of the University of California Radiation Laboratory, became director of its program. The installation had had little publicity—it was not until January, 1954, that the AEC disclosed officially that weapons research had been going on at Livermore, with 1,500 persons employed.

A sharp difference of opinion arose over the significance of Livermore. Some went so far as to claim that its establishment was one of the all-important achievements in the history of atomic energy, symbolizing the final success of those who favored the thermonuclear program. Others pointed out that the early H-bomb successes were all the result of work at Los Alamos, and that Livermore's contribution was minor, although its young and potentially outstanding scientists would doubtless make a brilliant record as the laboratory grew and matured. This view was supported by Dr. Edward Teller, who publicly

stressed the primary importance of the Los Alamos scientists in
the work which lay behind early H-bomb successes.

Whatever the initial importance of Livermore, there is no
doubt that the Joint Committee favored the establishment of a
second weapons laboratory to push the thermonuclear program.
In its 1951 Report to Congress, after the Eniwetok tests had
given rise to increasing optimism about thermonuclear possibilities, the Joint Committee stated:

> The Committee specifically suggests that early consideration
> be given to the possibility of a second weapons development labo-
> ratory to supplement Los Alamos at least in certain engineering
> phases.
> As this suggestion indicates, concern is felt over the increasing
> burdens imposed upon Los Alamos . . . [and] results [of Nevada
> and Eniwetok tests], achieved by Los Alamos, create incentive
> to pursue so many lines of endeavor simultaneously as to create
> difficult problems for any single laboratory.[23]

The creation of the Livermore installation, a move in harmony with this recommendation, was one of the achievements
for which the Joint Committee took a large measure of credit.
Certain statements of the Committee and its staff, in fact, gave
the impression that the initiative was wholly the Committee's.
The facts are not that simple, however. The story behind the
establishment of Livermore began toward the end of 1951.[24]
Work on the H-bomb had been slow and uncertain until the
Eniwetok tests in the spring of that year, when results were
obtained which had a bearing on possible thermonuclear systems.
Chairman Dean has stated that he and the other Commissioners
decided it was time to bring together all the people with knowledge of hydrogen weapons and, as he put it, "get them all
around a table and make them all face each other and get the
blackboard out and agree on some priorities." [25] This was done

at a series of meetings in June, 1951, at the Institute for Advanced Study at Princeton. To those meetings, Dr. Edward Teller brought a whole new theory, a new approach to the problem of producing thermonuclear weapons. After the two-day session, everyone was convinced that, in Mr. Dean's words, "we had something for the first time that looked feasible in the way of an idea."

By this time, it was plain that Dr. Teller was the key man. His long enthusiasm for thermonuclear research and the experience which it had given him, together with his unquestionably superior theoretical capacities, made it imperative that his services should be retained.

Unfortunately, it became apparent by late 1951, if not before, that Dr. Teller was dissatisfied with arrangements at Los Alamos. In part, the difficulty seems to have been caused by disagreements between Dr. Teller and Dr. Bradbury, the AEC's director of the Los Alamos Scientific Laboratory, upon how and to what extent thermonuclear research should be incorporated into the program at Los Alamos; and in part, it was caused no doubt by Dr. Teller's temperament, which made it unlikely that a harmonious relationship could be established between him and a number of his fellow scientists. In any case, his unhappiness at Los Alamos did not abate, and on several occasions he left and was only persuaded to return through the efforts of Chairman Dean.

At the same time, there were reports that the GAC was not facilitating thermonuclear work, and even that scientists both within and without the GAC were actively working to prevent the success of the H-bomb.

As a result, the question of a second weapons laboratory, where Dr. Teller could work satisfactorily on the H-bomb, became a significant issue during the winter of 1951–1952. Dr. Teller himself was actively working for this. Dr. Oppenheimer has revealed that the AEC asked the GAC for its opinion on this several times during the period. He recalled that most of the members opposed a second Los Alamos—meaning a second full-scale laboratory in the desert—and suggested that if Los Alamos could not do the whole job, some of the more routine work should be moved to Sandia. The GAC feared that a full-scale laboratory would seriously weaken Los Alamos, and would create serious problems of recruitment. Dr. Oppenheimer testified that the GAC, in contrast, favored the conversion of some existing facility to carry on testing work on thermonuclear systems—a small, specialized laboratory rather than an "across-the-board" installation of the same magnitude as Los Alamos. Livermore, he said, was under consideration as a site, and the GAC endorsed the idea.

Chairman Dean's testimony before the Gray Board [26] pointed out that a second laboratory meant different things to different people. He himself felt that it must be some place already established and some place where Teller would work efficiently. The only possibility he could see was under Dr. Lawrence at the Berkeley Radiation Laboratory or at the Livermore site 30 miles southeast of Berkeley. In expressing opposition to a second Los Alamos, in a letter to the Joint Committee, Mr. Dean was thus not opposing *any* sort of a second installation, but only the full-scale integrated laboratory recommended by some.

On the Commission, Chairman Dean's limited approach to a second weapons laboratory was not shared by all his colleagues. Commissioner Murray's viewpoint was very similar to Dr. Teller's, that is, strongly in favor of a second installation and without serious reservations as to the possible harmful effects on Los Alamos. These two men wrote a joint letter to the GAC, dated December 19, 1951, urging approval of a new laboratory.[27]

The Air Force—and the Department of Defense—also favored the establishment of a new installation. David T. Criggs,

who was a consultant at various times to the Air Force, the
Armed Forces Special Weapons Project, the Corps of Engineers,
and the California Radiation Laboratory, testified before the
Gray Board that the Air Force in 1951 was dissatisfied with
H-bomb progress and seriously considered establishing an independent Air Force weapons laboratory, a step which was
thought to be permissible under the Atomic Energy Act.[28]

It appears, then, that the AEC's solution to the controversy—
the Livermore installation—was opposed by no one. Moreover,
the establishment of *some* sort of second laboratory was favored
not solely by the Joint Committee, but by members of the Commission, scientists, and the military. What weight the recommendations of each should have is a question too difficult to
answer from the available evidence.

However, it is true that one of the important factors in the
agitation for a new laboratory was the Joint Committee. Its
voice was unified and insistent, and undoubtedly it was one of
the most influential in securing a decision to go ahead with the
project.

■

In its new role of initiator and prodder, the Joint Committee received expert and enthusiastic support from its staff. Often the
staff of a Congressional committee is ignored, for its work is
done in the background, quietly and anonymously. Yet members of the staff can have a significant impact on the direction of
the work done by the committee itself, and on the agency or
agencies with which the committee deals.

Beginning in 1949, the staff of the Joint Committee did take
on just such a significant, though often hidden, role in the
atomic energy program, and during the Dean period it was particularly active. When Senator McMahon assumed the chairmanship of the Committee, he brought new leadership to the

staff, and according to interviewees, he delegated considerable responsibility to it and placed much confidence in it. Generally speaking, the influence of the staff was felt in two directions: first as a policeman watching the Commission's operations, and second as a participant in policy decisions.

Even an active Congressional committee staff cannot review all the aspects of an agency's work. It must rely in general on spot-check techniques, rather than on a continuous investigation of administrative activities. Its work cannot be thorough, and hence the staff must depend on unexpectedness and on its ability to penetrate at any time to any level of the agency with questions and criticisms.

With an active and trusted staff, however, these methods can be of great help to a committee, giving the members confidence that they have "policemen" on the job, and that the probing and checking will keep the organization alert and efficient. With this confidence, the committee members themselves can give their attention to larger issues.

Members of the Joint Committee could certainly feel such confidence in their own staff during the Dean period. The staff was expert and active; it dealt competently with all phases of the Commission's activities. And the checking was aided, interviewees say, by the willingness of the AEC to give access to its own files. It is true that the AEC, on a few occasions, suggested to the Committee that the staff investigators were somewhat in the way, hampering the progress of work, and that it might be wise to suspend work temporarily while some employees concentrated on obtaining the specific information which was desired. But on the whole, there was remarkably little friction between the staffs of the Commission and the Committee, the files were open to all, and the members of the Committee had no reason to complain of lack of cooperation.

But the effect of a staff directly upon the thinking of its committee members, and consequently on the direction of their interests and activities, can be equally important. We have seen already how, in the early days of the atomic energy program, the staff of the Joint Committee had much to do with the Committee's insistence upon questions of security. In the Dean period, the most influential staff figure was the Executive Director, William L. Borden. Mr. Borden was a young lawyer, not long out of Yale Law School, when Senator McMahon brought him to the Joint Committee as staff head. He already had an intense interest in atomic energy, and during his first year at the Law School had written a book, entitled *There Will Be No Time,*[29] on the strategic and policy implications of the A-bomb. The point of this book, which is said to have impressed Senator McMahon greatly, becomes significant when one considers the Joint Committee's activity in urging a faster program development during the Borden tenure. The author subtitled his work *The Revolution in Strategy,* and outlined what he considered the clear implications of this revolution. The advent of atomic weapons, he felt, solved the problem of destroying enemy industrial power. His reasoning is summarized in this paragraph:

> The trend is toward a return to eighteenth century warfare and the classic principles of Karl von Clausewitz, because once again the key to victory lies in defeating hostile military forces. Victory will not be now primarily by destroying civilian concentrations and then waiting for the opponent's armies and navies to crumble for lack of supplies. This process is so time-consuming that the belligerent who relied upon it might find himself forced to surrender long before home front paralysis made itself felt in the field. Paradoxically, warfare remains a struggle between rival industrial systems. *But the struggle takes place before hostilities begin, and industrial supremacy is measured in terms of stock piles available for immediate use.*[30]

Once hostilities start, in other words, there will be no time for further preparations. The next war, according to the author, may be a one-hour affair. The emphasis which this theory puts on preparedness and superior military strength at all times is obvious.

In keeping with the thesis of *There Will Be No Time,* Mr. Borden felt very strongly that this nation lost three and one-half years by not pushing ahead immediately in 1947 with an all-out H-bomb program. In his work as staff director, he threw his influence in the direction of more rapid program development, thus complementing and intensifying the attitude already held by the Committee.

Perhaps it is too much to say that the staff under Mr. Borden infected the Committee with an ideology of atomic preparedness. But the Borden viewpoint was highly articulate and deeply felt, and can hardly have had less than a substantial influence on the thinking of the Joint Committee.

■

What can now be said of the relationship between the AEC and the Joint Committee? Many interviewees have said that it was "close," "harmonious," but a more accurate description seems necessary.

Criticism of one group by the other was obtained in interviews; however, this tended to be superficial. The Atomic Energy Commission sometimes thought the Joint Committee was irresponsible in advocating faster and greater accomplishment because the Joint Committee was not accountable for money or administration. At other times, the AEC felt the Joint Committee tended to steal AEC ideas and take credit for them. And generally, the AEC felt that the Joint Committee staff gave their bosses, the Congressmen, too much credit in order to flatter them. Also, the AEC thought the Committee staff was often meddlesome merely in order not to be caught napping by the Committee members.

On the other hand, interviews revealed that the Joint Committee members were annoyed by a lack of "horse sense" in arrangements for such matters as the housing at Savannah River. The Joint Committee staff sometimes found minor irregularities and exposed them. In one such case, a staff member discovered what appeared to be a kickback on a 1951 Cadillac in return for concessions made in an AEC contract.[31] Thus the Joint Committee functioned in what it thought to be a properly critical way.

Yet these criticisms did not reach to the basic relationship which was developing. The Joint Committee was now as a matter of course consulted about all policy matters that would issue in public statements, operating decisions with political overtones, and major operating decisions affecting the basic direction of the atomic energy program. In short the Joint Committee had become less and less an outside body, and more and more part of what may be called the inner control group—in a sense, a collective executive made up of the five Commissioners and the eighteen Congressmen on the Joint Committee. The Joint Committee members identified themselves with the program. They were exhilarated by the prospects of the program. In fact, their involvement in vital matters apparently impressed them with the need to assume a greater sense of responsibility and at the same time a greater willingness to exert influence in policy-making. In part, the atomic arms race, which developed from 1950 on, presented to them dramatically the importance of their role. In part, their awareness of the absence of organized public opinion, lobbyists, and special interest groups caused them to rely on their own reasoning powers for guidance in public policy.

The AEC accepted this new partnership for several reasons. Naturally, it feared any further Hickenlooper inquiries. Moreover, secrecy of itself prohibited the cultivation of public opinion as a counterpoise to the Joint Committee ideology. The lack of an effective clientele from which to draw support also made the Joint Committee's friendliness more desirable. And most important of all, agreement on common goals made it natural to enlist the support and guidance of an interested and informed Congressional committee. Truly executive-legislative barriers had been lowered; the Joint Committee and the AEC worked together as an inner control group for the nation's atomic energy program.

V

Defense of Agency and Program

In general, the preceding chapter reviewed the new roles of the AEC and the Joint Committee in the period of the Dean chairmanship. But one particular function of the Joint Committee became so prominent that it has been singled out for separate attention in this chapter. More and more the Joint Committee acted as the defender of the AEC against public criticism, and the defender of the program against appropriations cuts or restrictions.

At the basis of this defense was the Committee's identification with the agency and the program. However, it should be made clear that Chairman Dean well saw the value of such a defense; he conducted the AEC's Congressional relations with this end in view and encouraged the Joint Committee to pursue this role. Whatever combination of stimuli was present, the whole Committee (not only Chairman McMahon, in whom this feeling had developed earlier) came to acknowledge the identification.

The role as defender of the *agency* will be explained first, and then the role as defender of the *program*.

■

Any large government organization which has branches spread throughout the country—and the AEC was no exception—will sustain a certain amount of local criticism, in addition to the larger issues which may be raised against it. Individuals write letters to their Congressmen; the local press conducts campaigns.[1] In the Dean period, the Joint Committee clearly assumed the task of defending the AEC against such public criticism. While the program was expanding rapidly and new installations were being built in many parts of the country, there were local allegations of inefficiency, lax security, extravagance, and so forth. Many of these were investigated by the Committee. It is plain to see from the spirit of these investigations that the Committee was just as interested in exposing false criticism as in discovering real causes for grievance.

What did the Committee consider unjustified criticism? We have seen how the Committee came, during several years, to place absolute pre-eminence upon the atomic and thermonuclear programs, and more and more this view dominated the Congressmen's evaluation of AEC's achievement. Whenever criticism of the AEC was based simply on criteria of local expediency, or on any other criteria which could be overridden by the broader considerations of urgency, the Joint Committee was quick to defend the Commission and to exonerate it publicly.

A number of instances can be cited. On one occasion, for example, the Committee had to deal with a letter from a Congressman, who brought charges against the Commission on the basis of information he had received from two private individuals.[2] The charges involved the Paducah project and alleged discrimination by the AEC against one of the informants, improper handling of security, and various other improper practices, including downright dishonesty. Senator McMahon replied after extensive investigations by the Joint Committee staff. The Senator pointed out that the serious charges could not be substantiated, that only one or two irregularities of a minor nature had been discovered. In reply to the charge of discrimination, Senator McMahon stressed the fact that the atomic enterprise was a huge one, with hundreds of firings, dismissals, job terminations, and the like. He exonerated the Commission by reminding the Congressman that his informants were contractor employees, and that the AEC should in any case not be condemned since employees of this contractor were in exactly the same position as employees of any ordinary company doing business in its own way.

A more highly publicized instance of public criticism of the Commission and subsequent Joint Committee defense occurred in 1952, when the press commented unfavorably on a $756 weekly wage alleged to have been paid to a plumber at the Nevada Test Site, then under construction. The Joint Committee held public hearings,[3] which were little more than an opportunity for the AEC to explain the situation. The alleged payment was admitted, but the Commission assured the nation that it was an isolated instance, arising from the urgent nature of the work, and not evidence of widespread extravagance.

Another more recent instance occurred when Representative Kelley of Washington charged that numerous secret documents had been misplaced at Hanford. Chairman Cole of the Joint Committee immediately asked the AEC to investigate, and upon receipt of its report, quickly issued statements to the press which exonerated the AEC from any real carelessness.[4]

The threat to the AEC from public criticism was minor in comparison to the threat provided by budget cuts and restrictions, originating mostly in the House Appropriations Committee. It goes without saying, of course, that the appropriations groups, and other Congressmen as well, did not agree with the Joint Committee that the restrictions and reductions actually were a threat to the program. The point, however, is that the Joint Committee decided to do battle in behalf of the AEC's budget estimates. This aspect of the Joint Committee's defense can be documented in great detail. Various techniques have been used by Joint Committee members in attempting to exert pressure on the appropriations groups against budget cuts or language restrictions (e.g., procedural stipulations and limitations on items like personal services). These include direct appeals to key appropriations personnel, informally by letter, telephone, or consultation, and formally by appearance at Appropriations Committee sessions. Beyond this, the Joint Committee members have gone to the floor of the House and Senate to attempt a modification of the work done in the Appropriations Committees by alteration of the money bills.

Instances of Joint Committee defense of the budget may be found as early as mid-1948, although the backing then came mainly from one or two of the stronger advocates, such as Senator McMahon, and scarcely foreshadowed the later, unanimous defense of the Dean period. In connection with a 1948 supplemental bill, the House subcommittee, through Chairman Wigglesworth, expressed dissatisfaction with what it called extravagance of operation in the AEC and complained of lack of cooperation by the Commission.[5] While two Joint Committee members, Representatives Cole and Van Zandt, concurred in the charges of extravagance, Representatives Holifield and Durham spoke in defense of the AEC.[6]

A cut of $58 million in Commission funds nevertheless went through the House, and was accepted by the Senate subcommittee. On the floor of the upper chamber, Senator McMahon took strong issue with the cut, which he felt "may be nothing less than calamitous" for the whole atomic energy project.[7] A week later the Senate agreed to an amendment by its Appropriations Subcommittee restoring $20 million. This failed to satisfy Senator McMahon, however. Receiving permission to reopen debate, he protested against "an uninformed, unconsidered, and . . . reckless exercise of power to reduce a budget estimate for an agency . . . as vital, if not more vital to national defense, than any other. . . ." [8] His amendment to restore the full amount was rejected by voice vote.

In early 1949, the AEC requested more than $1 billion in cash and contract authority for the fiscal year 1950. The House Appropriations Subcommittee recommended a total reduction of $77 million—hardly a crippling reduction of funds.[9] The subcommittee went into great detail in its report, specifying the programs to be cut and the respective amounts. Weapons and reactor development were left substantially alone, but funds for source and fissionable materials were reduced considerably. The specific cuts were softened, however, by a proviso that diversions *could* be made from one program to another in response to needs which might develop after the hearings on the bill.

On the floor, Representative Durham did not take issue with the work of the House subcommittee, but presented a detailed description of the manner in which the requested funds were to be spent, and said he would "earnestly recommend" favorable action by the House, which was granted.[10] When the bill came to the Senate the subcommittee of that chamber wrote into its report the direction that the cuts (in total amount the same as the House allowed) be taken in programs *other* than source and fissionable materials, weapons, and the military phases of reactor development.[11] Senator McMahon objected to this, saying that no distinction can be made between military and nonmilitary fields for purposes of applying budget cuts. He agreed, however, to the total amount of funds, and to a rider limiting AEC freedom to start construction projects.[12]

Two months later, the Soviet atomic explosion had been reported by President Truman, and the urgency that characterized the Dean years was beginning to appear. Senator McMahon at that time introduced for the Joint Committee a bill to amend the construction rider, making it inapplicable to "technical facilities to be used in the production of the end product of the Commission." [13] In its report, the Joint Committee pointed out the urgency of the AEC program, and the fact that in many cases, "in order to obtain the necessary drive, [it is necessary] to proceed immediately with construction in situations where time permits only one preparation of incomplete plans and specifications." [14]

On the floor, Senators McMahon and Hickenlooper spoke in favor of the amendment. Senator Millikin, too, rose to support the bill—"There is no alternative to it, unless we wish to lose very valuable time. . . ."—but he pointed out that he was not satisfied with the AEC's conduct of its fiscal affairs and thought the restrictive rider a good thing when it was originally adopted. The amendment was enacted without serious opposition in either chamber.

In 1950 the AEC requested and received the first really sustained Joint Committee campaign to defend the AEC from an allegedly serious threat to its financial welfare. The controversy centered upon the fixed fees paid by the AEC to community contractors at Oak Ridge and Los Alamos. After complaining without effect of the seemingly high rate of these fees, the House subcommittee wrote a provision into the appropriations bill for the fiscal year 1951, restricting the amount payable as a fee for community management to $90,000 per year, and for the operation of a community transportation system to $45,000.[15] These amounts were half the fees then being paid to the contractors at Oak Ridge.

Before the House could take action on the recommendations of its subcommittee, the Senate subcommittee held its hearings.[16] The AEC was quick to point out the proposed rider and to characterize it as a very serious matter; the Commission warned that its enactment could easily lead to direct government operation of the community services at Oak Ridge and Los Alamos, which would mean a diversion of government employees from important posts and would substantially affect the whole program.

The Joint Committee first took action when Senator McMahon was invited to testify before the Senate subcommittee on the AEC budget. Most of his remarks were in opposition to the community management rider. A few days later, while the Senate Committeemen still considered the bill, Senator McMahon called a meeting of the Joint Committee and the Commission to discuss the matter.[17] Chairman Dean appealed to the members of the Joint Committee to convey to the appropriations people the importance of the principles which were at stake in the community management rider—something he felt the AEC itself had failed to do. He suggested that it would be wise to appoint a panel of experts to study the problem and recommend a permanent solution. For their part, the Joint Committee members were equally convinced of the undesirability of the rider, and they asked the AEC to prepare briefs or letters containing information which they could use during the coming struggle on the floor of Congress.

The Joint Committee's first opportunity came when House floor debate reached the discussion of AEC funds.[18] Representative Holifield promptly offered an amendment to delete the rider altogether. After a show of opposition from the appropriations people, Representative Cole offered a substitute amendment which would allow the limitation to take effect only after the existing contractual obligations had expired. Three other Joint Committee members engaged in the debate. Representative Hinshaw rose to support the Holifield proposal or, if that were unacceptable, the Cole amendment. Representative Van Zandt produced the letter which had been prepared by the AEC. The fifth Joint Committee member to participate, Representative

Durham, defended the AEC and went on to support the amendments. They were defeated, however, Cole's 64 to 27, and Holifield's 86 to 19.

A month later, the Senate subcommittee still had not reported, and the AEC met again with the Joint Committee.[19] Chairman Dean again pointed out the grave implications of the rider, but the Joint Committee scarcely needed further arguments on that score, and most of the meeting was occupied with a discussion of means which might be used to convince the Senate appropriations group of the same view. Representative Kilday wondered whether or not it would be a good idea to offer a bill to forestall "rider legislation." Senator McMahon, however, felt that private conversation between "some of us" and Senator O'Mahoney would suffice, and that plan was adopted.

It is not possible to tell what effect the Joint Committee's "conversations" may have had, but the fact is that the Senate subcommittee finally did recommend the elimination of the rider, on the ground that it would interfere with AEC operations under the existing contracts. The report suggested emphatically, however, that a timetable be established for disengaging the towns from AEC management, and directed the AEC to give notice of cancellation to its Oak Ridge and Los Alamos community contractors, and to negotiate new contracts with lower fixed fees for the time while disengagement was being achieved.

The Senate accepted its subcommittee's recommendations without debate. In conference, however, the provision was reinserted in the bill, with the language slightly clarified. The Joint Committee made no further attempt to challenge this, and the rider was enacted into law.

The following year, the AEC requested omission of the rider, but Representative Gore's questioning of Chairman Dean disclosed the fact that new contracts had been signed in keeping with the provision, and that the dire effects predicted by the

AEC and Joint Committee members had not materialized.[20] Later, at Oak Ridge, a no-fee contract was signed with Management Services, Inc., for community management. The House subcommittee members made pointed references on several occasions to the fact that the Joint Committee's judgment on this issue had been faulty.[21]

The most outstanding examples of the Joint Committee's battle to save Commission requests for funds came in 1952. There had been minor skirmishes in 1951, it is true—principally over reductions in personnel. Representatives Price and Holifield, and later Senators McMahon and Knowland, took the floor of House or Senate to defend the Commission. But not until the huge requests of 1952—one regular, one supplemental—did the Joint Committee make its most concentrated efforts in behalf of its agency.

In January, the regular AEC request totaled more than $1.3 billion. The House subcommittee cut operating expenses by $92.5 million and plant and equipment funds by almost $82 million, reducing the total to $1.14 billion.[22] In addition, the subcommittee added provisos that no funds could be used to begin any new construction project (1) for which an estimate was not included in the budget, or (2) the currently estimated cost of which exceeded by 35 per cent the estimates included in the budget. These provisions replaced the more liberal ones in the 1950 bill.

The House members of the Joint Committee went into action when these recommendations came to the floor. Representative Durham first made a statement on behalf of himself and all the other House members of the Joint Committee. In it, he opposed the recommended cut in funds and the two riders "which might wrap a strait jacket around the most vital new projects." He went on to suggest some specific results of the cuts in terms of reduced programs.

Next, Representatives Price, Jackson, and Holifield, all of the Joint Committee, offered in turn three different amendments, designed to restore funds and to ease the language restrictions. In arguing for their proposals, the Committee members stressed the long and exhaustive consideration given by the Joint Committee to the AEC program, and compared this with the brief and inadequate Appropriations Committees' hearings. Nevertheless, the three amendments were rejected, and the bill was approved in both chambers, with the cuts and language restrictions intact.

In May, 1952, the AEC's biggest expansion program was submitted to Congress in a supplemental budget request for more than $3 billion. The request was the outcome of the processes which had been set in motion the preceding year by the Joint Committee's resolution on the desirability of more concentration on the development and production of atomic weapons.[23] In the Congressional debates which followed, the Joint Committee engaged in its most significant and most successful defense of the AEC.

The first action on the request was taken by the House Appropriations Subcommittee, which recommended an appropriation of $1.5 billion—a cut in the requested amount of 50 per cent.[24] That is, the budget for plant and equipment, on which the expansion principally depended, was cut from $3,018,600,000 to $1,450,000,000. The subcommittee also attached a proviso which came to be known as the "funds-to-complete" rider:

> *Provided further,* That no part of the foregoing appropriation shall be available for the construction of any building, utility, or other specific portion of a project, unless funds are available for the completion of such building, utility, or other specific portion of such project.[25]

The subcommittee in its report suggested that substantial amounts of money could be saved by the prompt formulation of plans and specifications, and invited the AEC to make such plans and then to return for the financing of the rest of the expansion program.

When the bill came to the floor, Representative Durham spoke for the Joint Committee by moving to strike the funds-to-complete proviso.[26] He argued that no one can determine final costs far in advance on facilities of a type that has never been built before. Representatives Price, Hinshaw, and Elston supported the amendment, the first two pointing out that the Joint Committee had been responsible for suggesting the expansion program, and that Congress should therefore approve it. The appropriations people took a strong stand in favor of their rider, however, and the Durham motion to strike it was defeated, 92 to 29.

The bill next came before the Senate Appropriations Subcommittee, where extensive alterations were made in it.[27] The total cash allowance was the same, but the Senators (1) increased the amount budgeted for operating expenses, (2) added $2 billion in contract authority to the sections for plant and equipment (which made a total appropriation to the AEC, both cash and contract authority, of more than $3.6 billion), and (3) eliminated the funds-to-complete proviso. This version was accepted by the Senate without debate.

With the report of the first conference committee, the debate began in earnest. That committee restored the funds-to-complete rider and reverted to the $1.45 billion allowed by the House for plant and equipment. At this point, President Truman was persuaded to take a hand, and he wrote identical letters to the House and Senate, urging defeat of the rider.[28] The Joint Committee chose to take its stand on the floor of the Senate, where there seemed to be more sympathy for the AEC and more respect for the Joint Committee's opinions. The battle was joined on July 5, 1952, a Saturday. Congress had planned to adjourn that very evening, since the Republican National Convention opened the following Monday, July 7. When the House adopted the conference report and the bill reached the upper chamber, Senate members of the conference committee anticipated the strong objections of the Joint Committee, and they took the floor to explain that the House conferees were adamant and simply could not be persuaded to soften their stand. Several of the Senators pointed out that the House conferees had agreed to an interpretation of the rider which would not be unduly restrictive.

Senator McMahon was in the hospital, suffering from the cancer which was to take his life a few weeks later, and Senator Hickenlooper spoke in his place, representing all eighteen members of the Joint Committee. He assured the Senate that the rider would in fact have a disadvantageous effect on American defensive strength, and he urged the Senators to return the bill to the conference committee. In support of his statements, Senator Hickenlooper revealed that the Joint Committee had formally agreed on a resolution condemning the proviso, and he also read into the record a similar statement from Senator McMahon.

AEC personnel have said that the Senate vote on the conference report was the closest shave the Commission ever experienced, at least in budgetary matters. The vote was a tie, which had the effect of sending the bill back to conference.

From this point on, events occurred rapidly, and maneuvering behind the scenes makes it difficult to follow them. It was already early morning, the Congressmen were anxious to adjourn, and informal procedure was the rule. The conferees met quickly. Soon the House spokesman, Representative Thomas, appeared with a proposal to raise the plant and equipment figure to $2 billion, and to amend the funds-to-complete rider so that it could be interpreted as liberally as possible. The House accepted this, but Senator Hickenlooper had received a prior report of it in the Senate, and immediately he stated that it would not be satisfactory. The debate went on until the House action on the second conference recommendation came formally before the Senate. A motion to accept this recommendation was defeated, and the same conferees were appointed again.

Negotiations between the two chambers continued until approximately 5 A.M., when an arrangement was reached whereby the disagreement would be adjusted in conference and reported on at noon on Monday—this was to be the only business considered before adjournment. At that time, a new recommendation was accepted by both chambers. The funds-to-complete rider was retained, but the cash appropriation for plant and equipment was fixed at almost $2.9 billion, an amount which the AEC agreed would be enough to carry forward the expansion program. (The original request had been for $3.02 billion.) Senator Hickenlooper's all-night stand had finally been successful.

Though shorn of detail, this account of the Joint Committee's defense of AEC budgets is enough to show the clear pattern of the Committee's aims. At this point, it is not necessary to evaluate the Committee's actual effect on the appropriations legislated by Congress for the AEC: sometimes the Committee's efforts were effective, and sometimes they were not. The significant point is that the Committee was willing to make a spirited and repeated defense of the AEC in spite of difficult and powerful opposition. The Committee members had assumed their share of responsibility for the atomic energy program, and they were unrelenting in their insistence that the program go forward as rapidly as possible.

Whatever the objective observer might conclude about the

extent of the Joint Committee's influence on AEC appropriations, the Committee itself had often expressed in the past dissatisfaction with the limitations of its role. It had tried several means to enhance its effectiveness, and one had been the attempt to place ex officio members on the Appropriations Committees. Such ex officio members were to sit with the House and Senate subcommittees when the AEC budget came under discussion. The device seemed to offer a chance to bring the *expertise* and the persuasiveness of the Joint Committee to bear on the Appropriations Committeemen directly and in the early, formative stages of the budget process, when the greatest effect might be expected.

In the Senate, the need for the ex officio device was less apparent than in the House. From the very beginning, representatives of the Joint Committee occasionally sat in on deliberations of the Senate subcommittee (at its invitation). Early in 1951, by means of a resolution introduced by Senator Bricker, the Senate formalized the arrangement by voting to place three ex officio Joint Committee members on the Senate Independent Offices Subcommittee to participate in consideration of the Commission's requests for funds.[29] Interview data indicate that the effect of this move, though difficult to measure, has been, as it was hoped, to enhance the influence of the Joint Committee.

It should be remembered, of course, that the Joint Committee enjoyed considerably more respect among the members of the Senate subcommittee than among their colleagues in the House. The House Independent Offices Subcommittee, which not only lacked confidence in the Joint Committee but cherished a strong tradition of independence, stood firmly against the ex officio device. Several unofficial attempts to win the point were made by the Joint Committee before the 83d Congress convened. In 1953, Chairman Cole made an official overture in a letter to Representative Taber, Chairman of the Appropriations Committee.[30] The intent in all cases, of course, was the same, to support the AEC by introducing part of its inner control group—representatives of the Joint Committee—into the Appropriations Committee's hearings. These overtures were always rebuffed because the House Appropriations Subcommittee wanted to deal with the AEC in the same way that it dealt with any other administrative agency, that is, to put the agency officials on the carpet and test their control of their agency through their ability to answer the questions of the subcommittee members. The subcommittees do not want other Congressmen running interference for administrative agencies.

Another means by which the Joint Committee has had hopes of increasing its control over the appropriations process is that of exercising the power to pass on the authorization of AEC appropriations. Mention has already been made of the 1949 proposals to give the Joint Committee the power to authorize all sizable AEC projects.[31] This seemed particularly desirable after the natural gas pipeline controversy. At that time, when the Joint Committee wrote up and introduced a bill for such authorization, the AEC expressed itself as against such an extension of the Joint Committee's power. The AEC's opposition was attributable to several factors. First, the delay that would be entailed in the final appropriations for new construction by a prior stage of authorization would probably inhibit the AEC from getting forward with the program. Second, the AEC felt that the Joint Committee was not qualified to judge such managerial problems as the location, size, and specific form of new construction; already the AEC was annoyed with the Appropriations Committees members who wanted to make sure that complete plans and specifications were drawn up before new construction was begun. In other words, the AEC believed that purely administrative decisions should rest with its own personnel.

The bills introduced in 1949 died in committee, and no more was heard publicly about authorization for three years, during which time the new relationships of the Dean period were established. In 1952, however, the Joint Committee held hearings on a number of proposed amendments to the Act, among them proposals for authorization.[32] It was learned that Senator McMahon in 1951 had written to the AEC and requested a new statement of its views on the authorization problem.[33] Mr. Pike had replied for the Commission, pointing out a number of possible difficulties, omissions, and undesirable features which, he said, should be discussed with great care before final action on the measure.

At the 1952 hearings, this proposal and three other types of authorization procedure were analyzed by the Joint Committee.[34] Budget Director Frederick J. Lawton appeared and argued against the proposals. In trying to convince him that authorization was desirable, members of the Joint Committee took some pains to explain their reasoning. They did not, however, discuss the problems which might be provoked by an uncontrollable Commission or by further extravagances and ill-advised investments (such as they considered the natural gas pipeline to be) which, without authorization, they were powerless to prevent. Instead, they discussed their difficulties with the Appropriations Committees and complained of their inability to influence the appropriations people against action which would delay or even cripple the atomic energy program. They emphasized their feeling of responsibility for the program. At one point, Representative Holifield said this:

> Our whole concern in this thing is that we have ridden herd pretty closely on this program. And in most instances we have guided the program and suggested certain phases of development in the program.
> Then when the Commission tries to set up its budget and

sustain that budget before the Appropriations Committee, they have been unable to do so.[35]

From these hearings it appears that the Joint Committee desire for authorization power in the Dean period was a product of its desire to protect the AEC from the growing interference of the Appropriations Committees, and not a result of its fear of being unable to control the AEC. This is an important distinction.

At the same time, the position taken on authorization in 1952 by Chairman Dean is interesting because it corroborates the other evidence that Mr. Dean believed it highly desirable to maintain a harmonious relationship with the Joint Committee. He believed that the Committee, if it worked closely with the AEC, had confidence in the AEC, and shared a feeling of responsibility for the program, would be a valuable ally. The Commission's job could be much easier if a powerful Congressional body were on its side, aiding it and defending it against threats such as those which might arise in the Appropriations Committees.

At the hearing, Mr. Dean said that, if authorization were to come, he would much prefer authorization of the entire budget, rather than of merely individual construction items which happened to exceed $500,000. He made it clear that he would rather have the Committee scrutinize the whole program—give, as he put it, "a careful look" to the "impact of that program" and the "significance of it in the years ahead."

The value of this, he felt, lay in the use that the Joint Committee could make of the processes of review and authorization. The outcome, he hoped, would not be simply this or that piece of legislation for funds, but rather a thoroughly informed Congressional committee "so that the rest of the Congress then could look to the joint committee" and "get behind us when the appropriation time came."

In spite of all the consideration given to the subject, the Joint Committee was unable to obtain the authorizing power until the summer of 1954, when Congress passed the revised Atomic Energy Act. Even then it came only because the members of the Committee continued to favor it and work for it, both in Congress and out.

■

The Dean period closed with a transitional interval in agency-committee relations, which lasted roughly from the end of July, 1952, until the departure of Chairman Dean in June, 1953. As a result, the pattern of relationships characterizing the period was established before the end of the first two years.[36]

There are several reasons for setting apart the months following July, 1952. First of all, the nation was involved in a Presidential election throughout most of the rest of the year. Congress naturally remained out of session, and its committees experienced the slackening that comes with both recess and election time. The Joint Committee staff stayed on the job, but the Committee could hardly carry on in the normal way.

A second factor bearing on the last months of the Dean period was the death of the Joint Committee chairman, and the subsequent uncertainty about who would replace him. Senator McMahon was hospitalized all through the funds-to-complete controversy and the Democratic national convention, where his name was placed before the delegates as a possible candidate for President of the United States, a tribute to his Senatorial leadership in atomic energy and foreign affairs. Senator McMahon did not live until the election; he died on July 28 in a Washington hospital, at the age of 48.

As a result of Senator McMahon's death, when the new 83d Congress convened in January, the Joint Committee was disturbed by an internal dispute which added considerably to the inefficacy caused by the absence of the Senator from Connecticut. When the Committee met again after the long recess, it undertook to choose a new permanent chairman to take over from Representative Durham, who had been acting as chairman in place of Senator McMahon. In attempting to do so, however, the members ran into a deadlock. The Senate members felt that Senator Hickenlooper was the man for the chairmanship, and voted for him unanimously. The House members took the view that a Representative should be in line for the job after the Senate's long tenure with the Hickenlooper and McMahon chairmanships of the first six years. (There was also some talk of an alleged early agreement that the chairmanship was to rotate between the chambers.) As a result, the House members voted just as unanimously for Representative Cole, and the outcome was an 8 to 8 tie, the two candidates not voting. Various negotiations to settle the matter all ended without success. The House members refused to back down, insisting that they should have a turn at the chairmanship, and the Senators refused to yield their traditional precedence over the lower chamber. For three months of 1953 the dispute continued. Not until April was the deadlock broken, when Senator Hickenlooper stepped aside and Representative Cole assumed the chairmanship.[37] Representative Durham had continued as acting chairman but could hardly show strong leadership as a temporary Democratic chairman in a Republican Congress. For this reason, the Joint Committee was not nearly so effective from July, 1952, until April, 1953, as it had been previously.

Finally, the position of the AEC chairman, Gordon Dean, became uncertain with the advent of a new Administration. During the Joint Committee struggle over its own leadership, Mr. Dean resigned his chairmanship of the Commission on February 10, 1953. He agreed, however, to stay on as chairman for three months longer, and he ultimately left the chairmanship on June 25, only five days before the end of his three-year term.

Mr. Dean's position became increasingly uncertain when it was revealed, early in March, that Rear Admiral Lewis Strauss was to be appointed as a special assistant to President Eisenhower to advise him on atomic energy matters. It was a matter of speculation whether Admiral Strauss was merely being placed in position to move quickly into the AEC chairmanship upon the departure of Mr. Dean, or whether the post of special assistant was to be a permanent one, a new link in the chain of command above the AEC. Late in June, of course, President Eisenhower did name Admiral Strauss to chair the Atomic Energy Commission. In any case, the intervening period had been one in which Chairman Dean had not been able to speak with authority for the new Administration.

For these reasons, the final months of Gordon Dean's chairmanship did not add to or change the AEC-Joint Committee relationships developed during the first two years of his tenure. How, then, may those relationships be characterized in the Dean period?

There is plenty of evidence that the Joint Committee by the time of the Dean chairmanship had adopted a strong advocacy of the AEC's program. Again and again, the Committee goaded the Commission for more speed and defended the program from outside threats. Statements from Committee members and staff personnel, both public and private, would lead one almost to the belief that the Joint Committee has been responsible for all the major developments in atomic energy during the past several years.

That, of course, would be an exaggeration. Congressmen are not reticent in evaluating their own achievements, and there is no reason to think that the Joint Committee offers an exception.

One can attain a balanced view if one imagines a continuum. At one end are the substantive Congressional committees which have little direct contact with the agencies and departments within their purview. At the other end are the committees which deal more closely with their agencies and directly influence their policies.[38] The Joint Committee on Atomic Energy of the later period must be placed far toward the latter end of the continuum, perhaps farther than any other committee of Congress.

This does not mean that a Congressional group was actually running the nation's atomic energy program. The Commission still was in charge. In fact, the Commission frequently made decisions in which the Committee had no hand whatever or with which the Committee openly disagreed.[39]

The new Commission-Joint Committee relationship definitely did mean, however, that a legislative group had established an almost uniquely close working arrangement with an agency, the legislators taking an intense interest in the program, acquiring extensive knowledge of it, feeling real personal responsibility for it, and vigorously pursuing its development.

In its eagerness to get forward with atomic development, the Joint Committee has sometimes advocated a program beyond that which the agency itself desired. Sometimes the Committee has been impatient with what it thought the slowness of the AEC; sometimes there has been a certain rivalry between the Committee and the AEC over which should have credit for popular decisions.

There are several ways to look at such an attitude. One might be that the Joint Committee members wanted to win political favor by taking credit for new developments in atomic energy. Interviewees have said that Senator McMahon especially, in his role as leader of the Committee, benefited from being known as "Mr. Atom" and from his continual association with the achievements in atomic energy.[40] Other Committee members, of course, do not share the chairman's limelight, though they do obtain a certain amount of publicity at hearings and Congressional debates.

It has also been suggested that the Joint Committee's role was made easy by the fact that it did not have to assume responsibility for the administrative and financial details of the program, that it could take credit for successful policies without risking criticism for administrative failures. But, on the whole, this view does not accord with the facts. The Committee risked a good deal of criticism, on more than one occasion, by taking a strong public stand in favor of specific aspects of the AEC program.

Whatever the explanation, the fact is that the Joint Committee emerged at the end of Gordon Dean's chairmanship as one of the strongest and most influential committees in Congress and the one which took the most active part in the affairs of its agency. Not since the middle years of the New Deal, the years of strong agricultural committees in both houses of Congress, has there been a case of legislative and executive groups working so closely and intensively toward the same goal.

Conditions within the Executive branch contributed to the growth of the Committee's attitude. The AEC, under Chairman Dean, showed a tendency, not to withdraw from the Executive, but to rely much less heavily than it had before upon the other agencies and departments within the Executive. The GAC, which had been a strong influence during the first two years, suffered a loss of prestige through its opposition to the thermonuclear project which removed it from the area of general policy, although its advice was still sought regularly on technical and scientific matters. The Department of Defense, though in general harmony with the AEC and the Joint Committee, was probably less enthusiastic about the atomic program than either of them. Defense officials were no longer working for greater military control of atomic weapons research, and were merely keeping up with developments. The Military Liaison Committee split into groups which tended to protect the interests of the three separate services and never exerted a unified influence on decisions of policy.

President Truman did not interfere with the AEC during the chairmanship of Mr. Dean. The President was consulted on all major issues—on the average, three times a year—but the initiative for atomic policy came neither from the White House nor from the National Security Council.

With no strong influence from the Executive branch, the AEC turned naturally to the Congressional group for support at the highest level. The Joint Committee was at the summit of its power.

VI

The Changing Forces

During the final months of Gordon Dean's chairmanship of the Atomic Energy Commission, the Republican Administration under President Eisenhower assumed control of the federal government, and Washington underwent the turmoil which inevitably accompanies a major change in political power. In January, 1953, the Joint Committee came under Republican control, but in January, 1955, it reverted to Democratic control. Mr. Dean remained as chairman into June, 1953, and in July he was succeeded by Lewis Strauss, the former Commissioner who had previously ended his service in 1950. The period from 1953 through 1955 can conveniently be called the Strauss period.

Recent events are always the most difficult to evaluate. The patterns of history do not become apparent until their cycles have been completed. It is impossible to make any conclusive judgments about the new relationships which have arisen between the AEC and the Joint Committee on Atomic Energy in the period 1953–1955. But certain new forces and new directions can be seen.

In the Strauss period, the observer can find many indications that the Joint Committee attempted to maintain its position as part of the inner control group of atomic energy. This intent appeared clearly in the series of events leading up to the Atomic

Energy Act of 1954, in certain provisions regarding the Joint Committee which were written into this statute, and in events subsequent to its passage.

The desirability of supporting a program of peacetime atomic power was the original consideration which developed into the comprehensive amending legislation of 1954. The AEC's program for civilian atomic power had gathered momentum slowly during the early years of the Commission's work. From 1947 until April, 1950, there had been one—and only one—project which had no military aspect whatever: a power-breeder reactor in process of development at Knolls Laboratory. The reactor was never built; in 1950 work was discontinued, and the AEC turned the experience it had gained to the task of constructing an atomic submarine.[1]

During the following months, however, the Commission received proposals from two industrial groups (Monsanto Chemical and Dow Chemical–Detroit Edison) which aimed at major industrial participation in the study and development of nuclear reactors that could be used to produce not merely plutonium but electric power as well. After discussing the proposals, the Commission in January, 1951, evolved what has been called the "Industrial Participation Program," which set forth the conditions under which the first step might be taken: a study of the AEC reactor development program by technical groups from the industrial concerns involved.[2]

On May 16, 1951, the Commission announced agreement with several groups of industrial concerns for studies of the possibility of private participation in the power development program. These studies were completed a year later, and in October, 1952, a second round of industrial reactor studies was begun.

During this time, of course, the Commission's own work on reactor development went forward. In place of the pessimism of the very first years was the AEC's first reactor development plan, announced in a speech by Dr. Bacher on March 17, 1949.[3] Dr. Bacher revealed that work would proceed on four new reactors, to form the basis of this nation's reactor development program. One was a submarine thermal reactor (STR); the second, originally a civilian power-breeder reactor on which work had been done at Knolls Laboratory, became, a year later, a submarine intermediate reactor, without peacetime power aspects. The third was a materials testing reactor (MTR), and the fourth an experimental breeder reactor (EBR). At this same time, the Reactor Development Division was created by the AEC.

One commentator ascribes this turning point in the reactor program partly to the criticisms of the Industrial Advisory Group in a December, 1948, report, and partly to pressure from the military for submarine propulsion units.[4] Whatever the reasons, the AEC had a program that would stimulate civilian power development, although the wisdom of assigning such high priority to military propulsion has been sharply questioned by some. In any case, Gordon Dean could truthfully state:

> We are going after the submarine reactor first. But in doing so, we are at least building a reactor that will produce useful power, and the dividend in knowledge that we gain will have a direct and immediate application to our effort to produce commercial civilian power.[5]

It was late in 1952 when the Joint Committee began to take an interest in civilian power development that went beyond merely keeping informed of AEC work (its statutory function) and urging continued efforts. From that time on, through the years of the Strauss period, the Joint Committee remained an active participant in the involved process of creating a power policy which would succeed at the earliest possible date. The first real move came on August 19, 1952, when Acting Chairman Durham wrote to the AEC, stating his intention to recommend early the following year that the Joint Committee hold a series of meetings on industrial participation, and requesting from the AEC a statement of views on the problem.[6] The Commission replied that it was then considering the problem in a series of conferences and would draw up a statement when its policy had crystallized. By the end of the year, the Joint Committee staff had prepared an extensive Committee Print of material, including speeches, reports, articles, and the like, all bearing on atomic power and private enterprise.

After the deadlock over its chairmanship early in 1953, but before the AEC policy statement was submitted, the Joint Committee became interested in the civilian power aspects of the new Eisenhower budget, which did not reach Congress until the middle of May. The entire federal budget, it will be remembered,was scaled down by the incoming Eisenhower Administration. Among various reductions in the AEC's budget requests was one in particular which seemed inadvisable to the Joint Committee members, especially Chairman Cole.[7] This was the elimination of an authorization to construct a pilot plant power reactor. Chairman Cole went to Chairman Phillips of the House Independent Offices Subcommittee and urged the restoration of this item. Later he spoke before the full subcommittee and said that he and the Joint Committee considered this elimination a dangerous slowdown in the preparations to construct a pilot model of a pressurized water reactor for commercial power.

Chairman Cole's overtures were apparently well received by the House subcommittee. Mr. Cole's standing was high with members of the subcommittee and with its chairman, Mr. Phillips, and the Cole arguments were persuasive. Chairman Dean of the Commission also argued against killing the provision, when the AEC appeared before the subcommittee, and his opinion undoubtedly was influential.[8] In any case, the House appropriations group decided to write into the bill a passage which would allow the AEC to go ahead with the construction of a civilian atomic power plant, provided it could be done within the total appropriated funds.[9] An important exception was made to the construction riders so that the project could be started even though funds for its completion were not available. In effect, the language of the bill was more than permission. It was direct encouragement to start with the reactor power plant, which the Eisenhower budget had eliminated. Of course, this did not mean an increase in the dollar amount of the year's appropriation, but it was a commitment to provide appropriations for the construction in future years.

Five months later, Commissioner Murray revealed the first result of this provision. On October 22, 1953, he announced that the AEC had embarked on a program to construct a full-scale power plant that would produce a minimum of 60,000 kilowatts of electricity. The AEC's reactor development division, Mr. Murray went on, had assigned immediate responsibility for the job to Admiral Rickover, the Navy's reactor expert. Westinghouse, having worked with the type of reactor chosen (pressurized water reactor), received the principal contract for the power reactor. The Duquesne Light Company contracted to build and operate the power station at a site on the Ohio River, 35 miles northwest of Pittsburgh.

In announcing the new reactor, Commissioner Murray made reference only to the Commission's decision that it was time for full-scale construction to be undertaken. Chairman Cole issued a statement the same day, however, which presented this policy decision in a different light. His statement read in part:

When the Joint Committee on Atomic Energy first saw the President's proposed budget on atomic energy for the coming

year, we realized that it made no provision for getting on with
development of a full-scale atomic power plant. As a result of
our review of this situation, we got into touch with the House
Appropriations Committee and explained the situation to them.
Through the close cooperation of the two committees there was
included, entirely on Congressional initiative, an authorization
to permit the start of construction this year of our first atomic
power plant. The Members of the Joint Committee and Congressman Phillips and his colleagues on the House Appropriations
Committee can take real pride in having been the originators of
this first major step. . . . It is gratifying indeed to see the Atomic
Energy Commission moving so swiftly in carrying out the will
of Congress in this project.[10]

Although this statement ignores the fact that the AEC also
favored retention of the pilot plant provision and argued for its
restoration before the subcommittee, there is undoubtedly a good
deal of truth in the assertion that the Committee's influence was
exceedingly important in bringing about the prompt construction
of the reactor. The Committee's success, in fact, is particularly
striking because it shows that the House Appropriations Subcommittee members had become susceptible to persuasion by
the Joint Committee—a definite contrast to their earlier lack of
confidence in the Joint Committee.

During the time when the budget was under consideration, the
Joint Committee undertook a series of twelve executive hearings
on the problem of private participation in atomic power development. On June 24, the hearings became public. At fourteen open
meetings, which lasted until July 31, more than fifty individuals
appeared to testify.[11]

In its twenty-six open and closed hearings, the Joint Committee used as a focal point for discussion the policy statement
requested by Representative Durham in 1952 and submitted by
the Commission at the end of May, 1953, together with an
AEC-proposed draft of new legislation aimed at promoting

private initiative in atomic energy by establishing the right of private ownership of fissionable materials and reactors and making other fundamental changes in the basic statute. The proposed legislation—alleged by Representative Holifield to lack Budget Bureau clearance—was not published, and received only informal Joint Committee consideration.

At the close of the hearings, Representative Cole summarized what the Joint Committee had done and predicted what might be done in the future. He first emphasized the comprehensiveness and diversity of the opinions expressed by the many witnesses—running all the way from encouragement of all-out private power development to insistence that only government development should be allowed. He then pointed out that a careful analysis of the testimony and other pertinent information would be necessary as preparation for considering possible legislation in 1954, and would be made by the Joint Committee.

After citing several points of substantial agreement among the various witnesses, Chairman Cole revealed that he had sent a request to the Commission, reading in part:

> 1. Even though the Commission has concluded that the time has not yet arrived when "any industrial, commercial, or other nonmilitary use of fissionable materials of atomic energy has been sufficiently developed to be of practical value," as set forth in section 7(b) of the act, it might, nevertheless, be of considerable assistance if the Commission were to prepare an estimate of the "social, political, economic, and international effects of such use" as now appear. . . .
>
> 2. There have been a substantial number of references by witnesses . . . to the indefiniteness of Commission plans for research and development in the field of atomic power components, pilot plants, and prototypes. It would seem appropriate that plans for Commission activity should be set forth in a concise manner so that all interested companies, groups, organizations, or individuals can henceforth have no doubt about the Federal program. . . .[12]

Two members of the Joint Committee, Representatives Holifield and Price, took a particular interest in civilian power policy. Representative Holifield delivered two addresses on the subject in the House, the second consisting of an analysis of the AEC policy statement.[13] Finally, at the close of the hearings on July 29, Representatives Holifield and Price introduced a resolution in the House and the former submitted a statement setting forth the viewpoint of the two Congressmen.[14] The Holifield statement reviewed his opinions of public sentiment to amend the Act to allow fuller participation by private enterprise in atomic power development. He expressed his conviction that basic changes in the Act would be "premature and ill-advised," and his strong opposition to any action that would "entail huge Government subsidies to private firms or restrict the participation, through patent devices or otherwise, to a small segment of industry." He took the position that the AEC should proceed with reactor development and technology "until private industry was willing and able to invest its own funds on an independent footing and to participate on the basis of equal opportunity for all."[15]

The Holifield-Price joint resolution was intended "to promote the peacetime application of atomic energy and the early development and practical use of atomic power." It provided for (1) advancement of the AEC reactor development program; (2) publication by the AEC of the greatest possible amount of information relating to civilian uses of atomic energy; (3) submission of an AEC report on the use of atomic power before enactment of any new legislation, in accord with Section 7(b) of the Act; (4) a continuation of Joint Committee study and investigation of the problems; (5) submission of a report to Congress by the Joint Committee of findings and recommendations.

There seemed to be substantial agreement among all parties on one point at least: that atomic power problems were complex, with no simple and easy solution, and that much further study would be necessary before new legislation could be formulated.

Meanwhile, the Joint Committee maintained its interest in AEC's progress toward atomic power technology. On February 5, 1954, the Commission submitted to the Joint Committee its proposed five-year power reactor development program, of which the already-announced PWR was a part. During February and March, the Joint Committee's Subcommittee on Research and Development held hearings on the program, and addressed pertinent questions to a number of nuclear scientists and engineers.[16] The subcommittee's conclusions were that the Joint Committee should support the program and should review it regularly. In addition, the subcommittee suggested that the Joint Committee confer with the AEC before further action on the PWR, to ensure that both groups agreed on its continuation, appreciated its limitations, and understood clearly what it might be expected to accomplish. (Such a meeting was held on March 12, 1954, when the AEC gave a detailed presentation on the PWR, and assured the Committee that every possible new development would be incorporated to make the reactor less costly without delaying its completion.) The report of the subcommittee was adopted by the full Joint Committee on March 23, 1954.

Having made certain that the Commission's reactor program would be vigorously pursued, the Joint Committee continued, early in 1954, to consider proposals for amending the Act to permit the participation of private industry in power development. On February 18, executive policy was finally established by a special Presidential message to Congress proposing amendments to the Act.[17] As a result of recent world events, President

Eisenhower did not limit himself to this aim, but recommended steps to achieve others as well:

1) Widened cooperation in certain specified areas with our allies;

2) Improved procedures for controlling and disseminating atomic energy information; and

3) Encouragement of broadened participation in developing peacetime uses of atomic energy.

With his message, the President submitted to the Joint Committee legislative proposals embodying these aims. But the Joint Committee asserted its own initiative, and disregarded the President's proposals by writing its own bill. Chairman Cole, in debate on the measure, explained the Committee's procedure. The President's bill, he said, was designed to carry out the three objectives, and would have made the international atomic pool possible, although it did not introduce the idea specifically. But it was so broad, and gave to the President "such rather complete, unlimited, and unrestricted authority, both in the domestic and in the international field," that Representative Cole refused to introduce it, feeling certain it would not be acceptable to the Committee, nor to the House.

Mr. Cole went on to say this:

> Thereupon the vice chairman and I and others . . . sat down and drafted our own bill. It had been my personal purpose and thought to treat these 3 phases of the amendments . . . in 3 separate bills. However, as we got into this subject, we discovered that the three problems were very interlocked and interwoven. We realized also that the act itself was in dire need of being overhauled and modernized and brought up-to-date. We therefore concluded that all 3 of our objectives, along with the overall revision, would be treated as 1 bill.[18]

The Joint Committee's work resulted in two companion bills, introduced by the Committee chairman and vice-chairman on

April 15 and 19, 1954, and referred back to the Committee for hearings.[19] In these deliberations, the Committee met almost daily and held a number of public hearings, at which witnesses from industry and from the Commission and other governmental units were heard. After weeks of work, new bills incorporating a number of revisions were introduced. The Joint Committee reported the new companion measures unanimously, though there was considerable feeling that certain of the provisions would need alteration on the floor of Congress.[20]

These events, which culminated in a new Atomic Energy Act, show that the Joint Committee was exceedingly active in the work of shaping the legislation and its underlying policy. Chairman Cole took pains to point this out to his colleagues in the House, when he said:

> This bill reflects the culmination of . . . 2 years of effort. If ever there was a bill that was figuratively hammered out on the anvil of the legislative process, this bill represents such a piece of proposed legislation.
>
> At no time have there been any instructions, given or accepted, by the administrative end of the Government, the Chief Executive or the Executive Department. Neither have we done other than to invite criticisms and recommendations of the Atomic Energy Commission.[21]

Mr. Cole's statement on the floor of the House was substantiated by Admiral Strauss when he said during the public hearings on the bill that:

> The record should show some place that this is not our bill . . . we are . . . the beneficiaries, but not the authors.[22]

On the whole, the bill which was passed by Congress was the same one which the Joint Committee reported out on July 12.[23] In contrast to the McMahon Act, the new legislation places a much greater emphasis on the peaceful uses of atomic energy and makes a determined attempt to separate atomic weapons from other devices which also happen to utilize nuclear materials. Thus, the AEC's monopolistic position has been curtailed somewhat; its direct and continuing control of *all* atomic plants and materials has been replaced by provisions which permit the private ownership of production and utilization facilities (e.g., reactors and their components as determined by the Commission) [24] as well as source materials (e.g., ores, concentrates, and metals) [25] and byproduct materials (e.g., radioactive reactor products other than fissionable materials).[26] Under license, private persons may use but not own special nuclear materials (e.g., plutonium and uranium enriched with the isotope U-235 or U-233).[27]

On the other hand, the responsibilities of the Commission have been increased several-fold by its new regulatory functions, i.e., the licensing of private production and utilization facilities, source and byproduct materials, and the use of special nuclear materials. In addition to licensing, the Commission must also establish standards and regulations for the private atomic industry, and inspect and supervise to see that these standards and regulations have been applied. This does not mean that the Commission is going out of the atomic business, because for a decade or so it will still be the principal producer of all atomic materials, both of the special nuclear and byproduct varieties.

Not only did the Joint Committee write the new Act, but it also insisted upon provisions to which the AEC was opposed. The strongest exception was taken to certain provisions which introduced the Joint Committee itself into the administration of the Act; but there was also some opposition to the creation of a new division of inspection within the internal organization of the AEC.[28] In all these cases, the Commission was unanimous in its opposition. Yet the Joint Committee ignored its wishes. The Joint Committee's position was as strong as ever.

On some other issues concerning the bill, the AEC was divided. Disagreements within the Commission occurred concerning (1) the description of the chairman's role and functions and (2) the propriety of entering into a long-term contract with a private utility to furnish electric power to the TVA, known as the Dixon-Yates contract.[29] These issues will be described in some detail later. Here it is sufficient to note that Commissioners Murray, Smyth, and Zuckert, appointees of President Truman, opposed Chairman Strauss and Commissioner Campbell, appointees of President Eisenhower. In doing so, they found support from the Democratic members of the Joint Committee, and as a result, the Committee accepted certain amendments to the draft of the bill. But these changes cannot be attributed to the strength of either the Commission or the Committee.

In drafting its own comprehensive revision, the Joint Committee made a number of changes which reinforce the impression that the Committee had no intention of foregoing its influential role. In fact, several of these provisions are really assertions of the Committee's desire to participate in the administration of the Act.

First are the provisions which underscore the requirement that the Committee shall be kept fully and currently informed. The Committee's report on the bill included a statement that it is the "intent of Congress that the Joint Committee be informed while matters are pending, rather than after action has been taken"—apparently an attempt to formalize the procedure which had become the informal rule during the Dean period. Furthermore, this obligation was extended to the Department of Defense, which must keep the Committee fully and currently informed on all matters within the Department's jurisdiction which relate to the development, utilization, or application of atomic energy. And the Committee also inserted a new provision to require any government agency to furnish any information requested by the Committee about that agency's activities in atomic energy.[30]

Originally the Joint Committee had even inserted a clause which provided that the Military Liaison Committee "shall keep the Joint Committee fully and currently informed on all military matters of the Department of Defense which the Joint Committee deems to relate to atomic energy, including any disputes or disagreements between the Commission and the Department of Defense, which relate to atomic energy." [31] But at closed sessions with the Joint Committee, Defense Department representatives reportedly argued that such a provision would infringe the principle of the separation of legislative and executive powers, and it was dropped. With both the Commission and the Department under statutory mandate to give the Committee complete information, however, the loss of the provision scarcely seems a handicap to the Committee.

Second, the Joint Committee added a clause which provided that during the first sixty days of each session of Congress, the Committee should hold hearings to receive information on the "development, growth, and state of the atomic energy industry" —a provision which seemed designed solely to require the Committee to do its own job more thoroughly.

Third, the Committee inserted itself into the procedures for determining what constitute "source materials" and "special nuclear materials." [32] The Act specifies that such determinations shall be made first by the Commission, next sent to the President for his assent, and finally laid before the Committee for thirty days, presumably to inform the Committee of what has been done. However, this provision might give the Committee, which has ready access to the sources of publicity, an effective veto over the decisions of the Commission and the President.[33]

Fourth, to a certain extent the Committee injected itself into foreign policy. The new Act permits the government to enter into cooperative agreements with other nations or with regional defense organizations, either to develop nonmilitary applications of atomic energy, or to exchange information on the defensive use of atomic weapons.[34] In the case of the nonmilitary agreements, the AEC is the responsible negotiator. In the case of military agreements the Department of Defense and the AEC join in the negotiations. In either case, the agreements must be approved by the President and must then lie before the Joint Committee for thirty days before they can take effect.[35]

The Commission and the Department of Defense joined forces to oppose the requirement that such agreements should lie before the Committee, but they met with little success, and they were effectively defeated when the Secretary of State refused to support them.[36]

Fifth, the Joint Committee acquired an additional mechanism of control as a result of the controversy on the floor of the Senate over the long-term utility contract with the Dixon-Yates combination.[37] Actually, as reported out by the Committee, the section authorizing the Commission to enter into long-term utility contracts was the same as an amendment to the McMahon Act which had been approved in the previous session. However, because the Commission's use of this authority to act as a broker between the TVA and private utilities caused great opposition, this section was changed by several qualifying provisions. Among them is a stipulation that any long-term utility contract entered into for electric services at the Oak Ridge, Paducah, and Portsmouth installations must be submitted to the Joint Committee for a period of thirty days.[38] Thus, without planning it, the Joint Committee gained an additional control.

Sixth, the Joint Committee acquired in the new Act the power of specific authorization for AEC expenditures for the "acquisition or condemnation of real property" and for "plant construction or expansion." [39] The Committee's long campaign to establish a procedure whereby it could pass on specific enabling legislation has been described already. The Commission's reaction when it heard of this newest proposal was the same as it had been earlier. In a letter and subsequently at the hearings, the AEC strongly urged the deletion of this provision on the ground that it would seriously delay vital atomic energy programs. [40] A memorandum submitted to the Committee pointed out that the absolute need for flexibility in the 1955 budget militated against the relatively rigid procedure of the enabling proposal. As a matter of fact, because precise construction plans hinged upon the results of various recent tests, the AEC had been able to persuade the House Appropriations Committee to palliate its construction rider in order to preserve the necessary flexibility, and the memorandum emphasized this. The victory would be wasted, the memorandum went on, if the authorization proposal were enacted. The Commission hoped that a budget presentation to the Joint Committee before the Appropriations Committees called for testimony—a practice followed "in previous years"—would be enough to keep the Joint Committee informed and make the enabling legislation unnecessary. The plea was of no avail, however, and the Joint Committee recommended the enabling provision to Congress.

The authorization power gained by the Joint Committee in this provision is a rather narrow one. It applies only to plant construction and real property acquisition. It is by no means program authorization. The Appropriations Committees did not oppose the provision and apparently did not feel that it was a threat to their own power. Perhaps also the close relationship between Chairman Phillips of the House Appropriations Subcommittee and Chairman Cole of the Joint Committee forestalled any conflict.

All of these powers served to place the Joint Committee in an exceedingly strong position from which to exercise the initiative in atomic affairs. Its insistence on these powers strongly supports the view that its leadership under the Cole chairmanship of 1953–1954 remained undiminished.

However, at about this time there occurred a widely publicized series of events which at first glance seem to challenge the conclusion that the Joint Committee maintained a high degree of initiative. These events began with the withdrawal of J. Robert Oppenheimer's security clearance, which had been kept active to allow him to act as an AEC consultant whenever the occasion might arise. Subsequently, the case was considered by a special review board (the so-called Gray Board), and written appeal was made directly to the AEC for final action by the Commissioners, following a recommendation by the General Manager.[41] The proceedings themselves were conducted entirely within the AEC. The repercussions of the case, however, were very wide; the action taken against Dr. Oppenheimer was considered to represent a theory of personnel security which some found abhorrent and others vitally necessary.

Although the case was initiated by a letter of charges against Dr. Oppenheimer prepared by the former executive director of the Joint Committee, the Committee and its staff remained entirely in the background during the proceedings. But no conclusion can be drawn from this failure to take an active role. The Committee had no opportunity to take a stand until the proceedings were completed on June 29, 1954, with the Commission's final decision. At that time the Committee was busy with amending the Act, and had no time to undertake hearings or investigations unless they were absolutely necessary. Procedurally, the case was handled in a perfectly regular and extremely thorough way, and there is no reason to believe that the Joint Committee members seriously opposed the decision which the AEC majority felt compelled to make, in spite of Commissioner Smyth's vigorous dissent. The Oppenheimer case, therefore, scarcely indicates a failure of initiative by the Joint Committee, and the other evidence from this period is almost wholly to the contrary.

■

One of the most significant developments in atomic energy under the Eisenhower administration has been the increasingly active role of the Chief Executive and his advisers. In part, this has been caused by the new Atomic Energy Act of 1954. The increased importance of Executive branch units outside the AEC is clearly indicated in the duties assigned to the President and the Department of Defense in the new Act. Retaining his duty to set annually production rates of special nuclear materials (Section 41b), to determine when and how much of these materials the AEC should deliver to the military (Section 91b), and to consent at least annually to the quantities of atomic weapons to be made, the President in the Act was specifically delegated other duties. First, the President was named as the final arbiter regarding agreements for cooperation with other nations in the use of special nuclear, source, and byproduct materials, as well as production and utilization facilities (Section 123). He has the same role in regard to international arrangements (Section 124). Second, he was required to decide in what cases the AEC was authorized to share nonmilitary restricted data with other nations (Section 144a). Third, his approval is necessary, should the Commission want to classify other substances as "source materials" or as "special nuclear materials" (Sections 51 and 61).

The powers of the Department of Defense were expanded to meet the new and enlarged military applications of atomic energy. Once the President has authorized the Department of De-

fense to manufacture or acquire any atomic weapons or utilization facilities, the AEC is forbidden to interfere and is denied
the authority to require a license for such facilities (Section
110b). Although the AEC retains title to the special nuclear
materials used by the Department, the latter obtains its special
nuclear materials by a determination of the President (Section
91b). Joint powers are created to govern the domestic release of
restricted military data (Section 142c), and the President may
authorize the Department to arrange to release such data to
another nation with the assistance of the AEC (Section 144b).
Finally it was made clear that the Department could take to the
President for settlement all matters of controversy with the
AEC (Section 27b).

More than the new basic statute was involved, however, in
the growth of top-level policy initiative. Various interpretations
of this trend have been made, but all agree that one event of
late 1953 was a pre-eminent cause of the President's new concern for atomic policy. That event was the Soviet Union's
achievement of a large-scale thermonuclear or H-bomb reaction.
On August 8, 1953, Malenkov announced that the United States
no longer had a monopoly on thermonuclear weapons. Eleven
days later, Washington and Moscow both revealed that recent
Russian tests had included fission and fusion (H-bomb) reac-
tions.

The realization that the United States' success in producing
the hydrogen bomb had been matched by the Russians only a
short time later gave rise to profound misgivings throughout
America. In Washington the significance of the Soviet success
was appraised and reappraised. This appraisal was the beginning
of a growing realization in the Executive branch that world
events demanded a more active and forceful policy by the
United States, if atomic war was to be avoided. Out of this
realization came a number of vigorous decisions by the highest

executive echelons. This occurred in both defense and foreign policy, the latter incorporating the active use of the peacetime aspects of the atom.

In the area of defense, certain concrete results appeared soon after the Soviet achievement of the H-bomb. Civil defense came suddenly to the fore with the establishment of Project Lincoln, a study carried out by the Massachusetts Institute of Technology of our actual and potential ability to survive atomic attack.[42] The project report advocated a vast expansion of continental defense measures (radar, industrial dispersion, etc.). Even more fundamental was a reappraisal of American military priorities, begun in the fall of 1953. Some observers reported the development of a new approach to defense, in keeping with which the nation should strictly limit the production of conventional weapons and rest United States security on atomic weapons.[43] This theory was debated at the end of the year, and out of it came the so-called "new look" in American defense policy, with emphasis on air power and nuclear weapons—offering to potential aggressors the threat of "massive retaliation." [44]

The newly emphasized possibility of all-destroying atomic war had other repercussions. When the Eisenhower-Churchill Bermuda conference was held in December, 1953, the respective delegations included on their agendas the problem of increasing the exchange of information between the two nations in order to build a more solid defense line. Some steps toward this end had already been taken, and data had been shared on the effects of atomic weapons on human beings and their environment.[45]

At the end of 1954, the North Atlantic Treaty Organization held a conference in Paris. Its objective was to work out arrangements for the use of atomic weapons by the NATO Supreme Commander with or without agreement among the participating governments. Negotiations, which were in the hands of the Defense and State Departments, produced an agreement between the North Atlantic Treaty powers to share information on atomic weapons.[46]

The President and his advisers did not limit their efforts in atomic affairs to defense, however. They also undertook a positive program aimed at lessening the need for defense by exploiting the peacetime aspects of the atom to increase international well-being and to foster friendship among nations. By all odds the most significant outgrowth of this program was the President's atom pool proposal, first announced in an address he delivered before the United Nations' General Assembly on December 8, 1953.[47] Mr. Eisenhower suggested that an international atomic energy agency be established by the UN. The nations which possessed atomic energy programs would then pool fissionable materials with this agency, which would distribute them to meet the needs of agriculture, medicine, and other peaceful activities throughout the world. The President invited the Soviet Union to participate in the plan.

During the succeeding months the United States engaged in diplomatic negotiations with the USSR. The results of these negotiations were meager, however, for the Soviet response appeared to be chiefly negative. As a result of this failure to achieve an understanding with the USSR on the UN atom pool, the United States felt it should arrange a substitute plan for sharing the peaceful benefits of atomic energy. This feeling was intensified as a result of a March 1 weapons test, the great significance of which became clear during subsequent months.[48]

This test indicated that a "uranium" bomb could be easily built by using relatively abundant natural uranium in conjunction with a thermonuclear weapon. In such a combination, the fusion reaction induces fission in the natural uranium. The first test gave an explosion about twice as great as had been expected, too great for the instruments to measure accurately. It was soon realized that such a weapon could be easily and cheaply expanded to almost unlimited size, dwarfing even the H-bomb. This knowledge gave renewed impetus to the need to develop the peaceful use of the atom, and to make this a basis for increased international understanding and good will.

Within the limits imposed by the new Atomic Energy Act of 1954, the President and his advisers drew up modified plans for developing a peaceful atomic program. At the UN General Assembly meeting in September, 1954, Secretary Dulles revealed American plans for a program in 1955. The United States, he said, was negotiating bilateral agreements with seven western nations, under which the United States would train scientists and technicians from these countries and supply nuclear materials. Mr. Dulles called on the General Assembly to establish an international agency to act as a clearinghouse for such negotiations.

This program, now called the Atoms for Peace plan, was embodied in a resolution introduced in the General Assembly by the United States.[49] The resolution, which would have given what amounted to a UN mandate to the plan, was debated for two weeks and subjected to continuous criticism by the USSR and other nations. Then Mr. Lodge revealed that the United States was allocating 100 kilograms of fissionable material to implement the plan, and Great Britain offered twenty additional kilograms.[50] This concrete manifestation of American and British determination to carry through the plan countered the opposition effectively. Mr. Lodge promptly worked out with Russia's Vishinsky a compromise resolution supporting the plan. Under its terms, the UN would convene by August, 1955, an international scientific conference on atomic energy, which would create an international agency to facilitate and supervise bilateral exchanges of information and materials. This agency's relationship to the UN was left to be settled later. This resolution received unanimous UN endorsement, although the USSR retained certain doubts and said it might not participate.[51] Early in 1955, plans for the conference got under way and the United States proceeded to conclude agreements with other nations for the sharing of information and materials. By June, the number of such agreements reached twenty-two.[52]

On June 11, 1955, President Eisenhower announced a new phase of the Atoms for Peace program. He said the United States would be willing to contribute one-half the cost of medical and research reactors for friendly nations, and to give them, "within prudent security considerations," the technological assistance needed to build and operate, at these nations' own expense, commercial reactors capable of supplying power for modern industry.[53]

To assist the negotiations required for the Atoms for Peace plan, the President appointed a special representative on international atomic matters, Mr. Morehead Patterson. It was Mr. Patterson who made the announcement in April, 1955, that a preliminary draft of a statute for an international atomic energy agency had been drawn up and circulated to a number of governments. He also attended the San Francisco Conference of the Atomic Industrial Forum to enunciate the Administration's policy of encouraging American business to build nuclear power plants abroad. Another Presidential emissary was Robert LeBaron, ex-chairman of the MLC, who was sent to South America to survey the possibilities there for international cooperation in the development of atomic energy for peaceful uses.

Although the AEC was doubtless not totally ignorant of the planning connected with the Atoms for Peace program, it is quite clear that the main impetus came from outside the Commission. The impression that the AEC played a secondary role in this program is strengthened by the fact that the many speeches, announcements, and press conference comments on the plan came exclusively from the top executive echelons.

Another incident illustrated the fact that policy on the international aspects of atomic energy was formulated at the Presidential level. This concerned the plan to build an atomic-powered merchant vessel, a so-called "peace ship," which could demonstrate to people in foreign ports the United States' peaceful applications of atomic energy in nuclear propulsion and radioisotope work in medicine and commerce.[54] The Joint Committee hearings on authorizing this and other capital outlay for the AEC revealed that the merchant ship idea had been conceived in the National Security Council, although Admiral Strauss, a regular participant in that body's deliberations on the atom, declined to reveal any particular person whose "brainchild" it was. The NSC then sent a directive to Chairman Strauss for an urgent study of the proposal. The study was quickly completed by the AEC's Reactor Development Division, but the other Commissioners did not know that the study was going on and were never able to consider the matter before Admiral Strauss reported to the NSC on April 7. At that meeting the proposal was adopted, and two days later a Presidential directive assigned high priority to the merchant ship as part of the Atoms for Peace program.[55]

It was world events, then, that gave heightened significance to atomic policy. Commissioner Murray expressed the change succinctly. "With the advent of Fusion Joe, as I call the Soviet thermonuclear test shot of last August," he said, "atomic energy has finally forced itself into the high councils of our government." [56] Furthermore, propaganda rivalry among the big powers naturally centered upon atomic power and other peaceful applications of atomic energy as the most attractive aspects of atomic development for the rest of the world. All of this activity was conducted in our government at the highest executive level, usually by special units and officials created by the President, and the Atomic Energy Commission found itself in a decidedly secondary position in such matters of atomic policy.

The top executive echelons also took a more active part in domestic atomic matters. President Eisenhower made revision of the Atomic Energy Act an important phase of his legislative program. He had already submitted his special message to Congress on February 18, 1954, and had asked for a wide program of information-sharing and increased participation by private industry in atomic power development.[57] But probably the most controversial step taken by the President occurred in the spring of 1954 when he ordered the AEC to proceed with negotiations with a private utility combination to obtain power for the TVA and thus compensate it for the amounts taken by the AEC at the Paducah installation.[58] This power, amounting to 600,000 kilowatts, was to come from a new plant in West Memphis, Arkansas, to be built by the Mississippi Generating Company, a new corporation controlled by two utility holding companies, Middle South Utilities Company and the Southern Company. It was thought that this replacement power could be fed into the TVA to provide enough power for the load growth of the area without any TVA plant expansion. In any case, new power generating facilities were seen to be necessary; a decision had to be made whether TVA should build them, or whether private utilities should build them and deliver their power output into the TVA system.

After informal conversations between Chairman Strauss and other government officials, the Acting Budget Director in December, 1953, wrote to the AEC and requested an exploration of the possibility of obtaining a large block of private power. Out of the ensuing negotiations grew the proposal of Middle South and Southern, known as the Dixon-Yates proposal. Details of the negotiations were submitted to the Bureau of the

Budget, together with the Commission's views on this and on a later proposal made by a group headed by Walter von Tresckow, a New York financial consultant. On June 16, 1954, Mr. Hughes of the Bureau of the Budget informed the Commission that the whole matter had been considered, including the possibility of expansion by the TVA, and that the President had asked him to "instruct the Atomic Energy Commission to proceed with negotiations with the sponsors of the proposal made by Messrs. Dixon and Yates with a view to signing a definite contract. . . ."

This directive set off a wide controversy; it was charged that the Administration was overriding the Commission's will in an attempt to undermine the TVA. While Commissioners Strauss and Campbell supported the proposed contract, the others expressed varying degrees of dissatisfaction with the President's order.

General Nichols, General Manager of the Commission, took the public position that the issue was one for decision at the Presidential level. In effect, he was admitting the President's authority to direct the Commission on issues other than those entrusted to him in the Act. After the contract had been approved by the AEC, Chairman Strauss said in a press conference that he wished that the TVA had negotiated the contract directly but that it was a Presidential order for the AEC to do so and hence he had had to proceed.[59] The legal question of the degree of AEC independence is not important here. Rather, the incident is one more clear indication that the President was determined to take a hand in policy matters which involved the AEC.

In the developments which ensued, the Republican-appointed AEC continued to follow the Presidential order and completed the negotiation of the contract with Dixon-Yates. The Republican-controlled Joint Committee waived the 30-day period of waiting and permitted the contract to become effective immediately.[60] The Democratic-controlled Joint Committee in 1955, by a straight party vote of 10 to 8, recommended that the Administration cancel the Dixon-Yates contract.[61] Thereafter the conflict was carried on in the debate over the President's budget request for an appropriation to construct transmission lines from the site to the TVA connecting lines. Although the House Appropriations Committee converted this request into an item for a new TVA steam plant, the full House, supported later by the Senate, approved the President's request.[62] The fact that the President was able to win approval for his domestic power policy against the wishes of the majority of the Joint Committee clearly indicated a lack of Committee power in politically charged matters of this kind.[63]

■

The President's closer dealing with atomic policy has, of course, affected the role of the AEC, and the change can probably be seen most clearly in the position of the chairman. All the evidence indicates that Admiral Strauss was very close to the President; indeed, he was a member of the circle of Mr. Eisenhower's highest counselors.

Even before he became chairman of the AEC, Admiral Strauss had been President Eisenhower's special adviser on atomic energy, and he continued to act in that capacity even while he carried on his duties as chairman of the Commission. Soon after he was appointed to the chairmanship, Strauss began to attend all meetings of the National Security Council, at the invitation of the President.[64] Early in 1954, Chairman Cole of the Joint Committee introduced a bill which would have made the AEC chairman a permanent member of the Council.[65] Representative Cole commended the President for his "sound custom" of inviting Admiral Strauss to attend the meetings, but he felt that the importance of atomic energy required the Commission chairman to become a member with full and permanent status, although later he changed his mind.[66]

These moves were particularly important because President Eisenhower was making more active use of the National Security Council than ever before in its history.[67] The Council regularly met for three weekly briefing sessions which ranged widely over the policy decisions confronting the Administration.

Beyond this, there were other indications that Admiral Strauss was prominent as a personal adviser to the President and as the top staff expert on atomic energy. He attended the Bermuda conference with the President and Secretary of State Dulles, and represented the government in talks with Lord Cherwell, Mr. Churchill's scientific adviser. He was reportedly one of the two chief advisers to Mr. Eisenhower on the atomic pool plan, the other being C. D. Jackson, then the President's assistant on psychological warfare.[68] At Bermuda, Press Secretary Hagerty announced the impending United Nations address, and said that Admiral Strauss and Lord Cherwell had been working on it ever since their arrival there.

In the spring of 1955, Admiral Strauss clearly was the only AEC Commissioner who was involved in the planning for the atomic-powered demonstration merchant ship. It was established at subsequent hearings by the Joint Committee that no Commission consideration or discussion occurred before the final National Security Council action. Notification to the other Commissioners of the impending consideration of the matter by the National Security Council occurred a day or two before the Council's meeting at which the policy was formally approved. Admiral Strauss explained this as a result of an inadvertent breakdown in communications within the Commission in addition to a sudden advance in the date of the meeting of the NSC.[69] Regardless of the reasons for the lack of consultation inside the Commission, the episode clearly illustrated that the role of the AEC chairman in the executive councils had become somewhat separate from his role as chairman of the Atomic Energy Commission.

It can be said with assurance, then, that the Strauss period was characterized by a new relationship between the President and the chairman of the AEC, with a resulting enhancement of the position of the latter. In the earlier period, of course, there was some contact between Chairman Gordon Dean and President Truman, and Mr. Dean could have been regarded in a sense as an adviser to the President on atomic energy.[70] But the contacts were sporadic and there was no consistent policy of initiative at the level of the President. Also, Mr. Dean played down his own position by working closely with his fellow Commissioners and acting consistently as spokesman for the policies evolved among the five, each voice having equal weight. All in all, the new relationship unquestionably differed substantially from prior relationships between the President and AEC chairmen.

Accompanying this trend was a new development in the chairman's position within the Commission itself. Gordon Dean, it will be recalled, worked with his fellow Commissioners closely and harmoniously. Interviews with Mr. Dean and others who worked with him gave evidence of his theory that it was of great importance for the AEC to function as a Commission, with all five Commissioners bringing their talents and viewpoints to bear equally on policy decisions. The chairman, of course, had to represent the Commission alone at times when it would have been inappropriate for all five members to be present, and he also naturally conducted a large share of the correspondence. In such cases, however, Mr. Dean made a policy of acting as a spokesman for the group, having consulted with his four colleagues in advance.

Admiral Strauss departed somewhat from the practice of his

predecessor. It may be that he adopted a different conception of his role mainly because, in his relations with the President, he enjoyed a position which was different and in some respects larger than the chairmanship had been before. But causes in matters of this kind are difficult to ascribe from the outside.

It has been reported that Admiral Strauss's methods began to provoke disagreement soon after he assumed the chairmanship in 1953, and that feelings ran higher and higher as the months went by.[71] In any case, the issue came into the open in May, 1954, when the Joint Committee came to consider a proposal written into the draft of the bill to amend the Act (reportedly on the initiative of Chairman Cole, principally, and Senator Hickenlooper). This proposal would have designated the chairman "principal officer of the Commission." [72] It caused a 3 to 2 AEC split between Truman appointees Smyth, Murray, and Zuckert, on the one hand, and Eisenhower appointees Strauss and Campbell, on the other. The various Commissioners appeared before the Joint Committee to testify concerning the "principal officer" provision, but in doing so they recorded their feelings about the manner in which the present chairman was filling his office.

The opposition to Admiral Strauss argued that he was unquestionably exceeding his powers by ignoring the other Commissioners and by failing to consult with them or keep them informed on major policy decisions. Commissioner Murray asserted specifically that "there have been some" major decisions from which the other four Commissioners had been excluded. Other instances had occurred, he said, when the four lacked access to atomic energy matters. Commissioner Smyth felt that Admiral Strauss had less confidence than former chairmen in him and that there was less informal consultation than there once had been. Commissioners Smyth and Murray joined Commissioner Zuckert in opposing any revision of the Act which would give the chairman more power or destroy in any way the co-equal status of the five Commissioners.[73]

Commissioners Strauss and Campbell supported the proposed amendment to the Act and cited the recommendation of the Hoover Commission that administrative responsibility should always be vested in the chairmen of government commissions. Admiral Strauss denied that he had failed to consult with his fellow Commissioners or failed to keep them informed. He said that he had not made any commitments to President Eisenhower without consulting his four colleagues.

The split between AEC members appointed by Mr. Truman and those appointed by Mr. Eisenhower was paralleled by a split in the Joint Committee, more or less on party lines. The Republican members favored the proposal, while Democrats, notably Representatives Holifield and Price, opposed it.[74]

On June 9, it was reported that the Joint Committee had resolved its conflict over the provision. Unanimously the group approved a section which said specifically that the Commissioners have "equal responsibility and authority" but denoted the chairman as "official spokesman" and charged him with the "faithful execution" of the Commission's policy decisions.[75] Chairman Cole said that he had never intended to alter the co-equal status of the members but merely to make the chairman a spokesman for all, as the compromise provided. Other Joint Committee members noted approvingly that the chairman's duties were delineated for the first time, the original Act having been silent on the point. All the Commissioners approved the compromise fully except Commissioner Murray, who had complained of non-access to atomic information and who felt that the new bill failed to state clearly that all five members should have equal access.

That his fears were not entirely unfounded is borne out by the fact that Admiral Strauss learned of General Manager Nichols' desire to resign, and then held it on a personal basis until General Nichols' decision was irrevocable. To the question of Senator Gore: "You do not think that a matter so important as the prospective resignation of the General Manager of the Commission is of sufficient importance to justify your confidence in your fellow Commissioners?", Mr. Strauss replied, "Not so long as I had it on a personal basis." [76]

Disagreement within the Commission occurred again in the matter of the "peace ship." The one remaining Commissioner appointed by President Truman, Commissioner Murray, was clearly annoyed with the chairman's handling of AEC consideration of this matter, and he made it plain in his testimony before the Joint Committee on the stages of development of the idea.[77] Significantly, the former Republican chairman of the Joint Committee, Representative Cole, was the one member who unswervingly, and embarrassingly for Chairman Strauss, insisted on going to the bottom of this episode. Representative Holifield summarized the Democratic concern with the conduct of the AEC's operations at the Commission level in this statement:

> We also feel, from the testimony that has been given, there was a lack of consideration of this between the members of the Commission even on the limited time element that was involved, in view of the answers that have come from some questions. And it brings up the old topic of whether the Commission is functioning as it should function, with a complete interchange of information among the Commissioners.[78]

■

It will be recalled that two trends within the Executive branch characterized the Strauss period. First, the focus of initiative in atomic policy appeared to be moving away from the Commission to some extent and in the direction of a new system of power centered upon the President and the National Security Council. Second, this new focus of initiative seemed to include the AEC chairman but to exclude the AEC as a whole. Chairman Strauss gained in influence, therefore, at the expense of his fellow Commissioners. Whatever the precise degree of this development, Admiral Strauss unquestionably exercised leadership and initiative in a way different from that of previous chairmen. This stemmed from his own personality, marked by independence and forcefulness, from the confidence placed in him by the President and most of the Congress as a result of his record on atomic energy policy, from the President's reliance on him for advice since early 1953, and from the Soviet H-bomb and succeeding world developments which put atomic energy policy in a category of most crucial significance.

The Joint Committee experienced difficulty in dealing with the new center of power—the President and his advisers, including Chairman Strauss. It was true that the Committee continued to give support to the AEC chairman. It was true that the Committee's Republican majority originated the proposal to denote him the "principal officer" of the Commission, and that Chairman Cole favored giving him a permanent seat on the National Security Council. Nonetheless, there was evidence of a certain independence on Chairman Strauss's part, not unnoticed by the Joint Committee.

This was discussed during hearings on the new Atomic Energy Act. Chairman Cole asked Admiral Strauss if there had not been recent instances when the AEC had resisted the principle that it must keep the Joint Committee fully and currently informed. When Chairman Strauss suggested that it was simply a matter of delay rather than resistance, Mr. Cole reminded him that for the first time in its history the Joint Committee had been forced to adopt a formal resolution to get information from the AEC. The press reported that the information consisted of minutes of Commission meetings, to be used in assessing the charge that Admiral Strauss had acted without consulting his colleagues on the AEC.[79]

There were further indications of the difficulty which the Joint Committee experienced in the new executive arrangements. At the hearings on amending the Act, Representative Holifield questioned Chairman Strauss on his relationship with the President as special adviser on atomic energy affairs. Several times Chairman Strauss flatly refused to give substantive answers to Representative Holifield's questions. Replying to a query on whether he had been consulted regarding the international atomic pool plan, he stated that he thought the question was one on which he should not be pressed. Later he stated again his feeling that he "must not testify on the subject of consultation by the President, however important or trivial the item." [80]

Again, on the first day of the "60-day hearings," held under the requirements of Section 202 of the Atomic Energy Act of 1954, it developed that the Joint Committee had not been informed of the decision of the General Manager to resign because both the chairman and the General Manager thought it was desirable "that it be not announced until [the] successor has been selected. For purposes of morale it seemed a good thing to do. That purpose was defeated by the leak of the information." [81] Eventually, because of the leak to the newspapers, Chairman Anderson of the Joint Committee heard the news from a newspaperman.[82] This incident leads to the further conclusion that the arrangements within the Commission itself were of such a nature that they prevented the Joint Committee from being a complete part of the inner control group.

During the "peace ship" controversy, Representative Cole indicated the Joint Committee's realization that it had to deal with a new, higher center of power and that it might have difficulty in getting its views accepted. Mr. Cole wrote a letter of protest directly to the President, rather than to the AEC, suggesting revisions in the plan. At the authorization hearing, he expressed some concern over the fact that no reply to his letter was made either by the President's office or by the AEC.[83] He took this to mean that the Executive branch had not agreed with his ideas and had abruptly discarded them. Chairman Strauss suggested that the AEC had not received a copy of the letter and that it had gone from the White House to Mr. Nelson Rockefeller, the President's adviser on psychological warfare. Later Chairman Strauss said he thought the AEC did have the letter after all. In any case, it can be seen that Representative Cole found it difficult to discover just where to direct his irritation. It was obviously not easy to determine who was responsible for the failure to respond to his objections, and whether complaints to the AEC might be unjustified because responsibility lay with higher authorities. Although this particular instance was not regarded very seriously, it did show that the Joint Committee might be hampered in attempts to bring its influence to bear on subsequent issues of greater moment.

Another factor, in addition to the intrusion of high executive elements in questions of atomic policy, tended to reduce the influence of the Joint Committee. This was the return of politics to the scene. The development of political overtones in many aspects of atomic policy affected both the Commission and the Committee, but since the Committee, composed of two parties, is a fundamentally political group, it was affected to a somewhat greater degree than the theoretically nonpartisan AEC.

Political factors became important, first, because traditionally controversial issues arose within the area of atomic policy. The success of thermonuclear devices and the "uranium" bomb in the weapons program had removed some of the urgency from questions of national defense, and attention could be turned to the civilian power field. Here open disagreements arose over the traditional Democratic-Republican issue of public power versus private power.

The disagreement was at the heart of the debate in the Senate, including a filibuster, on the proposed omission from the new Atomic Energy Act of the traditional "preference clause" favoring public and cooperative bodies in the distribution of public power.[84] It was related to the Dixon-Yates controversy, in which, it will be recalled, the AEC and the Joint Committee were thrust into politics by the President's insistence that the AEC become an instrument for the Administration's power policy.

Political elements came into prominence, not alone because hot partisan issues arose, but also because Presidential intervention tends to increase the likelihood of partisan byplay, whatever the issue. The President is leader of his party, and Presidential policy is considered the policy of the majority party. The opposition party is more likely to take issue with top-level executive decision-making than with the same decision when it is made by a relatively nonpartisan agency like the AEC. The Administration's "peace ship" proposal is a case in point. Considered part of the Republican program, it became a major political issue in the area of international policy.

The opening up of traditional partisan issues and the appearance of political controversy over the Administration's policy-making tended to weaken the influence of the Joint Committee in two ways. First, the Joint Committee itself split over political issues, thus hampering its own effectiveness by its inability to take a unanimous stand. For example, the Joint Committee split twice on strict party lines over the Dixon-Yates dispute. The Republican-controlled Committee of the 83d Congress voted 10 to 8 to waive the requirement that the contract lie before the Joint Committee for thirty days, and later the Democratic-controlled Committee voted 10 to 8 to recommend that the contract be canceled.

The patent provisions of the 1954 Act, though not so controversial, presented another instance of sharp Committee conflict. The Committee as a whole supported a five-year compulsory licensing provision. Four members disagreed. Two Republican Representatives, Cole and Van Zandt, asserted that the provision went too far. Compulsory licensing, they maintained, amounts to "Socialism run rampant." Two other members, Democratic Representatives Holifield and Price, felt that the provision did not go far enough. In their view, compulsory licensing was absolutely necessary, but for a period of at least ten years, rather than five as recommended by the majority. Because the Joint Committee was so divided, it was forced to accept the President's recommendation on this issue.[85]

On the "peace ship" authorization, the Joint Committee originally took a divided stand, but not wholly on party lines since at least one Republican, Representative Cole, opposed the plan. In the Senate, however, the issue was so clearly political that all the members from the Senate side of the Joint Committee voted on a strict party basis, as did all the other Senators but one. Such a strong political atmosphere is bound to have an effect on a committee whose members might otherwise take a unanimous stand or at least split only on the merits of the case, uninfluenced by party needs and political labels. Such an effect is indicated by the fact that Representative Cole, evidently the chief GOP critic of the original proposal, changed his stand and drew up new legislation authorizing the "peace ship." He said he did this not by Administration request, but only "on the strength of" accounts that the President still wanted the vessel. Although no behind-the-scenes negotiations have been revealed, it seems likely that Representative Cole was subjected to political pressure to accede to the strong emphasis of the Eisenhower Ad-

ministration on the "peace ship" plan. Subsequently the Director
of the Bureau of the Budget wrote a letter to Representative
Price in which he stressed the President's strong hope that the
"peace ship" proposal could still be passed before Congress adjourned.[86] Although Republicans of the Joint Committee generally lined up behind the President, the Democratic members
were successful in blocking the "peace ship," and Congress adjourned without taking action.

The growth of political motives in atomic energy weakened
the Joint Committee in a second way. Besides splitting the Committee itself, this development tended to bring other forces to
bear on the issues. Other units of Congress came into prominence. In the matter of nuclear propulsion, a strong pressure for
an experimental freighter developed from the merchant marine
interests. Over the objections of the members of the Joint Committee, who protested that the ship was premature and a drain
on resources which should go to the Navy, the Merchant Marine
Committee pushed the bill through the House. In the Senate the
bill was bracketed with the "peace ship" bill, and eventually
both of them went down to defeat when the Democratic leadership failed to give them priority. The episode revealed clearly
that the merchant marine pressure group was enthusiastically
favoring an atomic-powered merchant ship to keep ahead of
foreign construction. Already they were almost strong enough
to defeat the Joint Committee in a contest over atomic power
propulsion development.[87]

Presidential interest in atomic policy led to a politicization of
the atomic energy field, and we have seen how atomic policy
touched traditional political issues and pulled in other political
units, forces, and interests. In a sense each tendency reinforced
the other, and the result was a breakdown of the closed system
of AEC-Joint Committee policy-making. The Joint Committee,

being more subject to partisan splits, could hardly avoid a somewhat greater loss of influence than the AEC.

A division within the Joint Committee was also occasioned by President Eisenhower's nomination of Allen Whitfield to fill the unexpired term of Commissioner Campbell, and subsequently for a new term of five years beginning in July, 1955. Mr. Whitfield, a Des Moines lawyer and prominent Iowa Republican leader, was named to the AEC on March 16, 1955. The move brought an immediate Democratic outcry of "politics." Representative Price of the Joint Committee reportedly declared that the Administration was using the AEC "as a political dumping ground for job-hungry Republicans." The Joint Committee itself began an investigation of Mr. Whitfield's background and qualifications preparatory to holding a hearing on the nomination. In July, Chairman Anderson submitted twenty-four questions to the nominee for written answers. Mr. Whitfield asserted that these required him to produce personal records and the records of his law firm over a twenty-five-year period. He felt that to respond to some of the questions would involve a breach of legal ethics "incompatible with the proper relationship between clients and counsel," and he so informed Senator Anderson.

The Joint Committee also sent two special investigators to Iowa to inquire into Mr. Whitfield's background. When they reported that they had received very little cooperation, Senator Anderson authorized subpoenas to aid them in their search for information.

At this point Mr. Whitfield wrote to ask that the President withdraw his nomination. Even if confirmed, he said, he felt that his service might involve the AEC in further political controversy, which that important agency should not suffer. The White House withdrew his name the following week, and ended at least one threat to the nonpartisan character of the AEC.

■

It remains to pull together the various threads described in the preceding pages, and to give a comprehensive appraisal of the position of the Joint Committee in 1955, as it approached the end of its first decade. Having entered the Strauss period at the peak of its strength, the Committee worked hard thereafter to maintain and consolidate its position in the inner control group of atomic energy. During the early Strauss period the Committee was extremely active, especially in the development of military and civilian atomic power. It directed its attention both to the Commission's own reactor development program and to amending the Act to encourage the participation of private enterprise. In formulating the amendments, the Joint Committee wrote a comprehensive new bill, and included various provisions aimed at assuring a continuation of its own power.

After January, 1955, under the leadership of Democratic Senator Anderson, the Joint Committee continued to give evidence of the same initiative that had characterized the years preceding the 1954 Act. The Committee, for example, continued to urge the utmost speed in the AEC's experimental program for military nuclear propulsion. The several submarine reactor projects received warm support from Committee members. The group also continued to stress greater application of energy and money for research and development on the aircraft reactor project. Senator Hickenlooper spoke for the Committee in these words: ". . . I would just take this opportunity . . . to say again that which we have said many times, that I think this committee is very earnestly insistent that every possible thing be done which can be done within reasonable grounds, to get an atomic powered airplane in the air, and we should have had one in the air now." [88] Representative Price, in his capacity as chairman of the Research and Development Subcommittee, urged the Air Force to speed up development of a nuclear-powered airplane. He asked the Air Force "to consider again whether additional effort could not be applied." [89]

The military orientation of the Committee continued to be firm.[90] Its influence was felt on many other issues as well. Senator Bricker's Subcommittee on Raw Materials made a five-week trip in late 1954 to inspect atomic activities in a dozen foreign nations. In addition to discussions on uranium mining and refining, the subcommittee inquired how the bilateral agreements for cooperation under the 1954 Act might be expedited. In its report it urged that such agreements be entered into promptly "so that peacetime atomic developments may get under way on a broad scale." The subcommittee also offered various specific recommendations to facilitate this development. One such suggestion was that heavy water be made available to India for a large research reactor under construction. Within a few days the AEC announced the sale to India of ten tons of heavy water to meet this need.[91]

In the matter of peacetime applications of atomic energy, Chairman Anderson wanted to strengthen the Committee influence. Accordingly, shortly after assuming the chairmanship, he appointed an eight-member panel to measure the effect of the peaceful application of atomic power on all phases of United States life and to report its finding to the Committee by January 31, 1956. Robert McKinney, editor and publisher of the Santa Fe *New Mexican,* headed the panel which was made up of prominent businessmen and engineers. Subsequently Senator Anderson publicly asked whether the AEC was trying to produce energy from hydrogen isotopes. And after this program was revealed at the Geneva Conference in August, 1955, he took up the cause of greatly accelerating this research.[92]

A specific example of influence in a matter of peacetime policy involved the Subcommittee on Biology and Medicine. This group asked for as low a price for isotopes prepared for other medical and biological research as for those given for cancer research. The AEC subsequently changed its pricing to correspond with this recommendation.[93]

The effect of the Joint Committee's urging was strengthened by certain of the new duties and powers contained in the 1954 Act. As a result of these, particularly the authorization power, the Committee gained additional influence not only with the AEC but also with the Executive branch as a whole. This is especially well illustrated by the fact that a majority of the Joint Committee members, having reacted negatively to the President's "peace ship" proposal, refused to recommend authorization of the $21 million requested to carry out the plan. Strong Administration attempts to replace the item failed as the bill passed both House and Senate.[94]

The potential power of the authorization device was again demonstrated in the 1955 bill, in connection with the President's request for money to pay one-half the cost of medical and research reactors for foreign nations. The Joint Committee approved strongly of the plan, and recommended a $5 million authorization, $2 million more than the President requested. The Committee's figure passed both houses of Congress.

In exercising its new responsibility for reviewing authorizations, the Joint Committee also expressed its intention to formalize the procedures for the AEC to follow in the future acquisition or construction of plants, facilities, and property. The Committee said that it was time for the Commission to behave more like other government agencies in this respect.

Admitting that the AEC still required a certain amount of flexibility in budgeting, the Joint Committee nevertheless reduced the freedom that the Commission had had under the provisions of the 1955 Appropriations Act. That Act authorized the AEC to start any project for which an estimate was in the budget if the currently estimated cost of the project was within

35 per cent of that set forth in the budget estimate. The same Act allowed the Commission to begin a new project for which an estimate was not in the budget if the new substitute project was not of greater cost than the one that had been included in the budget.[95]

In the first case, the Joint Committee wrote into its authorizing bill provisions reducing the 35 per cent leeway to 25 per cent on projects not fully designed or containing novel technical aspects and to 10 per cent on projects which were well along in design or were in the nature of ordinary construction activity. As for the substitution provision, the Joint Committee was persuaded to retain the basic authority, but qualified it by four limitations.[96]

The 1954 Act also required the Joint Committee to hold hearings on the development, growth, and state of the atomic energy industry, within the first sixty days of each session of Congress. This resulted in an opportunity each year for industrial and other interested groups to offer comments, criticisms, or recommendations on the peacetime use of the atom. In 1955, for example, Mr. Francis K. McCune, Vice-President of General Electric, presented a lengthy statement in which he appealed for a freer distribution of atomic information. His remarks drew praise from the Joint Committee members, some of whom implied a criticism of the AEC for slowness in showing industry how to proceed under the new Act.[97] This sixty-day hearing requirement thus facilitated access to business and other groups and provided the Committee with ammunition to use in recommending action to the Commission.

The events since the 1954 Act was passed, then, demonstrate that the Joint Committee continued to desire a strong position in atomic policy-making. On the whole, the Committee could not maintain the degree of influence it attained in the Dean period. Its position became weaker in its total impact on the program, although its influence with the AEC remained extremely high.

The reasons for this decline have been elaborated in the preceding sections. One of the reasons is essentially that the President, the NSC, and Admiral Strauss took more initiative in atomic policy, with the result that the AEC found itself at a level below that of basic policy-making. Thus the Joint Committee, though it continued a close working relationship with the AEC, tended to lose contact with the seat of real policy-making. The other reason for the Joint Committee's relative loss of influence lay in the augmented political character of many issues in atomic policy. Because it divided within itself on these issues, and because it had to compete with other governmental and private groups which began taking an interest in the atom, the Joint Committee suffered a decline from the heights of the previous period.

Yet the Joint Committee by no means faded away after the advent of the Eisenhower Administration. Its prestige remained great and its several working relationships with the AEC continued in good order. The new Atomic Energy Act gave it an increased number of weapons to use in making its influence felt, not merely with the AEC, but to some extent with the top-level Executive as well. If it experienced a regression from previous heights, it remained in 1955 a highly respected, extremely active group, influential to a unique degree among Congressional committees.[98]

VII

The Appropriations Process

The Congressional procedures and techniques for appropriating the money required by the executive agencies of the government are close to any problem of policy and organization. The Appropriations subcommittees consider agency budgets once a year, generally speaking, although supplementary budgets may be considered more often. Each year the House subcommittee spends, on an average, one or two days with the budget of each major executive agency; the Senate subcommittee averages only half a day. The rest of the year brings little if any communication between the committee members and a particular agency.

From this brief encounter and with the help of very small staffs (one or two men for each subcommittee in the House and one man for several subcommittees in the Senate), these subcommittees must write the "language" which will serve as a control device for the forthcoming year. It is not an easy job: the language must not be so restricting that the agency will be unable to do its job well, nor so loose that the agency will be free to perform extravagantly.

Of course, the control of Congress over appropriations does not derive solely from the language of the appropriations bills. Each year in the committee hearing rooms, in the published committee reports, and in the chamber debates, Congress publicizes its intentions, and these extra-legislative expressions of

Congressional will exert a considerable force on the planning and thinking of executive personnel. These appear as criticism of existing arrangements, insistence upon clarity and specificity in plans, suggestions—even demands—for improved efficiency and economy, and analyses of performance records.

Before discussing the particular relationship between the AEC and the Congressional Appropriations Committees, it will be helpful to examine some of the factors which circumscribe the influence of these Committees. It should be remembered that, although the Appropriations Committees are basically responsible for setting the limits within which an agency must operate, room must be left within these limits for ordinary administrative initiative. An agency responsible for the execution of a complex aspect of public policy naturally cannot be controlled in all its workings by the yearly stipulations of the Appropriations Committees.

Nevertheless, the influence of the Appropriations Committees upon the executive program may be very great; often they are the principal policy-makers. Their influence of course varies from program to program and agency to agency. Part of the Committeemen's job is to gauge the degree of resistance which a particular agency can feasibly exert against the influence of the Appropriations Committees.

Any agency's power to resist the Appropriations Committees will depend on the degree of protection it can enlist. Many factors will determine this: the urgency of its program, the attitude of the public, the strength of the pressure groups which are for or against it, its record for honesty and administrative efficiency, and so forth. The military services, for instance, are in a relatively unprotected position (i.e., subject to appropriation control) during long periods of peace, but are in a strongly protected position during times of international unrest or outright war. The relative strength or weakness of most agencies vis-à-vis the Appropriations Committees changes continually, reflecting the changes in public affairs.

The degree of power exercised by the Appropriations Committees depends upon which of two areas of an agency's authority is being controlled. Generally speaking, the Appropriations Committees can wield a greater degree of influence in the area of administrative operations than in the area of program development. This contrast is so marked that there are a number of agencies whose programs are completely beyond the reach of the Appropriations Committees' influence, even though their administrative techniques have been sharply questioned and occasionally even condemned by the Committees. On the other hand, it is generally true that the agencies which have the least protection will experience Committee influence in both areas, although the influence will be stronger in administrative than in programmatic affairs.

The Appropriations Committees themselves, of course, must convince their respective chambers that the appropriations bills are in good order. Normally this is easy, because the size and complexity of the bills make it difficult to debate them on the floor. But usually there are two or three points in appropriations bills which encounter strong opposition each year. It is worth noting that the opposition usually occurs at points where the chambers believe the Committees have not realistically appraised the strength or weakness of an agency. In other words, if an unprotected agency is vulnerable to attack in Congress, there is almost always at least one legislator who is willing to see that the attack is made on the floor if it has not already been made in the committee.

Other subordinate factors may determine whether an appropriations bill will be challenged on the floor of the House or Senate. Almost any proposal which contains a major modification of policy is likely to be challenged. Similarly, a legal provision which seems too drastic a measure for an end which might be achieved through negotiation with the administrative agency involved, will probably meet with opposition. However, these are minor factors in comparison with the factors which derive from the agency's general power position.

The Committees are generally aware of these conditioning elements, and they function within them perspicaciously. Consequently, most appropriations bills are approved as they were written. But occasionally the Committees violate these conditions, and there ensues a political struggle which breaks out on the floor of Congress. Then the pressure groups, including the agencies of the Executive branch, must exert their influence behind the scenes. Although appropriations bills are generally passed without much difficulty, there are certain strong factors in the Congress itself which at times operate to limit the effectiveness of the Appropriations Committees.

These factors will be seen to operate in the case of the particular subcommittees involved in this study, namely, the Independent Offices Subcommittees in House and Senate. As their names suggest, these are concerned with the estimates and plans of a host of widely different agencies and programs. They study the important and often controversial budgets submitted by many large agencies such as the Veterans Administration and the Tennessee Valley Authority. The tasks confronting the Independent Offices Subcommittees as they sponsor these bills and take them to their respective chambers are highly diversified ones. Political controversy may erupt upon any number of their decisions. Each agency is likely to experience controversy with respect to its construction program, the adequacy and scope of its public services, the extent and liberality of its benefit and subsidy programs. In addition, in many of the postwar years, Congressional efforts at over-all budget coordination have been directed with particular force at these huge programs whose funds are annually carried in the Independent Offices money bills. These efforts at coordination are primarily accomplished by the imposition of formulas which effect a basic modification in the structure of the federal work program.

The House Appropriations Subcommittee on Independent Offices holds daily sessions in the winter months of each year to review the operations of the administrative agencies under its jurisdiction. It seeks to determine what financial plan of action is appropriate for the coming fiscal year, basing its decisions on the budget justifications and other verbal and written submissions made by the agency in question. Supplementary appropriations requests and deficiency requests are periodically received and, as in the case of the regular estimates, require justification by the agency. Preliminary to the hearings, a varying amount of spade work is done by the subcommittee's own independent investigators and staff personnel. The House Appropriations Subcommittee typically makes a careful and systematic study of the budget estimates, and its action and the immediately following action by the whole House are awaited before the Senate Committee begins its work.

The Senate Appropriations Subcommittee on Independent Offices also meets once a year for a general review of the agency's budget. In addition, it meets to consider supplemental or deficiency requests. The Senate unit, however, has traditionally been a review board or appellate body, giving primary consideration to appeals from House action. Most of its attention, then, is given to agency complaints about particular House-sponsored amendments or to agency pleas for changes in the language or amounts fixed by the House.

The agency usually comes prepared to explain the consequences of the House actions from which it is seeking relief. The Senate unit listens to these objections, examines their validity, and often hears the views of other interested parties. Of course, any Senator can introduce new considerations on his own initiative, so far as the agency's budget proposals are concerned, but in practice this is a very minor aspect of the work of the Senate subcommittees.

The Senate Appropriations Subcommittee does not engage in a systematic and thoroughgoing study of the agency's budget estimate, but takes a larger view, with the objective of ameliorating particularly onerous provisions made by the lower chamber. It is less likely than the House unit to come into conflict with the standing legislative committee which has jurisdiction over the agency in question. Partly in order to formalize an emphasis upon cooperation in the Senate between the Appropriations Committee in its appellate role and the standing legislative committee in its general policy-shaping role, the Senate Appropriations Committee has adopted a practice of permitting a number of legislative committees of the Senate to be represented ex officio when the Appropriations Subcommittees review requests from the relevant agencies. Such ex officio members are allowed to participate in the subcommittee's work, although they do not possess voting privileges. Since 1951, this form of ex officio membership has been granted on the Independent Offices Subcommittee to three Senate members of the Joint Committee on Atomic Energy.

These are the formal characteristics of the "division of labor" between the House and Senate Subcommittees which annually study the appropriations requests of the Atomic Energy Commission. Like other subcommittees, the Independent Offices Subcommittees have divided the tasks and now assume different roles in the production of appropriations bills.

VIII

The Formative Years: 1947-1950

Until this point, the history of the atomic energy program has been told largely in terms of the relationship between the Atomic Energy Commission and the Joint Committee on Atomic Energy. The story has been dominated by the progress of the Joint Committee toward a position of influence and leadership. On the other hand, the history of the relationship between the AEC and the Appropriations Committees, which will occupy this and the succeeding chapters, is the story of the failure of the legislative groups to attain a position of influence in atomic affairs. The fact is, the Appropriations Committees were notably unsuccessful in their attempts to force their values upon the AEC.

The first point to stress in any discussion of the relationships between the AEC and the Senate and House Appropriations Committees is the basic liberality and leniency which have marked all considerations of AEC budgets during the agency's first nine years.[1] At no time did the legislative leaders indicate any desire either to cut the program's scope or to slow its tempo. Instead, there was a long series of annual attempts to withhold substantial percentages of the very large budget estimates, attempts which failed when the cuts were restored in the supplemental appropriations usually enacted six or eight months later.

The reasons for this are complex and will require detailed analysis. In general, though, one can say that they are of two kinds: those arising from the unalterable nature of the atomic energy program, and those arising from conditions which might have been corrected by the people involved. The former, which are by far the most significant, consist chiefly of the urgent considerations of national defense which impelled the atomic energy program from the very beginning; no one could successfully urge a course which seemed to be contrary to those considerations. The latter, though they seemed important at the time, really were not. It is worth noting, too, that personalities and temperaments, which obviously were so significant in the affairs of the Joint Committee, were much less important in the relations between the AEC and the Appropriations Committees, partly because external factors overrode personal considerations, and partly because the people concerned met only two or three times a year and scarcely had time to develop personal affinities or animosities.

In the following pages the conditions which thwarted normal appropriations control have been ordered in a general way so that those subject to elimination by action on the part of the Committees and the AEC will be treated first. Those which are almost unalterable will follow.

■

The first problem which faced the Appropriations Committees in dealing with the AEC budget was the newness and technical complexity of the atomic energy program. During the period before 1947, appropriations for the program had been considered in a lump sum by a few Congressional leaders.[1a] Consequently no Appropriations Subcommittees had had an opportunity to become familiar with the program. With the creation of the Atomic Energy Commission, the Subcommittees on Independent Offices began to deal with a new agency and a program of which they knew very little.

The subcommittees were further handicapped, as they began to grapple with the atomic energy budget, by the technical complexity of the program. This factor was more evident in some phases than in others. Community operations, for example, were one aspect of the program the subcommittee members felt they could handle easily, if given the proper information by the AEC. Research, however, offered more complex problems—and research occupied an important place in the Commission's work.

The difficulties facing the legislators, who were eager to learn and do their jobs intelligently, can be easily seen by examining a typical instance, say that of Representative Wigglesworth and his investigation—which lasted perhaps five minutes—of a particular research project and the justification for it.[2] The incident occurred during a hearing in 1947 and dealt with a program of medical and biological research into the problems of radiation "sickness" and protection against it. The same circumstances can be observed in many investigations of facilities, production, and the weapons program, although the latter two would be partly off the record.

The session had been confined for perhaps half an hour to a general consideration of progress in the New York area. Representative Wigglesworth, Republican of Massachusetts, apparently tiring of generalities, singled out at random an item from the budget justifications. It referred to a contractual obligation and read, rather cryptically: "Payable to the University of Rochester, $1,300,000." Wigglesworth asked how the Committee could tell that the work to be done was not worth $300,000 or $3,000,000 rather than the amount the AEC did request.

The ensuing discussion quickly showed that the legislators were not themselves capable, as Mr. Wigglesworth's question had implied, of reviewing the contract from a substantive point of view. A number of medical and biological experts at the University of Rochester had devised and submitted a program for the continuing study of certain radiation problems which plagued the installations of the Atomic Energy Commission. Those facilities were, of course, in continuous use, and the immediate importance of this work was therefore unquestionable; furthermore in a world in which the potentiality of atomic warfare could not be dismissed, it was equally clear that this work on radiation safety problems had the most basic significance to military and public policy.

But though Representative Wigglesworth and the other legislators were certainly not presenting themselves as competent to judge the desirability or necessity of the program itself, the question remained a pertinent one. How could they know that this program should not cost $300,000 or $3,000,000? Accordingly, Representative Wigglesworth shifted his questions to the arrangements by which the project had come into being, been approved, been reviewed, and currently stood before them. The ensuing discussion revealed that the University of Rochester itself had formulated the proposal, which had then gone to the AEC Operations Office where the medical experts on the New York staff had given tentative approval to the program. Official consideration had first been cast in terms of the substance of the program and only afterwards had dealt with the question of its cost. Both on the substantive and the fiscal side, the Washington medical authorities of the program staff had reviewed the proposal. Thus the full authority of responsible experts in the university, in the New York regional office, and in Washington, was brought to bear in defense of the project.

Representative Wigglesworth, however, was not yet through with his inquiry. He had perhaps been convinced that the Committee could not pass on the substance of the program, and that it could not pass upon the competence of the experts who had determined the program's necessity and fixed its scope. What remained for the legislator to ask was again typical: what had been the extent of consultation with other public and private medical research organizations—the Public Health Service and the various research foundations?

Here again the discussion brought out the arrangements which the AEC had developed for providing adequate coordination of its plans with those of the Public Health Service and various private groups. The AEC's General Advisory Committee of scientists included, it was reported, several members who were also advisers to the Public Health Service.

In summary, then, three important points about the manner in which the Congressional committee members could and did seek to inform themselves on current AEC projects were revealed. The legislators could not hope to review the substance of the AEC commitment. They could and did insist upon adequate review and screening procedures, manned by competent personnel in the Atomic Energy Commission's organization itself. They could and did insist upon adequate coordination of the Atomic Energy Commission's program with parallel, overlapping, or competing programs carried on by other governmental agencies and by private groups active in the same field.

In time, of course, the newness and complexity of the program diminished somewhat and were no longer such impediments to the Appropriations Committees' control of the AEC budget. By 1949, the Committee members were considerably less handicapped by the unfamiliarity of the budget. Some aspects of the program did not seem new at all. Representative Case of the House Committee found that this was a real help to the legislators; in a discussion on the floor of the House, he remarked:

> . . . if you will take a segment of an activity which you do understand and to which you can apply some ordinary standards, you can find an index which will give a fairly reliable

guide in determining the efficiency of the spending operations
of any particular agency.[3]

He then went on to discuss various nontechnical aspects of
the program with considerable familiarity, indicating that he and
the other Committee members were feeling more at home with
the AEC and its program, and less thwarted by the fact that
that program did contain novel and complex features.

The Appropriations Committees, in the early years, were not
handicapped solely by their own unfamiliarity with the program.
They also faced the problem of an unsatisfactory budget presentation by the Commission. At the start, this was to some extent a result of the fact that the Commission itself had just taken
over the project and was in the process of organizing its operations. In 1947, when the House Committee asked the AEC to
come back at a later date with better information, the subcommitteemen were exceedingly critical of the Commission's records and of its knowledge of the present state of the program
and of future needs.[4] Mr. Lilienthal explained that the poor condition of the records could not be attributed to the AEC, but
was the responsibility of the Manhattan District, from whom
the Commission had inherited them.

The House report of the Deficiency Subcommittee in 1948
indicates acceptance of this explanation. This report acknowl-
edged that the Manhattan District's records and business arrangements "were in such condition as to give the Commission
an exceptionally poor basic program on which to work." [5]

The AEC committed itself informally to the correction of this
failing as rapidly as possible, and in the succeeding period the
records were considerably improved. Already in 1948, for example, Mr. Lilienthal reported that surveys had been made by
five independent accounting firms employed by the AEC, and
summaries of these were placed in the record.[6] The accountants

had suggested a number of reforms which would improve the methods then in use. In 1949, the House subcommittee urged the Commission to work toward further improvement of its accounting system and at the same time indicated that some progress had been made.[7] Early in 1950, the subcommittee again noted that the accounting procedures, which for the first time were on an accrued cost basis, had been improved, though the members felt further improvement was still possible.[8]

The need for secrecy was another factor which for a time hampered the effective presentation of the budget. It interfered with the work of both the agency and the subcommittee. During the first two years or so, the Commission was apparently uncertain of the extent of its obligation to communicate to the Appropriations Committees, and there was some resistance to requests for information. Interviewees have said that the AEC was once reluctant to disclose the number of employees in a cafeteria located at one of the atomic installations. The public record, too, shows evidence of the Commission's early resistance to providing the Appropriations Committees with information. In 1948, the House Committee wrote into its report the following criticism:

> . . . the Commission's refusal to furnish the Committee with information and appraisals of its various budgeted items, based on technical information which can be available only to the Commission, because of the scientific and secret character of the work involved, leaves much to be desired in establishing the confidence which the committee must have. . . .[9]

On the legislative side, the subcommittees for a time showed some reluctance to probe deeply into the sensitive, secret aspects of the Commission's work. In 1947, for example, the AEC brought certain top-secret information to the Senate hearing under armed courier. When Subcommittee Chairman Reed ques-

tioned the indefiniteness and lack of supporting detail in the
AEC's requests for funds, General Manager Carroll Wilson
said that the information had been prepared and would be given
to the Committeemen if they wished, but he emphasized the vital
importance of the information. The Senators were definitely reluctant to review such information, and Chairman Reed remarked that he had "no disposition to interfere with your secret
operations." [10]

On both sides, then, there was distinct uneasiness over the
possible consequences of mishandling secret information, and
often enough the Congressmen approved items in the budget
about which they neither knew nor wanted to know anything
more than the most rudimentary details. But in time these problems too were resolved. At the start of the 1949 hearings, Mr.
Lilienthal spoke at some length concerning the efforts which
were being made to give "a full disclosure of the details . . .
as those details are now known or are foreseeable," [11] and later,
when he appeared before the Senate subcommittee, he stated the
rule which he said the AEC had evolved to govern the distribution of information to several Congressional units:

> We have interpreted the statute in this way, that we should
> of course supply the Joint Committee, as we are required, with
> all information except such as it declines to hear or as the
> President says should not be supplied; second, that we should
> do the same thing with respect to the Appropriations Com-
> mittees, and this we have been doing.[12]

Interview data indicate that, in fact, the subcommittees were
satisfied with the Commission's later policies, as outlined by
Chairman Lilienthal. Although they became more confident and
more anxious to have a comprehensive review of the program,
secret and nonsecret, the AEC's continued willingness to channel all pertinent information to them meant that there were no
serious complaints on this score.

Other factors tended to create unsatisfactory budget procedures. The AEC could hardly present a full-year budget picture to the Committee, for in every year it made at least one
large supplemental or deficiency request. The AEC budget was
always, in effect, a tentative budget. Furthermore, in the early
years, the Congressional practice of the time required these supplemental and deficiency bills to be handled not by the House
Independent Offices Subcommittee, but rather by a special Deficiencies Subcommittee. This meant that the members of the
regular subcommittee did not obtain a full view of the agency
program, but only of that part for which funds were requested
at the time of the regular appropriation. In 1951, however, the
Independent Offices Subcommittee began handling all deficiency
and supplemental requests, as well as the regular requests, thus
solving that difficulty.

The task of reviewing the agency's activities was made harder
by the fact that contractors managed most of the AEC's operations. Thus the Committees often felt that they were not talking
to the people who really did the work and prepared the budget.
Representative Thomas' remarks, although they occurred in
1950, are indicative of this feeling:

> Your estimates are no more than your very best guess based
> upon what the prime contractor estimated. I believe the evidence
> shows so far that when it gets up here that you generally agree
> to the estimates of the prime contractor. Someone in the atomic
> group used the words that the estimates were high, wide, and
> handsome. I do not see why the committee has to take a pair
> of pliers and pull the information from your teeth as to what
> your contractors' fees are. Again you want to hide behind your
> security which is perhaps your best asset.[18]

All of these unsatisfactory conditions were amenable to correction. In some cases, active efforts toward improved procedures were necessary. The difficulties were partly eased by the

natural growth of familiarity and confidence among the Committeemen as a result of their repeated experience.

In any case, through the period ending in mid-1950, the Appropriations Committees were growing increasingly confident that they had established arrangements which would give them proper information, and that they were becoming sufficiently acquainted with the AEC's operations to deal competently with any evident deficiencies.

■

One must not conclude, however, that when the Committeemen increased their knowledge of the Atomic Energy Commission's program, they necessarily increased their power over it. In the preceding chapter, it was pointed out that this could be true only if the program were not protected by its fundamental importance to the national welfare. As a matter of fact, the program was protected by precisely this consideration, and it overshadowed all the others.

The enormous prestige of the program was an important factor from the very beginning. In 1947, when the Commission had presented a particularly hazy picture of its personnel requirements and estimated expenditures, Representative Wigglesworth was at pains to point out to the House how unsatisfactory the AEC presentation had been. In fact, he said, had it not been for the vital importance of the program, the House Committee would have voted no appropriation at all.[14] Nevertheless, the AEC received $175 million of its $250 million request. On the floor, Representative Thomas stressed the fact that this was not a cut, and that the AEC had been told to come back later for the rest, or more as might be necessary.[15] In neither of the first two years, in fact, was there any attempt to make substantial cuts in the AEC budget.

Following 1947, there was repeated insistence by the Appropriations Committees, in reports and on the floor of the House and Senate, that in criticizing the AEC or in recommending that a grant of funds be postponed or cut, the Committee members realized the great significance of the atomic energy program and were being extremely careful not to do anything which might damage the national security. Almost invariably the Appropriations Committees, in what little action on the AEC budgets they did take, attempted to separate the defense aspects of the program, leaving these untouched while making some reductions in others. In 1948, for example, the House Committee's report stipulated that the reductions were to be absorbed in items which would not affect the military phases.[16] Although the cuts were by no means severe, Senator McMahon of the Joint Committee felt compelled to take issue with the theory that, by leaving the military phases intact, the Appropriations Committees had not affected the rate at which the whole program could move forward.[17]

All in all, then, the extreme urgency of the AEC's mission made for leniency and liberality in respect to appropriations. To appreciate this fully, one must take into account the political situation in which the atomic energy budgets were approved. The AEC's first two years, of course, were the years of the Republican-dominated 80th Congress. When this Congress met in 1947, the GOP had working majorities in both chambers for the first time in over eighteen years. Republican expectations of victory in the 1948 Presidential election were high; many felt that the record made by the 80th Congress would be a definite selling point in the coming Presidential campaign. Accordingly, the Republican leadership in Congress stood for retrenchment of federal programs, reform in administrative organization, efficiency, and economy. Pressures began to build up in 1947 and more powerfully still in 1948 for a comprehensive and systematic application of the criterion of economy to all federal appropriations. In 1947, bitter and prolonged debates resulted; with respect to agriculture, internal improvements, and various domestic economic services, as well as in the fields of defense and foreign aid, the Republicans who dominated the Appropriations Committees stirred up controversy by sponsoring provisions which aimed at retrenchment and which sought to establish a Spartan budgetary program.

It is worth noting that the Joint Committee, which a year or two later was to protest loudly against suggestions of economy in the atomic energy program, was unable to muster a solid front in 1948. When Representatives Wigglesworth and Phillips of the appropriations group charged in public that the AEC was "extravagant," "unbusinesslike," and "lavish," they were joined by two of the ranking Republicans on the Joint Committee— Cole of New York and Van Zandt of Pennsylvania. And the partisan alignment of forces was highlighted when the Democratic members of the Appropriations Committee were joined in the debate by two influential Democratic members of the Joint Committee—Holifield of California and Durham of North Carolina—in opposing the Republican-sponsored recommendations.

Later, when the AEC appealed to the Senate for restoration of its $48 million cut, the Republican majority on the Appropriations Committee was somewhat more lenient. Nevertheless, the political alignment again consisted of party versus party rather than Appropriations Committee versus Joint Committee.[18]

The effectiveness of the atomic energy program's appeal, then, is all the more obvious in view of the political factors which might have been expected to give rise to severe treatment from the Appropriations Committee.

■

The patterns of interrelationship among these various factors were reaffirmed and crystallized by the events of 1949 and early 1950. By this time, the Appropriations Committees had developed a considerable confidence in their ability to deal effectively with the AEC budget. The new Democratic chairman of the House Independent Offices Subcommittee, Representative Thomas, had developed what many interpreted as a certain resentment toward what he considered the most pampered agency in government. It has been said that Mr. Thomas did not believe in atoms. In any case, he was particularly strong in his belief that there would be no harm in making the AEC conform to the disciplined, business-like methods which the Appropriations Committee tried to enforce in other agencies.

The AEC, in early 1949, became the subject of widespread attack from inside and outside Congress. It will be recalled that one of the most prominent issues concerned the AEC fellowship program, and that other issues involved rather startling overruns in the final cost of certain AEC construction projects, as compared with original estimates. This controversy surrounding the AEC doubtless heightened the feeling of confidence within the Appropriations Committees and their conviction that the AEC needed to be restrained.

The dissatisfaction of the Appropriations Committees became clear in two riders which they attached to the 1950 appropriations bill—one, the fellowship provision and the other, the first of a series of construction riders. Both have been described elsewhere, and the details need be of no concern here. The former, of course, had a decided impact on the fellowship program, but the latter is of more significance in illustrating the attempt of the Committees to curtail the agency's freedom of action.

The construction rider was approved, somewhat reluctantly, by the Joint Committee. In fact, the AEC itself had expressed acquiescence in it.[19] But three months after it passed, both the

AEC and the Joint Committee were united behind an amendment to weaken the rider.[20] The event which changed their position was the announcement, in September, 1949, of the first atomic explosion inside Soviet Russia. Immediately, the atomic energy program became more important than ever; the expansion of it became the nation's first necessity, and the amendment passed both houses easily.

Thus the increased desire of the Appropriations Committees to curb the AEC's excesses was almost immediately blocked by an event which no one could overlook. As the expansion program developed, the same conflict between the appropriations groups and the AEC continued. A good example was the controversy over the high fixed fees paid to community management contractors in 1950. The House Appropriations Committee wrote into its bill a restriction on the amount payable to these contractors.[21] The fees were obviously high, and yet the rider was passed only after bitter controversy. The Joint Committee and the Commission strongly opposed the rider and insisted that, even though it might not seem to affect the weapons program, it would really injure the whole AEC operation. Considering the state of world affairs, such an argument could not be lightly dismissed.

IX

The Expansion Years: 1950–1952

By 1950 the atomic arms race was under way in earnest. This meant that the Appropriations Committees had to work within the context of what may be appropriately called the expansion years.

The expansion years produced two conditions which were significant in determining the nature and importance of the role played by the Appropriations Committees. On the one hand, the greater urgency of the weapons and fissionable materials programs minimized the degree of control which these Committees could exercise over the AEC. On the other hand, the great expansion program meant that uneconomical construction procedures would be even more vulnerable to criticism by those who wished to reduce, or at least mitigate, the total dollar outlay. Thus, just when the force of world events acted to inhibit the Committees' power, the Committeemen felt the need for even greater power.

The Appropriations Committees were faced with potential extravagance which would be difficult to control. At the same time, they were confident that they knew how to deal with waste in the construction program. The results of this collision will be seen later in this chapter, when the story of the construction riders will be told. But first, it may be useful to consider an illustration of the House Appropriations Committee's new mood.

In the spring of 1950, the House Committee's new confidence was seen in its insistence upon the community management fee rider, in spite of predictions by the AEC and the Joint Committee that its passage would produce exceedingly unfortunate results.[1] The rider, it will be remembered, prohibited the payment of management fees in excess of $90,000 annually. The next year, when it became clear that the House subcommittee had been essentially right and that the rider had saved money without damaging the program, the alleged *expertise* of the AEC and the Joint Committee suffered a considerable humiliation.

In the appropriations hearings in 1951, Representative Gore, speaking for the subcommittee, was able to make fun of the AEC when it sought to secure elimination of the clause. He began the discussion by references to the unfavorable publicity he had received in his home constituency in Tennessee, due to statements by Commissioner Pike:

> *Representative Gore.* I might say that I was not only pleased yesterday to see the progress that has been made in this program but surprised, particularly since I remembered having seen a headline in a Tennessee newspaper quoting you Mr. Pike to the effect that if this limitation were approved, not only would it defeat the H-bomb but it would very probably ruin the atom bomb program as well.
>
> *Mr. Pike.* I was misquoted.
>
> *Mr. Dean.* When did that happen?
>
> *Representative Gore.* That was while this matter was in conference between the House and the Senate, very appropriately at that time. Of course, as I was in part the author of the provision, my constituents in Tennessee were very much disturbed that I was going to destroy either the H-bomb or the A-bomb, so I was heartened to see that the program is continuing, despite this terrible prediction.
>
> *Mr. Pike.* . . . I have had to eat crow before, but I do not think I ever made that statement.

Representative Gore. I must say that is a slightly liberal interpretation of what you were quoted as saying, but that was the impression left on my constituents.[2]

The weakness of the Atomic Energy Commission's case on this particular matter was further revealed by the ensuing colloquy.

Mr. Dean. I think we ought to say that our face is a little bit red on this, because the contractors in Los Alamos and the contractor at Oak Ridge have come down and met the arbitrary figure which the committee rider carried.

Representative Gore. Their faces may be a little red too, because they were making very dire threats that if this rider was approved, they just could not possibly operate, would not be interested to continue.

Mr. Dean. That was the evidence that we had at the time we came before your committee.[3]

These remarks indicate that the kind of negotiations which the AEC had engaged in with the management corporations had been more in the order of comfortable conferences than of hard bargaining. The legislators quite reasonably felt that, by forcing action as they had, some of the unnecessary generosity had been curbed, and—perhaps more important—the AEC had been given a lesson by the legislators in "how to drive a hard bargain."

The weakness of Mr. Dean's plea that the rider now be removed is apparent from the following quotation.

Mr. Dean. . . . it seems to us that the $90,000 fee should be arrived at in open negotiation across the table, each side trying to get the best bargain it can having some relationship to the actual service that is performed. I do not think the fee will go up if you remove the rider. So it is just a question of principle, should Congress say through a rider, that you cannot pay more than *x* number of dollars to a contractor.

Representative Gore. Well, the committee acted last year in this regard only because we had called it to the attention of the Commission . . . one year prior, expressing serious doubts and opposition to the size of the fee, but one year later the Commission had done nothing about it. Therefore the Committee felt that it must exercise some of its own prerogatives in placing the prohibition, and the only doubt the Committee had a year ago in placing the limitation in the bill was in the size of the fee. I really think I am qualified to say that the sentiment of the Committee favored a considerably smaller fee than the $90,000, but finally it agreed upon the $90,000 amount out of consideration for the possible disturbance of the program.

Mr. Dean. I am glad that it was not set lower than that, because I do not know what effect it would have had. I do not mean the contractors would have fallen out if it had been set lower than the $90,000, but I am glad it was not set lower than that.

Representative Gore. Is that all you wish to say?

Mr. Dean. I think so.[4]

The new attitude of the House subcommittee is clearly revealed in this exchange. The members were confident that they could analyze the administrative efficiency of the Commission in certain phases of its work. Yet even in recommending legislation to improve administrative practice, the subcommittee was careful not to do anything which could have a significant effect on the program. The members recognized that any such recommendation would clearly involve them in a struggle they could not win, because the programmatic aspects of the AEC's work were too well protected. But in other areas, those which could be sensibly argued to involve administrative efficiency rather than program accomplishment, the House subcommittee was now ready to act whenever and however the members thought action was necessary.

Much of the advice and urging pressed upon agency spokesmen by subcommittee members served merely to maintain the familiar Congressional stress upon general efficiency and money economy. Thus, the legislators would have had the AEC spend less on administrative personnel, seek in a variety of ways to run the various "government towns" more economically, and improve and perfect their methods of accounting so that the Congressional units concerned would be able to tell not only whether money was spent for legitimate objects, but how costly those various items of expenditure were.

An example of the familiar theme was provided by Representative Gore in the 1950 House hearings:

> What I have sought to indicate by my detailed examination of your department is the feeling on my part and on the part, I believe, of the Congress, and, I hope, the people, that as we move forward into a permanent atomic energy program, which, in the very nature of the undertaking, is expensive, exploratory, and experimental, that, nevertheless, we must diligently undertake to economize and minimize the cost to the people.[5]

These "thumbnail sermons" are familiar enough, occurring as they do throughout the Lilienthal years as well as during this later period. In the years after 1949, however, they seem to occur with greater regularity; and they are often references to specific subdivisions of the AEC rather than general exhortations.

Perhaps in themselves, such efforts at moral suasion do not change bureaucratic behavior very much. Nevertheless, taken in conjunction with the prerogatives and formal powers which appropriations subcommittees possess, these injunctions and urgings probably have a cumulative impact. By pronouncements of this kind, the desires of these powerful legislative units were made explicit, perhaps disturbing some of the complacency characteristic of most bureaucratic processes, sometimes spurring executive officials to better performances. These pressures may be thought of as designed to create an attitudinal change in administrators. That is to say, the Congressmen worked to inculcate in AEC administrators attitudes of increased concern for executive efficiency and managerial regularity.

■

With the appointment of Gordon Dean as chairman of the AEC, the Commission grew more responsive than it had been under Mr. Lilienthal's leadership to an administrative philosophy which condoned greater organizational centralization and more elaborate processes of executive control. Nevertheless, the House subcommittee felt it necessary to exert additional pressure in this direction. In calling upon the AEC to revamp its administration, the Congressmen had two related effects in mind: (1) to achieve, at top organizational levels, greater familiarity with field problems and developments, and (2) to secure, at those same top levels, an improved capacity for control and direction of the AEC program. An example of such prodding is provided in the 1950 Report of the House Appropriations Committee:

> During hearings on the bill, it developed that the members of the Commission were not well informed as to the finances of the agency. It was apparent that the people in the field made their own decisions without much control or advice from the Commission. The committee is of the opinion that this is a very unsound way of doing business, that the Commission should have a better knowledge of these affairs and the committee will expect better information from it in that connection during consideration of the 1952 budget.[6]

One of the means by which the Appropriations Committees normally exercise their control over the agencies and departments of the Executive is the budget hearing. In the hearings, the Congressmen are free to criticize separate items in the budget they are considering; and because the relationship between an agency and an appropriations committee is an annually recurring one, these criticisms become in effect suggestions or even commands to govern the agency's future plans and activities. The agency knows that in another year it must come before the Committee again, and that if the things which the Congressmen previously criticized have not been corrected, the agency's position at the hearings will be decidedly uncomfortable.

By 1950, the House Committee felt that the AEC should begin to conform to this pattern of governmental behavior. And, for one reason or another, the AEC disagreed. An incident which revealed this conflict involved a veterinary hospital at Los Alamos; the Congressmen called it the "dog and cat hospital." In 1950, the Committee members expressed their disapproval of this installation.[7] The next year, they learned that their criticism had been disregarded:

> *Representative Gore.* I believe . . . a year ago the committee expressed considerable opposition and doubt about the proposed construction of a dog sanatorium at Los Alamos. . . . Did you build that?
>
> *Mr. Morgan.* Yes, sir, we did. It was built and it is in operation.
>
> *Representative Gore.* What consideration was given to the doubts expressed in the committee about that?
>
> *Mr. Morgan.* There was considerable consideration given to those doubts, evaluated against what we felt was the need for research reasons and for the community also. . . .
>
> *Representative Gore.* My home town is trying desperately to build a hospital to look after some suffering humanity, but here, despite the opposition of the committee, we have an $85,000 Veterinary Hospital.
>
> *Representative Andrews.* . . . As I understand it, the committee denied any funds for it; is that right?

Representative Gore. . . . We did not specifically state in the committee report that it should not be built. In that, perhaps we erred.

Representative Thomas. . . . It was part of the budget, and the manager, without the agreement or approval of the committee, by virtue of the exercise of that authority, authorized its construction. Isn't that correct?

Mr. Morgan. It was built; yes, sir.[8]

Representative Gore thus explained it to his colleagues on the floor of the House:

The committee expressed objection in the report but did not specifically say that it should not be built. We did make a substantial reduction; and, as has been the custom of long standing, the comity between this agency and the committee was expected on my part, at least, to carry through and have the reductions we made apply to the specific item. The fact that it did not do so, I think, is a black mark against the Commission.[9]

The incident showed that the Committee's wishes still did not carry great weight with the AEC. This was a disturbing revelation of the Committee's weakness in the area of program decisions. Although the appropriation bill was reduced by the amount of the cost of the hospital in an amendment on the floor of the House, the fact remained that the bargaining position of the Appropriations Committees on matters of this kind was weak, considerably weaker than that obtaining with most other civilian agencies. This weakness was the source of the general feeling of frustration which the House subcommittee developed toward the AEC, a feeling which vented itself in the barbed exchanges with which the hearings abound during this period.

Another source of this feeling of frustration was found in the Committee's discovery of the true complexity of the AEC's operations, which they now were able to examine. It was as if they had learned enough to know how much they did not know about the AEC's activities.

In 1952, on a program involving research at Iowa State College, Representative Gore exclaimed in apparent exasperation, "This program is spread over a thousand places, all over the lot, not only research but everything. . . . How are we going to get the loose ends together, and how the Commission is going to do it, I do not know." Later he continued, "Chairman Dean, this discussion this morning illustrates conclusively, it seems to me, how impossible it is for this subcommittee, in a matter of a few days, or even a few weeks, to examine in detail all of these far-flung operations." [10]

An understandable reaction to this awareness was to wonder whether the Commission itself had developed the administrative techniques to control its own operations. Representative Gore said:

> One also gets the impression that it might be beyond the Commission, unless you have some systematic way of reaching determination of the budgetary needs and requests of these myriad operations. I would like to know what system the Commission has for arriving at the extent of the work, the supervision of the work, and the amount of money which you recommend to the Budget Bureau and to the Congress. [11]

When Representative Gore asked Mr. Boyer, the General Manager, whether he thought the Commission could keep control over its activities, Mr. Boyer replied confidently: "I might say that the top organization we have is responsible for directing these programs. . . . Our organization is built up with that purpose in mind, in order that we may determine the scope of the program. We must select capable contractors, and we must see that we get performance from them." [12]

Despite this optimistic evaluation, the House subcommittee

continued from time to time to probe into the Commission's techniques of control. To inspire in the management staff a genuine concern for control devices seemed to the Committeemen the most helpful pressure they could exert in their efforts to secure an adequate administrative performance.

■

Congressional criticisms of the AEC's plant and equipment program had for their objective a reform of the timing of the design and construction of new buildings and installations. In this period, the Congressmen on the Appropriations Committees became convinced (1) that the AEC's custom of beginning construction before plans had been completed was uneconomical and (2) that the traditional methods would lead not only to economy but to a faster rate of construction. Emphasis on these points was a prominent aspect of the hearings in 1950 and continued to mount until it erupted in the funds-to-complete proviso in the summer of 1952.

Before 1950, the subcommitteemen probably thought that the construction phase of the program would be transitional. They hoped that a more business-like atmosphere would appear when the first rush of construction subsided. But these complacent expectations were shattered by the news of Russia's mastery of atomic fission and by the quick expansion of our own atomic program. It was no longer possible for the legislators to think that the day was just around the corner when the construction phases of budget would diminish and operations would become the chief expenditure. Accordingly, the appropriations subcommitteemen were forced to become interested in the AEC's construction program.

By 1951, the subcommittee members again began to look forward to a reduction of building activities and a corresponding emphasis on operational expenditures:

> *Senator Saltonstall.* Then your operations, because of the new plants, will be continually going up for the next two or three fiscal years?
> *Mr. McCarthy.* That is right, sir.
> *Senator Saltonstall.* But your construction program should go down?
> *Mr. McCarthy.* It should go down.
> *Senator Saltonstall.* So that by 1955, we will meet the maximum of operations and the minimum of construction, unless we go into something new?
> *Mr. McCarthy.* Unless something new comes into the picture; that is right.[13]

Something new did come into the picture. On January 17, the President announced his approval of plans to expand the authorized capacity to produce plutonium and uranium-235. Appearing before the House Committee in early February, 1952, Chairman Dean pointed out that the regular estimates then before the Committee did not include requests for any funds to implement the proposed expansion program.[14] These would be forthcoming; spread over three years, they would aggregate between five and six billion dollars. Inevitably again, the emphasis in the expansion phase would be upon construction activities. In short, with one expansion after another, the Appropriations subcommittees of House and Senate repeatedly saw the day recede when the construction elements of the budget would diminish appreciably.

It will not be necessary to speak of all the attempts to solve the problem of costly construction procedures, but several successive attempts should be noted. All these attempts were in addition to the criticism which the Committee members continued to express in the hearings themselves.

The first attempt consisted of the requirement that construction plans be cleared with the Bureau of the Budget and reported to the Committees themselves.[15] This stipulation was obviously inadequate if the Bureau of the Budget took the AEC's point of view, and this turned out to be the case.

Next, a provision was inserted in an appropriations act to cut out the frills in the design of new construction work. The proviso read:

> That no part of the foregoing appropriations shall be used for any new construction project until after the Commission shall have notified all architects and engineers involved, that the plans for such project should be purely utilitarian and without unnecessary refinements.[16]

Without an unambiguous test of "utilitarian," such a requirement could scarcely be enforced.

The next attempt was a provision to prohibit the AEC from beginning any new construction project which had not been included in the budget estimates, or from continuing any construction project for which the revised estimate exceeded the original estimate by 35 per cent or more.[17] The obvious loophole here was that high original estimates could be submitted, thus defeating both provisions. Nor would the provisions compel the AEC to complete plans before beginning construction.

Finally, the most fundamental approach to the problem of the AEC's construction activities was an attempt to force the Commission to complete its designs before construction was begun. It appeared in the summer of 1952 when the Supplemental Appropriations Bill carrying the first installment of funds for the AEC's huge expansion program was reported by the House Appropriations Committee.[18]

As the Congressmen had come more and more to appreciate the problems of construction work, a number of them began to see a connection between the completeness with which construction work was planned and the device of a cost-plus-fixed-fee contractual form. If engineering and architectural design of a construction project were virtually complete in detail and specificity, the necessity for employing a cost-plus-fixed-fee type of contract would be substantially reduced. And to all Congressmen on the Appropriations Committee, a return to the lump-sum contract accepted in open bidding was the ultimate solution to the costliness of government construction programs. Furthermore, such contracts would obviate the necessity for administrative scrutiny of reimbursable costs, a task on which they felt administrators were always easy marks. In short, forcing the AEC to hold back the construction phases of its work until virtually complete plans were available was the key to more competitive governmental contracting.

Furthermore, such a restriction had great advantages in its own right. By forcing complete designing, it was felt that false starts, surplus materials, delays in scheduling parts' deliveries, and many other costly construction errors could be eliminated. Literally millions of dollars, Congressmen sincerely averred, could be saved by such a procedure.

The Appropriations Committeemen were clearly upholding three values in the American ethos, money economy, the efficiency of business forced to survive in a competitive situation, and precise managerial control. Yet to put these values into practice, a de-emphasis upon other values would have to be achieved. Such other values were speed, novelty, and up-to-dateness, which seemed necessary in the atomic energy program.

The values of the Appropriations Committees had substantial and widespread appeal in Congress, as the Appropriations subcommitteemen of House and Senate well knew. But those same legislators must also have known that, with regard to the Atomic Energy Commission's construction budget, many Congressmen were prepared to sacrifice the old-fashioned virtues in favor of speed in an experimental field where up-to-dateness meant everything.

The particular method used in this attempt at restriction has already been discussed in the description of the construction riders. It was to make a sizeable cut in obligational authority for new plant construction and to require that all the projects the AEC started be so completely planned that the final costs of all of them together would be within the appropriations granted.

The dramatic legislative history is recounted in Chapter V. The outcome was that the funds-to-complete requirement was retained in a bill which gave the AEC practically all the obligational authority it had asked for. Although the funds-to-complete proviso remained, the AEC had enough obligational authority to make liberal estimates and thus was not forced to delay the start of each project until design was complete.

The result was widely interpreted as a great victory for the Joint Committee on Atomic Energy and for those who believed that speed was the chief value in the atomic energy program. It is true that the funds-to-complete rider stands in every appropriation act which Congress has enacted since 1952. Given the long-range goal of moving toward a system of competitive lump-sum contracts, and given the corollary goal of improving the planning and supervisory control of the AEC over construction work, the Appropriations Committees may well have made some progress toward their objectives. However, they have failed to enforce their whole view, and the AEC's standard practice in dealing with new construction is still not what the Committees think it should be.

Originally, the Appropriations Committees had been frustrated in the full performance of their duties toward the AEC by secrecy which prevented them from analyzing the program and discovering its weak points. They were frustrated by not knowing what to do. But by 1952 they were convinced that they knew at least some of the deficiencies of the program, and their frustration was caused simply by the powerful opposition which was evoked by their attempts to introduce reforms. This was particularly true in the case of the House subcommittee; clearly its relationship with the AEC was not a happy one.

X

Republican Control

The election of President Eisenhower in November, 1952, resulted in a fundamental reprograming of the federal budget, intended to be in line with the aims expressed by the new President during his campaign. As finally submitted by the new Administration, the revised estimates reduced by nearly half a billion dollars the figure of $1.6 billion projected in the Truman budget for the AEC.[1] A substantial part of this reduction was in the contingency funds, which were included in the estimates to take care of variations in construction costs, and in the reserve which had been kept against the cancellation of certain electric power contracts. Certain cuts were made, as well, in a number of programs.

The House Appropriations Committee, then, received a budget which had already been pruned by the new Republican executive leadership. The Committee, of course, was also under Republican control, and Representative Phillips took over the Independent Offices Subcommittee chairmanship from Representative Thomas. It might be expected that the Republican Committee leadership would not wish immediately to embarrass its party by attacking the budget of the first GOP Administration in two decades. The change in party also had significance in the displacement of Representative Thomas. He was always considered by the AEC—and with reason—as a particularly for-

midable enemy, and his sponsorship of the funds-to-complete
rider in 1952, and his conception of it, had seemed to the Commission a serious threat.

In any case, the first year of the Eisenhower period brought a
lessening of tension, and fewer attempts were made to place new
restrictions on the AEC. The Committees made almost no reduction in the Eisenhower budget, indicating general satisfaction
with the reprograming carried out at the executive level.[2]
Their liberality, of course, must be seen in the light of these
executive cuts, which caused the AEC to express some concern.
Forced to live with the funds-to-complete proviso, the agency
did not wish to forfeit its contingency funds, which seemed a
good cushion against the proviso, but the Committees made no
restoration.

On the other hand, the Committees did show a sympathetic
interest in the program by their action in regard to the development of atomic power for civilian use. In reviewing the AEC
budget in 1953, the National Security Council eliminated work
on a large ship reactor, but the AEC obtained permission to
"come back with a rescoped program" aimed at the development
of a light pressurized water reactor adaptable to either large
ships or commercial power installations. This item amounted to
$7.9 million, and the Appropriations Committees approved it.[3]
Chairman Dean pointed out, however, that a separate provision
allowing actual construction of pilot models of a commercial
power plant was omitted from the Eisenhower budget. Chairman
Cole of the Joint Committee also took an interest, and he got in
touch with the House Committee to urge inclusion of an item for
pilot plant construction. As a result, the House Committee
wrote into the bill a provision allowing the expenditure of up to
$7 million of funds not otherwise committed and exempting
this work from the construction riders.[4]

On the whole, then, the seeming liberality of the Appropriations Committees and the lessening of tension between them and
the AEC in 1953 may be slightly misleading because of the
cuts which had already been made in the AEC budget by the
Executive. It must be remembered, too, that the funds-to-complete rider remained, and that an attempt to modify it, which
succeeded in the Senate Committee, was defeated in conference.[5]
Nevertheless, a relatively cordial relationship did appear between the Joint Committee and the House Appropriations Committee, and the House group seemed once again willing to listen
to the Joint Committee's strongly program-oriented point of
view.

■

With the budget for fiscal year 1955, there appeared a more
nearly "normal" Appropriations-AEC relationship as it had developed during the expansion years, and there seemed to be at
least the possibility that the Appropriations Committees would
exert a greater influence in the future. Representative Phillips'
cooperative attitude toward the Joint Committee must not be
taken to mean that he did not see a highly significant role for
the Appropriations Committees in holding the Commission as
closely as possible to efficiency and economy, always so
prominent among the Committees' criteria. At the start of the
fiscal year 1955 hearings, he said:

> Now I think you have come to the point where you can op-
> erate more cautiously, like all other agencies, on such matters
> as personnel, storage, and similar items.[6]

In its report on the AEC's request for about $1.3 billion, the
House Committee announced various reductions in the estimates
for operating expenses, the largest naturally being in Program
Direction and Administration, which was cut by $2,769,000.

But an even larger hidden reduction was made by requiring a decrease in inventories of $5,783,000.[7] In the Plant and Equipment Appropriation, the House demanded that the AEC use up available balances from previous appropriations—the total was $122,000,000—which the AEC had allowed as contingency funds against the possibility of overruns in construction projects. In other words, the House Committee was objecting to what it called "underruns." Also eliminated was $12,000,000 to provide for new uranium processing plants in case private capital did not build them within the next year. The impression that the House Committee was rather aggressive and confident is strengthened by a provision in the report that the Committee "will expect action to be taken [to dispose of Commission real estate and community operations] prior to presentation of next year's budget." [8] Furthermore, the two Committees in conference modified the Commission's request for a provision which would have authorized the rental of office space in the District of Columbia, allowing this only if no space were available in suitable government-owned buildings.[9]

Yet the impression of severity can be exaggerated. The House Committee was persuaded by the AEC to moderate the rider which provided that all construction projects had to appear in the budget. This was done by allowing substitution of new projects for the ones which appeared in the budget.[10] However, the AEC had a specific reason. With tests in the offing, some flexibility was desired so that substitute construction projects might be inserted, depending on the outcome of the tests. Thus the rider was eased not because of a change in heart by the House Committee and an acceptance of the old arguments presented ever since 1952, but because of a particular emergency. Still, the incident did indicate at least the continuation of the Committee's dealing softly with the AEC.

What of the relationship between the Appropriations Committees and the Joint Committee? Considerable harmony might be the proper characterization. They all seemed to agree that the AEC should push ahead in the development of civilian power. The Joint Committee seemed to be satisfied with the Appropriations Committees' treatment of AEC budget bills. The Joint Committee did not even register any open protest against the retention of the different construction riders. At any rate, the Committee members did not contest these clauses on the floor of the House in the debate on the Independent Offices Appropriation Bill for 1955. In fact, no debate involved the AEC. Even in the Senate, there was no debate concerning the AEC. No major issues disturbed the relationship between the two Committees. The Appropriations Committees seemed to support the general policy advocated by the Joint Committee, and the usual Appropriations Committees' reductions in small items appeared to be the standard and expected work of committees which are giving their attention to the details of administrative procedure.

Indicative of this harmony between the Appropriations Committees and the Joint Committee was the fact that the Appropriations Committees did not object to a change which the new Atomic Energy Act made in the division of prerogatives among the Committees in regard to the authorization power. The Joint Committee inserted into the bill an authorization power for itself "for acquisition or condemnation of any real property or any facility or for plant or facility acquisition, construction, or expansion." [11] As on the previous occasions when this increase in the power of the Joint Committee had been suggested, the AEC took exception to it. In the past the Appropriations Committees had supported the AEC, but this time they remained silent, and the new provision was enacted into law.

As a whole, then, the Republican period seems to offer no striking evidence of change, but rather a continuation of the

forces which have affected the entire history of AEC appropriations. Perhaps there is a slight shift in the direction of a more
normal Committee influence upon the agency, but if so, it is
nothing upon which one can base a view of the future. If international affairs take a permanent turn toward peace and reduced
tension, then of course the AEC's program will no longer enjoy
the same degree of protection as from its place in the national
defense effort. But no one can predict with assurance the future
pattern of international affairs, or the developments in the field
of atomic energy itself. And this means that no one can predict
what degree of authority the legislative groups may bring to
bear upon the atomic energy program. It is even conceivable
that the events of the future, either in the international arena or
in the nuclear laboratories, could produce a renewed urgency in
the atomic program which would surpass anything we have
known so far.

XI

Political Science and Atomic Energy

Anyone who writes of vital public affairs is faced with a lengthening and continuous march of events. He is forced to pick a stopping place which, between the writing and the final publication, recedes at once into the past. Our historical-analytical survey of atomic energy in government must end with the year 1955. It ends at a time when this nation is just beginning programs in atomic energy of the greatest interest and significance. Without less emphasis on atomic military preparedness, the nation and the world are looking hopefully and purposefully, as never before, toward the development of peacetime uses of the atom. On both levels, international and domestic, the Atomic Energy Act of 1954 contains provisions which are promising and significant. As these words are written, the history of this new Act is still in its early stages. Its operation will offer a most fruitful object for future research.

Yet the new Act marks no abrupt break with the past. Many of its provisions are identical with those of the 1946 legislation. Many more reflect developments in the eight-year life of that earlier Act, developments which, in the area of institutions and governmental processes, have been traced in the preceding pages. The present builds on the past—the future history of atomic energy can only be understood in terms of what has gone before.

One may gain a perspective on the events described in the

preceding pages by placing them against a background of general theory about the political setting in which all governmental agencies function. There is, first of all, a substantial environment of control which surrounds any agency, made up of spheres of influence which are normally in a state of flux. No agency in American government can operate in a political vacuum, although some are closer than others to such a condition. Rather, every agency with any significant policy-making or service functions is the center of a pattern of lines of influence.

A fundamental distinction should be drawn immediately between what may be called defense and nondefense areas. In the former, particularly in times of international tension, the processes of democracy are relatively limited by secrecy requirements. The governmental unit primarily responsible for military matters—the Department of Defense—operates in an environment that is generally limited to other governmental groups— the President and his advisers, the Department of State, the AEC, Congressional legislative and appropriations committees, and sometimes high-ranking individual Congressmen, to name those who first come to mind. Society as a whole, and its many pressure groups, cannot achieve much knowledge of aspects of military operation, nor have much impact on important weapons policy. To state this fact is not to deplore it—it is simply to admit that the necessities of secrecy limit military policy-making in many cases to a relatively small circle of governmental bodies.

It is in what may be termed the nondefense phases that the full play of democratic control processes is apparent. Without the requirement that important policy matters be kept from potential enemies, these phases may be subject to an extremely complex interplay of interested groups and individuals, working directly on agency personnel to influence the program, or working through other governmental units to achieve their objectives indirectly.

An agency is not a passive entity but rather takes on the role of active participant in this interplay of forces which shapes the policy of its program. Given their task by the legislature, agency personnel inevitably put the imprint of their own personalities and policy preferences on the work of their unit. They wish to see the agency achieve its organizational goals, as they themselves interpret them. Certain forces pressing on the agency may be considered by its leadership to be threats to the achievement of a desirable policy, and these leaders will meet such threats by appealing to other outside groups and interests for added strength in repelling the unwanted pressure. For example, an agency may seek executive support or active public approval to forestall the threat of a budget cut by the Appropriations Committees.

There are other reasons for agency participation in this struggle. Administrators conditioned by American political and social ideals often encourage the development of a complicated web of political communication and control simply because they have a conception of the proper functioning of a democratic society which puts a premium on control of the "bureaucracy." When a program has a peculiar significance for the safety or well-being of the nation, an administrator may be expected to be especially eager to have outside ties, because he is motivated partly by a psychological need to share some of his heavy burden of responsibility.

No agency is self-contained, then, but rather functions in a complicated political setting. Influence is brought to bear on it from many sources. Where the program is not in a vital defense area, influence may be shared among many outside groups as well as other governmental groups. Where secrecy is required, only the governmental units tend to participate, in a limited struggle among public officials.

In the governmental environment, agency relationships with Congress are fundamental ones. The legislature, after all, holds great and immediate power over an agency, primarily through its legislative and appropriating functions. By means of its committees, Congress may be the predominant source of influence on an agency and its program. But the legislative will, when it is in disagreement with an agency, is sometimes unable to enforce itself against the influence of other outside units, with which the agency may have close contact and to which it can turn for support, or against the vital importance of the agency's work to the national welfare. Conversely, public displeasure with an agency may result in attempts through pressure on Congressmen or the Executive to bring the agency to terms, or to weaken it or kill it altogether. These groups may be unsuccessful because of the close relationship between the agency and its substantive committees, which have come to share mutual conceptions of proper policy and procedure.

When secrecy limits an agency's outside ties to the governmental circle, Congressional committee importance tends to be at its highest. A vital defense program is relatively hidden in the high councils of the Executive branch and in the agency with primary responsibility. The general public necessarily remains ignorant to a great extent, and so does Congress as a whole. Only Congressional committees can demand and receive admittance to the inner circle.

■

The story of atomic energy, during the early years, is the story of the most vital defense program in history. The Atomic Energy Act of 1946 consequently provided for an unusual system of highly simplified control over it. It vested particularly great authority in the AEC, with provision for the continuing operation of the project largely in secret. Congress attempted to compensate for this power and secrecy by creating a particularly strong Joint Committee to carry on continuous surveillance of the agency. Thus, while the range of outside group contacts for the AEC was limited—private interest groups and the public generally seemed excluded by secrecy—there was a plan for greater than usual control by one outside unit in particular, the Joint Committee on Atomic Energy.

For a time the Joint Committee, learning about a new field and a new agency, limited its role to checking on AEC policy and action. More than that, its stress was on security by concealment, a viewpoint which conflicted with that of the Commission. In the highly charged political atmosphere of 1947 and 1948, it is not surprising that friction developed between a Republican-controlled Committee and the Truman-appointed Commission, headed by a man as controversial as David E. Lilienthal.

The Joint Committee-AEC relationship at first, then, was neither close nor fruitful. The Commission, disagreeing with the Committee on priorities, needed support not only to maintain its own conception of proper policy against Committee opposition, but also to escape part of its terrible responsibility by sharing the job of decision-making.

Normally an agency has several directions in which to turn in such a case. Public support is one possible recourse, and Mr. Lilienthal did make some attempt to cultivate popular favor by discussing in public those aspects of the program which could be brought into the open. Yet he was seriously limited, and the important decisions had to remain the responsibility of the Commission.

Nor could the AEC turn to Congress or Congressmen outside the Joint Committee. The Appropriations Committees' task, as we have seen, precluded any continuous and fruitful interrelationship with administrative agencies. Those Committees were uninformed about atomic energy and had neither the time nor the staff to become informed quickly. Further, their orientation was in the direction of frugality, efficiency, and careful planning, which the Commission felt were secondary to getting forward with a strong and aggressive program. Other Congressmen, potentially more sympathetic in some cases, were equally uninformed and equally unable to do much toward correcting this condition.

Within the executive branch, the Commission once more found little opportunity for close and harmonious outside relationships. The President, hampered somewhat by a National Security Council that was not functioning fully, took no more than a routine role, fulfilling his statutory responsibilities and meeting with the Commissioners on rare occasions, but leaving the responsibility and the problems in large measure up to them. In addition, no cooperative relationship developed with the military, partly due to unforeseeable circumstances which left the Military Liaison Committee far from being the coordinating body envisaged in the Act.

The Commission then found only one outside source to which it could go for support and advice. This was the General Advisory Committee, whose members knew more about atomic energy than the Commissioners and were eager to share the AEC's problems and support it in its policy decisions. Temporarily, then, the GAC moved in to fill as best it could the void in which the AEC found itself. During most of the Lilienthal period, the GAC was extremely close to the Commission and highly influential.

The GAC, however, could not maintain its unusually strong position. Its decline dates from late 1949, when news of the Soviet A-bomb brought into question the adequacy of United

States atomic military power. The General Advisory Committee was unable to adapt itself to the idea that every possible effort was necessary, including a strong thermonuclear program, in order to maintain American supremacy. When the decision on the H-bomb went against the GAC, it lost prestige and was generally pushed into the background on all but strictly technical matters.

Of the later history of the atomic energy project, the most spectacular aspect was doubtless the growth of the Joint Committee's influence. Although it was partly due to the Hickenlooper investigation, and to certain modifications of AEC behavior, which reassured the Congressional group, the emergence of the Joint Committee into a commanding position stemmed mainly from the beginning of the atomic arms race late in 1949, when it was discovered that the Soviet Union had the A-bomb. This, together with the tenure of Senator McMahon and Gordon Dean as chairmen of the two groups, resulted in much greater harmony of viewpoint and purpose. When those favoring the thermonuclear program gained the balance of power in both agency and Committee, a mutual trust and closeness developed which suggested that the Committee might be considered part of the inner control group of atomic energy.

This is obviously an unusual role for a legislative committee to play, even in matters of defense. Normally in executive-legislative relations, Congressional committees tend to avoid responsibility for program execution, and prefer to leave this to the agencies. Furthermore, legislative committees, in spite of their duty to maintain a continuous review, have usually found that the pressure of other work interferes.

The Joint Committee has been an exception to this rule. Because it was given wide authority and the right to a complete knowledge of the Commission's activities, secret and nonsecret, and because it dealt with one agency in one field, the Committee identified itself with the agency and the atom to an unusual degree. As the only legislative body with access to the atomic energy program, the Joint Committee has taken its responsibility most seriously in later years. Its members have realized the limited degree of control which secrecy allows other outside bodies to exercise, and they have come to realize too the vital significance of the atom for national survival and well-being. In a sense, they and the Commission seemed to be peculiarly isolated from other external groups, and they began to feel that the atom was in a real sense their "property" and their responsibility. Without other fields to deal with, and for some time without burdensome legislation to consider, the Joint Committee concentrated on atomic policy and administration with enthusiasm and determination and assumed the uniquely influential and responsible role which has made it one of the most important committees on Capitol Hill.

If the Joint Committee achieved an unusually influential role in atomic energy affairs, the Appropriations Committees have fallen somewhat short of attaining their normal degree of control over executive agencies. At the beginning they were limited by their unfamiliarity with the field of atomic energy. They were not long hampered by secrecy, for the AEC soon adopted the policy of acceding to any request for information, secret or not, and the Committeemen began to gain knowledge and self-assurance. However, when the Committees made attempts to curtail certain practices of the AEC which they thought were extravagant and wasteful, they found that the AEC was one of the least vulnerable agencies in the government, as a result of the importance of its work. Particularly after the first Soviet A-bomb in 1949 and during the period of expansion which followed, the Appropriations Committees faced a nearly insurmountable problem in attempting to control AEC expenditures. They made no effort to curtail the Commission's program, for there was no more vital program in the government. Indeed, so "protected" was the Commission that attempts to restrict its administrative procedures or other aspects of its operations often had to overcome formidable protests from both the AEC and the Joint Committee, who were likely to claim that restrictions of any kind would have a detrimental effect on the program.

Finally, the granting of the authorization power to the Joint Committee has not increased the leverage of the Appropriations Committees with the AEC in any way. In fact, it may have decreased it.

This history suggests that one should imagine a generally fixed degree of support and accompanying control which an agency must obtain from external sources. Without contact with any group whatsoever, it clearly cannot survive. If it refuses to be influenced by a particular group, it must compensate by accepting guidance and receiving support from other groups. The recession of one unit from a previously close relationship to an agency, creating what might be thought of as a "partial vacuum," will be followed by an expansion of the influence of those units that remain, thus filling the vacuum. An agency's "independence" from certain influences merely increases its dependence on others.

■

With the great 1952 expansion program and more recent successes with hydrogen weapons, attention is now turning to the peacetime uses of the atom. Atomic power, with its tremendous long-range possibilities, is a matter of growing concern to a great many economic interests in American society. The atom has also become an important factor in international policy, as we have seen. The growing significance of atomic energy for both private interests and the general public seems likely to bring the AEC far more completely into a normal pattern of governmental relationships than it has ever been before. One may already see the emergence of a trend toward the complexity that characterizes the pattern of control surrounding governmental programs with immediate economic and social implications. Previously there was no such immediate relationship, and the public made little effort to break through the secrecy enveloping atomic energy. In those units which could assume positions of influence, the importance of atomic energy to the nation's welfare tended to overshadow partisan political considerations, uniting groups which normally split into factions along more or less political lines. There was only one position to be taken by all parties on atoms for the military, and that was "the greatest possible speed toward the greatest possible atomic strength."

A wider variety of outside influences now impinges on the AEC in the increasingly important nonmilitary aspects of atomic energy. The outside controlling units are proliferating: witness the interest of industrial and utility groups in atomic power generation and the manufacture of reactor and generating equipment. Although secrecy is still present, these people do not fear to enter into the realm of the atom, but are actively seeking a new and important role—the creation, in fact, of a new atomic industry.

Within the government, the growing complexity is indicated by the interjection of other governmental units into the Dixon-Yates contract controversy, and by the increasing use of the atom as an instrument of foreign policy. These elements have begun to pull atomic energy outside the AEC-Joint Committee circle.

The peacetime atom means primarily atomic power, and the issue of public versus private power has been the subject of intense political controversy for many years. This means that the special interest groups on both sides of the issue (and others) will take politically opposite positions, and that such governmental units as Congressional committees, which are basically political and composed of members of both political parties, will tend to split along party lines. This political element has already been seen in the Dixon-Yates dispute and others.

The emergence of the peacetime atom may mean, then, some recession of the Joint Committee's extreme influence in the primary control group of atomic energy, as other units gain knowledge and influence. The Appropriations Committees may be expected to have a greater impact on atomic energy as emphasis draws away from the military, and a similar trend has already been noticed in the top-level Executive. Thus policy-making will go on outside the Joint Committee-AEC complex, and these two units will find other forces planning and influencing aspects of atomic energy policy. The Joint Committee, for example, showed some signs of jealousy because it had no part whatsoever in the formulation of the President's plan for an atomic-powered merchant ship.

At present, however, the Joint Committee's influence is still extremely high, and it would be rash to predict any substantial diminution. In the peacetime area secrecy is still important—it is easy to overemphasize the present extent of declassification because of the extreme concealment that has been the rule for so long. In this situation, many pressure groups are finding that they must depend on the Joint Committee to a considerable degree, since they themselves lack knowledge and leverage with the AEC. In the defense area, where the role of the atom continues to be crucial, research and development have resulted in advances and refinements—sometimes major changes in direction and emphasis—about which even the relatively informed outside observer can only speculate. The Joint Committee continues therefore to feel its great responsibility for making independent evaluations of progress. The Committee's emphasis, as a fully informed participant, continues to be on maximum atomic military strength, and its sense of the importance of this is undiminished.

In both peacetime and defense areas, the Joint Committee has great prestige because of its solid record of achievement and sound judgment, and Committee enthusiasm and initiative remain high. On the whole, one cannot escape the conclusion that the Joint Committee will remain a particularly influential participant in atomic energy affairs.

■

Atomic energy provides the political scientist with a historical example of the governmental process adapting itself to unusual needs by the creation of an unusual pattern of control. The atom required, and still requires, expert science, secrecy, and wise policy-making to a unique degree. This means that the democratic system of representative government has to adapt itself to a fluid program behind a wall of secrecy.

Our representative government requires institutions which provide opportunity for debate and development of opposing points of view, where "out-groups," i.e., those who do not have influence with the responsible executive agency, can register their protests. Thus, public control does not depend on each citizen's knowing the complicated details of any one public policy. Rather, effective responsibility means that vital decisions should be subject to independent criticism by experts. If such criticism is not effective when it is made directly to the responsible executive agency, there must be other channels through which it can flow.

In most cases, many individuals and groups are affected by governmental programs, and are well informed about them. In

these circumstances, there is no problem in obtaining outside
evaluation and criticism; generally, many voices are raised, both
praising and condemning the actions of administrative agencies
on various grounds. But where secrecy greatly limits the number
of potential critics, it becomes vitally important that forums for
amplifying and evaluating criticisms be made freely available at
all times. There must be a guarantee that anyone with informed
views and criticisms will be heard. No constructive criticism
should be ignored, since relatively little is available. If too few
are in a position to make informed evaluations, it may even be
necessary to create special new groups of outside critics and give
them security clearance, so that they may carry out an evaluation of the secret program.

Of all governmental programs, atomic energy has been the
one most in need of special arrangements to ensure outside criticism and control. The Atomic Energy Act provided for these
functions in part by the creation of special advisory committees
in two crucial areas. One statutory adjunct to the AEC was the
Military Liaison Committee. The great military importance of
the atom led to the establishment of this advisory group to represent to the Commission the viewpoint and judgment of the
Department of Defense and other executive units engaged in defense activities. The strong scientific and technical element in
the program gave rise to the second advisory unit established
by the Act, the General Advisory Committee of scientific experts appointed by the President.

There is a limit, however, to the usefulness of such groups.
The danger that minority views might be ignored by them is
shown in the case of the H-bomb decision. On that issue the
scientific minority was prevented from effectively expressing its
views by the fact that the GAC took a contrary position, almost
to a man. There are obvious risks in so formalizing one's technical advisers, for a small group of experts cannot always be ex-

pected to give the right answer, and may cut off consideration of more correct views if the system is too inflexible. Furthermore, specialists in one area do not necessarily have the perspective to give broad criticism and guidance, which is perhaps even more necessary than technical advice. Useful as these specialist groups have been, then, their creation did not exhaust the needs for outside control over the AEC. There remained a lack of sufficient, general, nontechnical evaluation from independent groups, open to receive communications from all sources of specialized knowledge and informed opinion.

The political units of the government normally serve this purpose. One such means of effecting broad control over an administrative agency is through the chief of the executive branch. This history of the atomic energy program has shown how provision was made for presidential responsibility in certain areas. In the H-bomb controversy, for instance, it was shown that the presidential function automatically served as a separate medium of policy evaluation. But, generally speaking, the high echelon of the Executive is too busy with the multifarious government programs to exercise continuous control over any single agency.

Our governmental system, which incorporates the principle of the separation of powers, depends heavily on the independent checks provided in various ways by Congress. Secrecy, however, prohibits the whole legislative body from filling this role of independent criticism of the Administration. In such situations, the committees which have access to the secret information acquire a special responsibility to serve as a point of protest for critical experts and as an evaluating post for any critical opinions that can be discovered. Under conditions of secrecy, this task is far from being a passive one. Instead, committees are required to be well-informed sleuths carefully looking for evidence of criticism among the limited group of persons who are behind the cloak of secrecy. Furthermore, they must take the place of outside critics in inventing policies alternative to those being followed by the agency.

These are not tasks which the normal busy legislative committees in House and Senate can easily fulfill. Neither can they be carried out by the Appropriations Committees, which are also pressed for time and preoccupied with budgetary efficiency and economy. Some special feature is clearly necessary if these tasks are to be undertaken with vigor.

The Atomic Energy Act of 1946 invented, and the Act of 1954 endorsed, a new institution for this purpose—a joint committee with full legislative powers and the prerogative to be kept fully and currently informed. From the foregoing account, this unit of public control has been seen to grow slowly in stature until it came to provide a tremendously valuable adaptation of our democratic system to the problems of secrecy. Its "jointness" made possible a close relationship of direct and immediate access to the AEC. As the single responsible Congressional body, it drew upon the best talents of members from both chambers and upon the best attributes of both chambers.

Although the Committee had few outside groups available to furnish criticisms of the AEC, it compensated for this lack by developing its own peculiar intelligence in the field. As a result, groups taking exception to existing policies made use of it as an effective channel in expressing their views, which otherwise might have been heard with much more difficulty.

Of course there is room for criticism of the Joint Committee. The Committee was slow in assuming its full responsibility. The Committee's judgment may have been wrong on specific issues over the years—the reader must make these evaluations himself. Nonetheless, it is clear that, in a vital secret program suddenly injected into the American governmental process, the structural device of a strong Joint Committee-Atomic Energy Commission combination provided a good means for enabling democratic government to survive the unusual stresses arising from the needs of atomic energy control.

Appendices

DATES OF SERVICE—ATOMIC ENERGY COMMISSIONERS [a]

Commissioner	Appointed to the AEC	Confirmed	Reappointed	Confirmed	Designated Chairman	Effective Date Resigned
Bacher[a]	10-28-46	4-9-47	…	…	…	4-21-49
LILIENTHAL[a]	10-28-46	4-9-47	…	…	10-28-46	2-15-50
PIKE[a]	10-28-46	4-9-47	6-19-50	7-10-50	2-14-50[b]	12-14-51
Strauss[a]	10-28-46	4-9-47	…	…	…	4-15-50
STRAUSS	6-24-53	6-28-53	…	…	6-24-53	…
Waymack[a]	10-28-46	4-9-47	…	…	…	12-2-48
DEAN	5-9-49	5-20-49	6-19-50	6-26-50	7-1-50[c]	6-25-53
Smyth	5-9-49	5-20-49	6-19-50 / 5-21-51	6-26-50 / 5-31-51	…	11-30-54
Murray	3-22-50	3-31-50	6-19-50 / 4-24-52	6-26-50 / 4-29-52	…	…
Glennan	8-11-50	8-22-50	…	…	…	11-1-52
Zuckert	1-21-52	2-4-52	…	…	…	6-30-54[d]
Campbell	7-14-53	7-21-53	…	…	…	11-30-54
Libby	9-30-54	12-2-54	…	…	…	…
von Neumann	10-23-54	3-14-55	4-1-55	…	…	…
Whitfield[e]	3-16-55	…	…	…	…	…
Vance	10-10-55	…	…	…	…	…

[a] The terms of the five original Commissioners expired July 31, 1948. By amendment of the Atomic Energy Act of 1946, the terms were extended to June 30, 1950. (Public Law 898, 80th Cong., 62 Stat. 1259, 42 U.S.C. 1802.)
[b] Commissioner Pike was never designated chairman, but served as acting chairman after Mr. Lilienthal's departure.
[c] Commissioner Dean served as acting chairman from July 1 to July 10, replacing Acting Chairman Pike whose reappointment had not been confirmed when his term expired June 30, 1950. President Truman named Mr. Dean as permanent chairman on July 11, 1950.   [e] Nomination withdrawn, July 12, 1955.
[d] Term expired.

Note: Chairmen are designated by names in capital letters.

TERMS OF ATOMIC ENERGY COMMISSIONERS

· 1947 · 1948 · 1949 · 1950 · 1951 · 1952 · 1953 · 1954 · 1955 · 1956 · 1957 · 1958 · 1959 · 1960 ·

Waymack | ** Smyth | Smyth | Smyth | * Libby

Lilienthal | Murray | Murray

Murray

Bacher | Dean | Dean | Strauss

Pike | Pike | Zuckert | *** | von Neumann

Strauss | * | Glennan | *** | Campbell | ** | Vance

* Vacancy

///// Chairman

DATES OF SERVICE—
AEC GENERAL MANAGERS

General Manager	Appointed	Confirmed *	Effective Date Resigned
Wilson	12-30-46	4-9-47	8-15-50
Shugg †	8-15-50	...	11-1-50
Boyer	11-1-50	...	11-1-53
Nichols	11-1-53	...	5-1-55
Fields	5-1-55	...	...

* *An amendment to the Atomic Energy Act, approved September 23, 1950, authorized the Commission to appoint and remove the General Manager. (P. L. 820, 81st Cong., 64 Stat. 979, 42 U.S.C. 1802.) Prior to this the President appointed the General Manager, subject to Senate confirmation.*

† *Carleton E. Shugg served as acting General Manager during the period between the departure of Carroll Wilson and the appointment of Marion Boyer.*

SENATE MEMBERS OF THE JOINT COMMITTEE
ON ATOMIC ENERGY BY YEARS

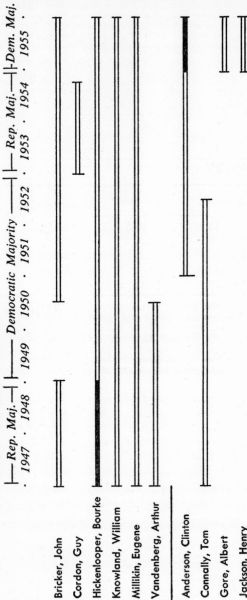

HOUSE MEMBERS OF THE JOINT COMMITTEE
ON ATOMIC ENERGY BY YEARS

Total membership — 9   ▬▬▬ = Chairman   ▨▨▨ = Acting Chairman

CHAIRMEN OF APPROPRIATIONS
SUBCOMMITTEES IN CHARGE OF AEC BUDGETS

1947–1948   Republican Congress

Subcommittees on Independent Offices:

Senate Chairman: Senator Clyde M. Reed
House Chairman: Rep. Richard B. Wigglesworth

1949–1952   Democratic Congress

Subcommittees on Independent Offices:

Senate Chairman:

1949–1950: Senator Joseph C. O'Mahoney
1951–1952: Senator Burnet R. Maybank

House Chairman: Rep. Albert Thomas

1953–1954   Republican Congress

Subcommittees on Independent Offices:

Senate Chairman: Senator Leverett Saltonstall
House Chairman: Rep. John Phillips

1955–1956   Democratic Congress

Subcommittees on AEC-TVA:

Senate Chairman: Senator Lister Hill
House Chairman: Rep. Louis C. Rabaut

SUMMARY OF CONGRESSIONAL ACTION ON AEC BUDGET ESTIMATES*

Fiscal Year 1947–Fiscal Year 1955

Fiscal Year	Amount Requested		Amount Appropriated	
	Cash	Contract Authority	Cash	Contract Authority
1947 Reg.	$ 605	$...	$ 565	$...
1948 Reg.	250	250	175	250
1948 Supp.	...	150	...	150
1949 Reg.	550	400	512	400
1949 Supp.	110	...	110	...
1950 Reg.	740	427	703	387
1950 Supp.	...	88	...	79
1951 Reg.	710	334	648	300
1951 Supp.	260	...	260	...
1951 Supp.	1,080	...	1,065	...
1951 Supp.	64	...	59	...
1952 Reg.	1,210	...	1,140	...
1952 Supp.	273	...	266	...
1952 Supp.	484	...	200	...
1953 Reg.	1,312	...	1,138	...
1953 Supp.	3,191	...	2,987	...
1954 Reg.	1,096	...	1,058	...
1955 Reg.	1,342	...	1,210	...
Total	$13,277		$12,096	

* All figures are given in millions of dollars.

PAST AND PRESENT AEC OFFICIALS, CONGRESSMEN, AND CONGRESSIONAL STAFF MEMBERS WHO WERE INTERVIEWED

JOINT COMMITTEE ON ATOMIC ENERGY

Senators

Bourke B. Hickenlooper   John Pastore
Eugene D. Millikin   Clinton P. Anderson
Richard B. Russell   Edwin C. Johnson

Senators' assistants

Mrs. Dorothy McRae (assistant to Millikin)
William Jaeger (assistant to Knowland)
George Ready (former assistant to L. Johnson)

Representatives

W. Sterling Cole   Melvin Price
Chet Holifield   Carl Hinshaw
James Van Zandt   Henry M. Jackson
Thomas A. Jenkins   (now Senator)

Joint Committee Staff

Corbin C. Allardice   Walter Hamilton
George Norris, Jr.   Kenneth Mansfield

Ex-Staff of Joint Committee

Fred B. Rhodes, Jr.   Harold Bergman
William L. Borden (2)

APPROPRIATIONS COMMITTEES

Senators

Homer Ferguson   Warren G. Magnuson

Representatives

John Phillips   Albert Thomas
Norris Cotton   George W. Andrews
Charles R. Jonas   Sidney R. Yates
Otto Krueger   Albert Gore
Francis Case   (now Senator)
    (now Senator)

ATOMIC ENERGY COMMISSION

Commissioners

Henry D. Smyth   Eugene M. Zuckert (2)

Assistants to Commissioner Thomas E. Murray

Gerard Smith   Comdr. James Dunford

General Manager

Marion Boyer

Assistant General Manager for Administration

James L. Kelehan (with Newton Steers)

Office of Industrial Development

Dr. William L. Davidson

Office of Classification

Murray L. Nash (Technical Assistant)

Special Assistant to General Manager
>   Edward R. Trapnell

Secretariat
>   Philip J. Farley (with Charles Sperry)

Office of the General Counsel
>   Harold L. Price (Deputy General Counsel)
>   George F. Trowbridge
>   Harold Green

Division of Finance
>   Francis J. McCarthy, Jr.   Philip Mullenbach (2)

Division of Security
>   Captain J. A. Waters, Director

Division of Organization and Personnel
>   Oscar S. Smith, Director (2)

Division of Information Services
>   Morse Salisbury, Director

Division of Construction and Supply
>   F. H. Warren, Deputy Director

Ex-Officials of AEC
>   David E. Lilienthal (Chairman)
>   Gordon E. Dean (Chairman)
>   T. Keith Glennan (Commissioner)

Everett L. Hollis (General Counsel)

Fletcher Waller (Director, Division of Organization and Personnel)

Carroll L. Wilson (General Manager) (2)

Adrian Fisher (General Counsel)

Joseph Volpe, Jr. (General Counsel)

BUREAU OF THE BUDGET

Frederick Schuldt

NOTES

Chapter I

1. The most authoritative account of the wartime project is Henry D. Smyth, *A General Account of the Development of Methods of Using Atomic Energy for Military Purposes under the Auspices of the United States Government* (Washington: Government Printing Office, 1945).

2. 60 *Stat. at L.* 755–775 (Public Law 585, 79th Cong., 2d Sess., Atomic Energy Act of 1946, approved August 1, 1946).

3. For the background of the Act, see U.S. Congress, Senate, *Atomic Energy Act of 1946,* Hearings before the Special Committee on Atomic Energy, 79th Cong., 2d Sess. The conclusions of the Special Committee are contained in U.S. Congress, Senate, Special Committee on Atomic Energy, Report to Accompany S. 1717, *Atomic Energy Act of 1946,* 79th Cong., 2d Sess., S. Rept. 1211 (April 19, 1946). See also Byron S. Miller, "A Law is Passed—The Atomic Energy Act of 1946," *University of Chicago Law Review,* XV (Summer, 1948), 799.

4. Some indication of MED organization and procedure is given in U.S. Atomic Energy Commission, *Second Semiannual Report of the Atomic Energy Commission* (Washington: Government Printing Office, 1947), pp. 4–6. See also the Smyth report, cited in Note 1, *supra.*

5. Testimony on the condition of the project at the time the AEC took command may be found in U.S. Congress, *Investigation into the United States Atomic Energy Project,* Hearing before the Joint Committee on Atomic Energy, 81st Cong., 1st Sess., pt. 19, pp. 770–777.

6. 60 *Stat. at L.* 755, 756–757 (Atomic Energy Act of 1946, Sec. 2a).

7. *Ibid.*

8. *Atomic Energy Act of 1946,* S. Rept. 1211, p. 12.

9. Richard O. Niehoff, "Organization and Administration of the United States Atomic Energy Commission," *Public Administration Review,* VIII (Spring, 1948), 96.

10. The principal exception to this was the Director of Military Application, whose direct contact with the General Manager remained unbroken.

11. Details on specific AEC projects and contractors may be found in the Commission's *Semiannual Reports,* 1947 to date.

12. The AEC's *Ninth Semiannual Report* (January, 1951) is mainly devoted to a discussion of AEC contract policy and operations. For an extended treatment of the economic and administrative aspects of the cost-plus-fixed-fee contract, see Richard A. Tybout, *Government Contracting in Atomic Energy* (Ann Arbor: The University of Michigan Press, 1956).

13. The programs and facilities of the AEC are most fully described in the *Semiannual Reports.* A good over-all treatment of the program is Gordon Dean, *Report on the Atom* (New York: Alfred A. Knopf, 1953).

14. 60 *Stat. at L.* 755, 756–757 (Secs. 2a and 2b).

15. *Ibid.,* 760 and 763 (Secs. 4c and 6a).

16. The McMahon Bill was S. 1717, and the May-Johnson Bill was H.R. 4566, both introduced in the 79th Cong., 1st Sess.

17. *Atomic Energy Act of 1946,* S. Rept. 1211, p. 11.

18. 60 *Stat. at L.* 755, 757–758 (Sec. 2c).

19. *Atomic Energy Act of 1946,* S. Rept. 1211, p. 12.

20. 60 *Stat. at L.* 755, 758 (Sec. 2d).

21. *Atomic Energy Act of 1946,* S. Rept. 1211, p. 11.

22. 60 *Stat. at L.* 755, 757 (Sec. 2b).

23. U.S. Congress, Senate, *Atomic Energy Act of 1946,* Hearings before the Special Committee on Atomic Energy, 79th Cong., 2d Sess., p. 39.

24. 60 *Stat. at L.* 755, 772 (Sec. 15a).

25. For the powers and functions of the Joint Committee, see *ibid.,* 773 (Secs. 15b–15e).

26. *Ibid.,* 775 (Sec. 19).

27. James R. Newman and Byron S. Miller, "The Socialist Island," *Bulletin of the Atomic Scientists,* V (January, 1949), 14–15. Mr. Newman had been White House adviser on atomic energy legislation and subsequently counsel to the Senate Special Committee on Atomic Energy; Mr. Miller had been the Associate General Counsel of the Office of War Mobilization, which acted for the Administration in securing atomic energy legislation in 1946.

Chapter II

1. Commissioner Bacher so characterized his previous connection with the Manhattan Engineer District in U.S. Congress, *Investigation into the United States Atomic Energy Project,* Hearing before the Joint Committee on Atomic Energy, 81st Cong., 1st Sess., pt. 19, p. 770.

2. This nomination and those of the five Commissioners were interim appointments by the President, i.e., made while Congress was not in session. Thus all six could take office on January 1, 1947, when the transfer of authority was made from the MED to the AEC, without waiting for Senate confirmation.

3. U.S. Congress, Senate, *Confirmation of Atomic Energy Commission and General Manager,* Hearings before the Senate Section of the Joint Committee on Atomic Energy, 80th Cong., 1st Sess.

For the story of the Lilienthal confirmation in greater detail than is given here, see Joseph P. Harris, *The Advice and Consent of the Senate* (Berkeley and Los Angeles: University of California Press, 1953), pp. 155–169.

4. On August 2, 1946, the day after the Act became law, nine members were designated in each chamber of the 79th Congress to serve on the Joint Committee. The Committee held one organizational meeting that same day, electing Senator McMahon chairman and Representative Thomason vice-chairman. Thereafter, it was inactive until reorganized in January, 1947. See U.S. Congress, Joint Committee on Atomic Energy, *Development and Control of Atomic Energy,* 80th Cong., 2d Sess., S. Rept. 850 (April 30, 1948).

5. *Congressional Record,* 80th Cong., 1st Sess., Vol. 93 (March 31, 1947), p. 2853.

6. *New York Times,* March 11, 1947.

7. These and succeeding quotations from the Senate controversy are from *Congressional Record,* 80th Cong., 1st Sess., Vol. 93.

8. See David Lilienthal and Robert H. Marquis, "The Conduct of Business Enterprises by the Federal Government," *Harvard Law Review,* LIV (February, 1941), 545.

9. U.S. Congress, Senate, *Confirmation of Atomic Energy Commission and General Manager,* Hearings, etc., pp. 7–8.

10. ". . . we on the Commission, vested with a kind of quite terrible responsibility, find in it [the Joint Committee] a great reassurance." David E. Lilienthal, "The People, the Atom, and the Press," an address before the annual convention of the New York State Publishers Association (AEC Release, January 19, 1948).

11. See U.S. Congress, *Labor Policy in Atomic Energy Plants,* Hearings before the Joint Committee on Atomic Energy, 80th Cong., 2d Sess.

12. *Ibid.,* p. 33.

13. *Ibid.,* p. 115.

14. At a press conference in 1948, for example, he said: "The Commission has been concerned from the outset, and particularly since this time last year, with finding a more effective way of increasing the area of public knowledge about this enterprise, since it is so peculiarly a public enterprise both as to ownership and the strong public interest of the people of the United States in it. . . .

"If this can be done, it seems to us not only in the public interest and in the interest of the press, but very much in the interest of the more effective functioning of the Commission's work." (AEC Release, July 24, 1948, p. 9).

15. David E. Lilienthal, "The People, the Atom, and the Press" (AEC Release, January 19, 1948).

16. See *Development and Control of Atomic Energy,* S. Rept. 850.

17. *Congressional Record,* 80th Cong., 1st Sess., Vol. 93 (March 28, 1947), p. 2805.

18. S. 1004, Bill to Amend the Atomic Energy Act of 1946, introduced by Mr. Knowland (March 31, 1947), 80th Cong., 1st Sess.

19. Quoted in *Congressional Record,* 80th Cong., 1st Sess., Vol. 93 (March 28, 1947), p. 2801.

20. This information was hardly of a substantial nature. The report on one, for example, consisted entirely of the fact that his brother once became a member of a Yonkers, New York, organization which was in some way affiliated with the Communist Party.

21. For a detailed description of the AEC's Personnel Security Program, see U.S. Congress, *Investigation into the United States Atomic Energy Project,* Hearing, etc., pt. 23, p. 976.

22. *Ibid.,* pt. 4, pp. 148–149.

23. 60 *Stat. at L.* 755, 767.

24. U.S. Congress, *Investigation into the United States Atomic Energy Project,* Hearing, etc., pt. 23, p. 942. The number of persons given emergency clearance is relatively small in comparison with the more than 100,000 candidates for clearance who were subjected to FBI investigation during these first two years. See U.S. Atomic Energy Commission, *Fifth Semiannual Report of the Atomic Energy Commission* (Washington: Government Printing Office, 1949), p. 121.

25. U.S. Congress, *Investigation into the United States Atomic Energy Project,* Hearing, etc., pt. 3, p. 105.

26. For a more complete account of Senator Vandenberg's discovery of and reaction to this wartime agreement on the A-bomb, see Arthur H. Vandenberg, Jr., ed., *The Private Papers of Senator Vandenberg* (Boston: Houghton-Mifflin, 1952), pp. 359–361.

27. *Ibid.,* pp. 361–363.

28. Information concerning these meetings is taken from the Daily Digest of the *Congressional Record,* 81st Cong., 1st Sess., Vol. 95.

29. See Mr. Lilienthal's statement in U.S. Congress, *Atomic Energy Commission Fellowship Program,* Hearings before the Joint Committee on Atomic Energy, 81st Cong., 1st Sess., pp. 1–4.

30. *Ibid.,* pp. 5–7.

31. *Ibid.,* p. 8.

32. This philosophy about administrative organization, it is interesting to note, seems in keeping with the role Senator Hickenlooper predicted the Commission would adopt, when he defended Mr. Lilienthal on the Senate floor against an attack by Senator Bridges:

"If the Senator is suggesting that Mr. Lilienthal overrides the provinces of employees or those under him, I do not believe Mr. Lilienthal is of that disposition. I think Mr. Lilienthal is a forceful executive. But I believe that, as a successful administrator, he will cooperate with his associates in the Commission and will certainly confine his activities to the establishment of general policy, and that the General Manager will be fully authorized and permitted to perform his functions as such." *Congressional Record,* 80th Cong., 1st Sess., Vol. 93 (March 25, 1947), p. 2532.

33. U.S. Congress, House of Representatives, *Independent Offices Appropriation Bill for 1949,* Hearings before the Subcommittee of the Committee on Appropriations, 80th Cong., 2d Sess., pp. 871–872.

34. This exchange occurred on the floor of the Senate:

Mr. Bridges. "Members of the military have complained to me, I shall not elaborate on what they have said or mention their names at this time. But when [Senator McMahon] says that no one in the military has complained about this matter, that is a broad statement. . . . He can only speak for himself."

Mr. McMahon. "I think that if the Senator has any observations to make regarding any specific complaints made by any responsible member of the military it is a proper subject to place in the Record at this point."

Mr. Bridges. "The military men I have talked with are opposed to Mr. Lilienthal. Of course, the President has nominated Mr. Lilienthal, and the fact that the President is the Commander in Chief of the Army and Navy could mean their careers would be prejudiced by taking a public position in opposition to the President. Therefore, I do not blame them for being silent." *Congressional Record,* 80th Cong., 1st Sess., Vol. 93 (March 25, 1947), p. 2536.

35. 80th Cong., 1st Sess.: S. 979; S. 1118; H.R. 2543; H.R. 2791; H.R. 3217. 80th Cong., 2d Sess.: S. 2388; H.R. 5909.

36. S. 1952, Bill to replace the AEC by eight military men

and one scientist, introduced by Mr. Cain (May 26, 1949), 81st Cong., 1st Sess.

37. For a report on this incident, see Walter Millis, ed., *The Forrestal Diaries* (New York: Viking Press, 1951), pp. 458–461.

38. During both sessions of the 80th Congress, two Senators and five Representatives held concurrently membership on the Armed Services Committees of their respective chambers: Senators Edwin Johnson of Colorado and Richard Russell of Georgia; and Representatives Sterling Cole of New York, Carl Durham of North Carolina, Charles Elston of Ohio, Lyndon Johnson of Texas (2d Sess.), R. Ewing Thomason of Texas (1st Sess.), and James Van Zandt of Pennsylvania. In addition Representatives Chet Holifield and Melvin Price had served on the Military Affairs Committee of the 79th Congress. Representative Elston probably went furthest in his feelings about the military; see *Congressional Record,* 79th Cong., 2d Sess., Vol. 92 (July 17, 1946), p. 9272.

39. See U.S. Congress, *Confirmation of Atomic Energy Commission and General Manager,* Hearings, etc., p. 13.

40. *Ibid.,* p. 25.

41. General Groves, who became a member of the Military Liaison Committee on January 31, 1947, had been Director of the Manhattan District, and naturally had an insight into the workings of the project that the new civilian commissioners could develop only with time. Whether or not he actually had questions to ask or advice to offer which embarrassed the Commission, it is clear that the possibility of this existed.

42. The original letter was dated November 14, 1946. See United States Atomic Energy Commission, *In the Matter of J. Robert Oppenheimer,* Transcript of Hearing before Personnel Security Board (Washington: Government Printing Office, 1954), p. 169.

43. *New York Times,* July 22, 1947.

44. See U.S. Congress, *Investigation into the United States Atomic Energy Project,* Hearing, etc., pt. 6, p. 262.

45. "The Commission frequently receives a Joint Chiefs' 'requirement,' as it is called, for a particular weapon or family of weapons, or a new reactor to produce a certain material, or a new production site, without any prior consultation between the Chiefs

and the Commission. This is wrong. Proper liaison between the Commission and the Joint Chiefs is lacking. It is really not furnished by the Military Liaison Committee. . . . This Committee was to function as the military watchdog of the newly created civilian Commission. What is needed today, however, is not watchdogging, but the unplugging of the channels of communication between the two agencies. Joint consultation at early stages could prevent many a questionable 'requirement' from being frozen at the Joint Chiefs' level." Gordon Dean, *Report on the Atom* (New York: Alfred A. Knopf, 1953), p. 140.

46. An illuminating discussion of the GAC is provided in Dr. Oppenheimer's testimony before the Personnel Security Board; see *In the Matter of J. Robert Oppenheimer,* Transcript, etc., p. 66.

47. *Ibid.,* p. 67.

48. *Ibid.,* p. 406.

49. See Ralph E. Lapp, *The New Force* (New York: Harper and Bros., 1953), pp. 50–51.

50. Dr. Oppenheimer was asked in the spring of 1942 by Dr. Compton to take over responsibility for work on the bomb itself. He accepted and began a series of conferences which led him to the conclusion that a central laboratory was necessary. Out of this grew Los Alamos. Here he served as director from late 1942 until October 16, 1945.

After the war Dr. Oppenheimer resumed his teaching career at the California Institute of Technology. In 1947 he became Director of the Princeton Institute for Advanced Study.

Meanwhile, he retained a very active role in atomic energy affairs. He testified on the proposed legislation under consideration in 1945 and 1946 for the domestic control of atomic energy. During the immediate postwar years he served as a member of a panel involved in preparation of the so-called Acheson-Lilienthal report on international control of atomic energy. His principal role in atomic energy affairs, however, was as the General Advisory Committee chairman.

51. See Dr. Oppenheimer's testimony, *In the Matter of J. Robert Oppenheimer,* Transcript, etc., p. 232.

52. See the testimony of various scientists associated with him since 1942. *Ibid.,* pp. 256 ff.

53. One interviewee asserted that Dr. Oppenheimer's influence on the program during the first two or three years was greater than that of any other single individual, David Lilienthal included.

54. See testimony of Dr. Wendell M. Latimer, *In the Matter of J. Robert Oppenheimer,* Transcript, etc., especially p. 663.

55. U.S. Congress, Joint Committee on Atomic Energy, *Argonne National Laboratory, Du Page County (Ill.) Site,* Committee Print, 80th Cong., 2d Sess.

56. See H.R. 6402, introduced by Mr. Johnson, and its companion, S. 2589, introduced by Mr. Hickenlooper (April 30, 1948), 80th Cong., 2d Sess.

57. See U.S. Congress, Senate, Report to accompany S. 2589, *A Bill to Provide for the Extension of the Terms of Office of the Present Members of the Atomic Energy Commission,* 80th Cong., 2d Sess., S. Rept. 1352, pt. 2, Minority Views (May 24, 1948).

58. For the House debate on the extension, see *Congressional Record,* 80th Cong., 2d Sess., Vol. 94 (June 18, 1948), pp. 8953–8954; for the Senate debate, see *ibid.* (June 19, 1948), pp. 9060–9067 and 9070–9072.

59. *The Forrestal Diaries* contains an interesting reference to the suspicion which Mr. Lilienthal engendered in Republican Joint Committee members. It describes a meeting between Forrestal and Senator Hickenlooper at which the latter stated his concern over certain of Mr. Lilienthal's public utterances, as follows:

"The Senator said he had come over to give expression to certain rather vague misgivings which he was experiencing in connection with the Atomic Energy Commission and its activities. He could put his finger on no one action or policy, but said that the character and number of speeches which Lilienthal was making, the emphasis upon the future possibilities of atomic power as a source of energy for industrial and general purposes, and his constant reference to control of atomic energy by 'the people,' all made a pattern with ultimate indicated objectives as follows: (1) the indispensability and therefore the perpetuation of Mr. Lilienthal in power; (2) the general underlying idea of statism." Walter Millis, ed. (New York: The Viking Press, 1951), pp. 379–380.

60. W. W. Waymack, "Four Years Under Law," *Bulletin of the Atomic Scientists,* VII (February, 1951), 51–56.

61. *Congressional Record,* 80th Cong., 2d Sess., Vol. 94 (June 19, 1948), p. 9062.

62. Senator McMahon may be an exception. As "Mr. Atom," he seemed to feel an extraordinary personal interest and responsibility regarding atomic energy, right from 1945. In the 80th Congress, of course, he was not Joint Committee chairman and could not make full use of his knowledge and enthusiasm.

63. In 1947 and 1948, Mr. Lilienthal addressed more than twenty-one groups throughout the country, whereas the other Commissioners collectively made about half as many addresses. Some of Mr. Lilienthal's topics were: "Atomic Energy Is Your Business"; "Democracy and the Atom"; "Atomic Energy and the Engineer"; "Atomic Energy and the American Farmer"; "The People, the Atom, and the Press"; "Atomic Energy—Where Do We Stand Today?"; "The Business Side of the Atom"; "Youth in the Atomic Age"; "Human Relations and the Atom"; "Teaching and the Atom"; and "Private Industry and the Public Atom." For a tabulation of Mr. Lilienthal's trips, see Exhibit 30, U.S. Congress, *Investigation into the United States Atomic Energy Project,* Hearing, etc., pt. 23, pp. 1056–1061.

Chapter III

1. Congress adjourned August 7, 1948, reconvened December 31, 1948, in accordance with H. Con. Res. 222, and adjourned on the same day, *sine die. Congressional Record,* 80th Cong., 2d Sess., Vol. 94 (August 7, 1948), pp. 10196 and 10250; (December 31, 1948), pp. 10264 and 10273.

2. U.S. Congress, *Investigation into the United States Atomic Energy Project,* Hearings before the Joint Committee on Atomic Energy, 81st Cong., 1st Sess., 23 pts., Appendix and Index.

3. U.S. Congress, *Atomic Energy Report to Congress,* Hearings before the Joint Committee on Atomic Energy, 81st Cong., 1st Sess.

4. The hearing also developed a dispute between Senator McMahon and Representative Holifield, on the one hand, and Senators Tydings and Connally on the other, as to the possibility of publishing stockpile figures. Senator McMahon favored this, and kept it a live issue over the succeeding months in spite of

President Truman's flat refusal, on February 9, to disclose the figures. This was not, however, so much an AEC-Joint Committee disagreement as a dispute between various Committee members themselves.

5. See *Congressional Record*, 81st Cong., 1st Sess., Vol. 95 (March 23, 1949), pp. 2997–3007.

6. *Ibid.*, pp. 3002–3004.

7. For Mr. Cole's remarks and the Lewis commentary, see *Congressional Record*, 81st Cong., 1st Sess., Vol. 95 (May 12, 1949), p. A2900. For Senator Hoey's remarks and the letter from Mr. Lilienthal on the awarding of the AEC fellowships, see *ibid.*, pp. 6081–6082.

8. See Senator McMahon's statement, *Congressional Record*, 81st Cong., 1st Sess., Vol. 95 (May 19, 1949), p. 6455.

9. U.S. Congress, *Atomic Energy Commission Fellowship Program*, Hearings before the Joint Committee on Atomic Energy, 81st Cong., 1st Sess., pp. 1 ff.

10. The full exchange is as follows:

Representative Elston. "You still have not answered what I am getting at. Are you going to keep Freistadt, a Communist, in this program if the National Research Council recommends that he be kept?"

Mr. Lilienthal. "I would like to see what the National Research Council's restudy of this question turns up. I believe that having it reexamined, we would be in a better position to say."

Representative Elston. "Suppose on reexamination they still decide to keep him, but the evidence that you have in your possession is that he is a Communist, as indicated by his own statement. Now, which would you do? Accept the word of the council and keep him in the program? Or would you get rid of him?"

Mr. Lilienthal. "I would feel obliged to accept the judgment of the council."

Representative Elston. "Even though you knew he was a Communist?"

Mr. Lilienthal. "Even though they knew he was a Communist."

Representative Elston. "Even though they knew it, and even though you knew it, you would keep him in school?"

Mr. Lilienthal. "I think this may well be an unlikely speculation. But you put it in that form, and I would say that rather than have the National Research Council withdraw from the program, which might be the result, the lesser of the two evils would be recommended." U.S. Congress, *Atomic Energy Commission Fellowship Program,* Hearings, etc., p. 36.

11. *Ibid.,* pp. 23–32 and 51–88.

12. For Senator Hickenlooper's statement as released by his office, see U.S. Congress, *Investigation into the United States Atomic Energy Project,* Hearing, etc., pt. 23, pp. 1112–1113.

13. *Ibid.,* pp. 1100–1101.

14. *Ibid.,* pt. 1, p. 3.

15. *Ibid.,* p. 14.

16. *Ibid.,* pt. 2, pp. 63–72.

17. *Ibid.,* pt. 3, pp. 104–141, *et passim.*

18. A jar containing several grams of uranium was discovered missing at the Argonne National Laboratory on February 7, 1949; it was reported to the FBI on March 28, reported to the Commission April 13, and to the Joint Committee on Atomic Energy on April 27. *Ibid.,* pt. 1, pp. 18–19.

19. A report submitted at a later date by Dr. Thiele summarized his final findings as follows: "The amount of U-235 in the missing jar was between 30.3 and 31.7 grams, and the amount of U-235 in the enriched material found in the scrap uranium was between 29.0 and 31.3 grams. Since these figures overlap it follows that the best available data do not indicate the loss of any uranium, by theft or otherwise, but neither do they exclude the possibility that some small amount may have been stolen. The attendant circumstances make it extremely unlikely that any was stolen." See *ibid.,* pt. 23, p. 120.

20. For Mr. Lilienthal's opening statements on the Commission's stewardship, see *ibid.,* pt. 19, pp. 763–769.

21. Other witnesses: Brig. Gen. James McCormack, Jr., Director, Division of Military Application, AEC; Mervin J. Kelly, Executive Vice President, Bell Laboratories, Inc.; Dr. Norris E. Bradbury, Director of Los Alamos Scientific Laboratory; Carroll L. Wilson, General Manager, AEC; Clark Center, General Superintendent, Carbide and Carbon Chemicals Corp.; James W. Parker, President and General Manager, Detroit Edison Co.; Isaac Harter, Chairman of the Board, Babcock and Wilcox Co.; Dr. Lee A.

DuBridge, President, California Institute of Technology; Dr. Enrico Fermi, Institute for Nuclear Studies, University of Chicago; Dr. Shields Warren, Director, Division of Biology and Medicine, AEC; Dr. Alan Gregg, Chairman, Advisory Committee on Biology and Medicine, AEC, and Director for Medical Sciences, Rockefeller Foundation; Joseph Volpe, Jr., General Counsel, AEC.

22. U.S. Congress, *Investigation into the United States Atomic Energy Project,* Hearing, etc., pt. 23, pp. 1120–1121.

23. U.S. Congress, Joint Committee on Atomic Energy, *Investigation into the United States Atomic Energy Commission,* 81st Cong., 1st Sess., S. Rept. 1169 (October 13, 1949), and pt. 2, Minority Views (October 26, 1949).

24. See "The Russian Explosion," *Bulletin of the Atomic Scientists,* V (October, 1949), 261.

25. Sec. 102-A. "No part of any appropriation contained in this title for the Atomic Energy Commission shall be used to confer a fellowship on any person who advocates or who is a member of an organization or party that advocates the overthrow of the Government of the United States by force or violence or with respect to whom the Commission finds upon investigation and report by the Federal Bureau of Investigation on the character, associations, and loyalty of whom, that reasonable grounds exist for belief that such person is disloyal to the Government of the United States." 63 *Stat. at L.* 634.

26. See U.S. Congress, *Investigation into the United States Atomic Energy Project,* Hearing, etc., pt. 23, pp. 1121–1173.

27. *Mr. Lilienthal.* "Mr. Cole, may I make this suggestion in the spirit of assisting the Commission's business? If we could be advised, say of an afternoon, of the subject matter that is to be presented the following morning, then only those individuals who are concerned with that subject need be here, but as long as we do not know until the hearings open even what the area is, it puts us at a great disadvantage not to have the people here to provide the information." *Ibid.,* pt. 3, p. 140.

28. See "Analysis of public opinion regarding the issues involved in the investigation into the policies and administration of the Atomic Energy Commission." *Ibid.,* pt. 23, pp. 1122–1173.

29. S. 1952, Bill to replace the AEC by eight military men

and one scientist, introduced by Mr. Cain (May 26, 1949), 81st Cong., 1st Sess.

30. H.R. 5534, introduced by Mr. Durham, and its companion, S. 2215, introduced by Mr. McMahon (July 7, 1949), 81st Cong., 1st Sess.

31. *New York Times,* July 15, 1949.

32. See U.S. Congress, *Investigation into the United States Atomic Energy Project,* Hearing, etc., pt. 5, pp. 195–196, and "Security and Intelligence, Personnel Clearances" (June 17, 1948), GM-80, U.S. Atomic Energy Commission, *General Manager's Bulletins,* amending General Manager's letter of February 14, 1947.

33. This is borne out by the issuance of several significant directives from the General Manager and Controller of the AEC: "Contract Manual" (January 27, 1949), GM-125, U.S. Atomic Energy Commission, *General Manager's Bulletins,* and "Cost Accounting" (January 10, 1949), Accounting Series, No. 5, U.S. Atomic Energy Commission, *Controller's Release No. 7.*

34. It is interesting to note Senator Vandenberg's feelings about the inquiry and Mr. Lilienthal. In a letter dated May 24, 1949, the Senator wrote:

"No one can make any sort of argument for educating young Communists at government expense—and least of all in atomic physics. I can't defend [Lilienthal] in this instance and I don't intend to try. Indeed I am inclined to think he has outlived his usefulness. But I don't intend to join the hysteria which would 'boil him in oil.' "

He expressed much the same feelings in another letter a few days later:

"Of course, Lilienthal is not guilty of 'incredible mismanagement' (at least not from anything I have yet seen or heard). But I increasingly feel that he is much too loose when it comes to national security." Arthur Vandenberg, Jr., ed., *op. cit.,* p. 358.

35. "Mr. Lilienthal Resigns," *Bulletin of the Atomic Scientists,* V (December, 1949), 328.

36. See U.S. Congress, Joint Committee on Atomic Energy, *Natural-Gas Pipe Line Oak Ridge, Tenn.,* Committee Print, 81st Cong., Ist Sess., pp. 1–2, and U.S. Congress, *Natural Gas Facilities for Oak Ridge,* Hearing before a Subcommittee of the Joint Committee on Atomic Energy, 81st Cong., 1st Sess., pp. 25–37.

37. U.S. Congress, *Investigation into the United States Atomic Energy Project,* Hearing, etc., pt. 10, p. 435.

38. Ralph E. Lapp, *The New Force* (New York: Harper and Bros., 1953), pp. 86–87.

39. See U.S. Atomic Energy Commission, *Eighth Semiannual Report of the Atomic Energy Commission* (Washington: Government Printing Office, 1950), p. ix.

40. For a discussion of the immediate postwar development of the H-bomb, see U.S. Atomic Energy Commission, *In the Matter of J. Robert Oppenheimer,* Transcript of Hearing before Personnel Security Board (Washington: Government Printing Office, 1954), especially Dr. Teller's testimony, pp. 711–712, and Dr. Oppenheimer's, pp. 949–950.

41. Representative Cole's statement is printed in the *Congressional Record,* 83d Cong., 2d Sess., Vol. 100 (Daily Edit., April 8, 1954), p. A2716.

42. See *In the Matter of J. Robert Oppenheimer,* Transcript, etc., p. 402.

43. Membership of the General Advisory Committee, 1949: Chairman: Dr. J. Robert Oppenheimer, Director, Institute for Advanced Study, Princeton, N.J.; Members: Dr. Oliver E. Buckley, President, Bell Telephone Laboratories, New York, N.Y.; Dr. James B. Conant, President, Harvard University, Cambridge, Mass.; Dr. Lee A. DuBridge, President, California Institute of Technology, Pasadena, Calif.; Dr. Enrico Fermi, Professor of Physics, Institute for Nuclear Physics, University of Chicago, Chicago, Ill.; Dr. I. I. Rabi, Chairman, Department of Physics, Columbia University, New York, N.Y.; Hartley Rowe, Vice President and Chief Engineer, United Fruit Co., Boston, Mass.; Dr. Glenn T. Seaborg, Professor of Chemistry, University of California, Berkeley, Calif.; Dr. Cyril S. Smith, Director, Institute for the Study of Metals, University of Chicago, Chicago, Ill.

44. At a 1954 hearing, Representative Holifield commented on the fact that Commissioners Dean and Strauss appealed to the Joint Committee on the H-bomb dispute. U.S. Congress, *S. 3323 and H.R. 8862, To Amend the Atomic Energy Act of 1946,* Hearings before the Joint Committee on Atomic Energy, 83d Cong., 2d Sess., pt. I, p. 291.

45. *New York Times,* October 4, 1953, Magazine Section, pp. 13 ff.

46. "Mr. Lilienthal Resigns," *Bulletin of the Atomic Scientists,* V (December, 1949), 328.

Chapter IV

1. H.R. 8103, introduced by Mr. Durham, and its companion, S. 3437, introduced by Mr. McMahon (April 17, 1950), 81st Cong., 2d Sess.

2. Section 2(a) of the Atomic Energy Act would have been amended to read, in part:

"After June 30, 1950, the General Manager shall be appointed for a 3-year term, and the first such appointment for a 3-year term shall be made with respect to a term beginning July 1, 1950."

3. *New York Times,* June 20, 1950.

4. U.S. Congress, Senate, *Confirmation of Sumner Pike to be a Member of the Atomic Energy Commission,* Hearing before the Senate section of the Joint Committee on Atomic Energy, 81st Cong., 2d Sess.

5. For the debate on the Pike confirmation, see *Congressional Record,* 81st Cong., 2d Sess., Vol. 96 (July 10, 1950), pp. 9755–9773.

6. *Ibid.* (June 23, 1950), p. 9163.

7. "News in Brief," *Bulletin of the Atomic Scientists,* VI (August–September, 1950), 287.

8. It is interesting to note a news story in the *New York Times* of August 10, 1950, which reported Carroll Wilson's hope that his departure was not the signal for a thorough shake-up in the AEC. He made this statement, the story went on, after Joint Committee members (unnamed) predicted that his departure would be followed by a " 'top-to-bottom house-cleaning' to rid the Commission of 'the Lilienthal influence.' " According to the story, sources close to Chairman Dean said he planned no wholesale replacement—and none occurred.

9. S. 3437, reported by the Joint Committee on Atomic Energy to the Senate (August, 1950), 81st Cong., 2d Sess.

10. A scientific minority, following Dr. Edward Teller, has

been in the ascendant ever since the H-bomb decision, which was in line with their recommendation.

11. *New York Times,* November 27, 1949.

12. See U.S. Congress, Senate, *Confirmation of Gordon E. Dean and Henry De Wolf Smyth as Members of the Atomic Energy Commission,* Hearings before the Senate Section of the Joint Committee on Atomic Energy, 81st Cong., 1st Sess., p. 23.

13. U.S. Atomic Energy Commission, *Memorandum for Information,* Transcript of Remarks of Chairman Gordon Dean, August 9, 1950 (AEC Release, August 11, 1950).

14. *Ibid.*

15. U.S. Congress, Joint Committee on Atomic Energy, *Development and Control of Atomic Energy,* 81st Cong., 2d Sess., S. Rept. 1041 (October 19, 1951), p. 7.

16. U.S. Congress, Joint Committee on Atomic Energy, *Report on Raw Materials,* 82d Cong., 1st Sess., H. Rept. 2449 (July 2, 1952).

17. Total amounts appropriated for the AEC are as follows:

Fiscal Year	Total
1949	$1,022,000,000
1950	1,169,000,000
1951	2,332,000,000
1952	1,606,000,000
1953	4,145,000,000

18. U.S. Congress, *Expanded Atomic Production Program,* Hearing before the Joint Committee on Atomic Energy, 82d Cong., 1st Sess. (The testimony of all witnesses except those speaking for the Navy was so uniformly of a classified nature that it did not lend itself to publication. The actual published hearing consists of non-secret excerpts from the meeting held with the Secretary of the Navy and the Assistant Secretary of Navy for Air.)

19. S. Con. Res. 46, introduced by Mr. McMahon (September 18, 1951), 82d Cong., 1st Sess.

20. U.S. Congress, *Expanded Atomic Production Program,* Hearing, etc., Appendix, p. 11.

21. *Congressional Record,* 82d Cong., 2d Sess., Vol. 98 (June 27, 1952), pp. 8349–8353.

22. U.S. Atomic Energy Commission, *Fifteenth Semiannual Report of the Atomic Energy Commission* (Washington: Government Printing Office, 1954), p. 13.

23. *Development and Control of Atomic Energy*, S. Rept. 1041, p. 5.

24. The story about the Livermore Laboratory, as well as other activities in which Dr. Oppenheimer figured, was revealed in U.S. Atomic Energy Commission, *In the Matter of J. Robert Oppenheimer*, Transcript of Hearing before Personnel Security Board (Washington: Government Printing Office, 1954), *passim*. This proceeding involved a review of the denial of Dr. Oppenheimer's security clearance as AEC consultant and was held before a specially constituted board, which took the name of its chairman, Gordon Gray, former Secretary of the Army and then president of the University of North Carolina. The other members of the Gray Board were Thomas A. Morgan, former president of the Sperry Corporation, and Dr. Ward V. Evans, Professor of Chemistry, Loyola University, Chicago.

25. *Ibid.*, p. 305.

26. See Chap. IV, n. 24, *supra*.

27. *In the Matter of J. Robert Oppenheimer*, Transcript, etc., pp. 311–312.

28. *Ibid.*, p. 755.

29. William L. Borden, *There Will Be No Time* (New York: The Macmillan Co., 1946).

30. *Ibid.*, pp. 72–73, italics added.

31. U.S. Congress, *Wage Payments at Nevada Test Site*, Hearing before the Joint Committee on Atomic Energy, 82d Cong., 2d Sess., Appendix.

Chapter V

1. U.S. Congress, *Wage Payments at Nevada Test Site*, Hearing before the Joint Committee on Atomic Energy, 82d Cong., 2d Sess., Appendix.

2. *Ibid.*, pp. 44–45.

3. U.S. Congress, *Wage Payments at Nevada Test Site*, Hearing before the Joint Committee on Atomic Energy, 82d Cong., 2d Sess.

4. *New York Times,* March 8, 1953.

5. U.S. Congress, House of Representatives, Report to accompany H.R. 6829, *Supplemental Independent Offices Appropriation Bill, 1949,* 80th Cong., 2d Sess., H. Rept. 2245 (June 8, 1948).

6. *Congressional Record,* 80th Cong., 2d Sess., Vol. 94 (June 9, 1948), pp. 7614 and 7624–7625.

7. *Ibid.* (June 10, 1948), p. 7714.

8. *Ibid.* (June 18, 1948), p. 8768.

9. U.S. Congress, House of Representatives, Report to accompany H.R. 4177, *Independent Offices Appropriation Bill, 1950,* 81st Cong., 1st Sess., H. Rept. 425 (April 11, 1949).

10. *Congressional Record,* 81st Cong., 1st Sess., Vol. 95 (April 14, 1949), pp. 4681–4682.

11. U.S. Congress, Senate, Report to accompany H.R. 4177, *Independent Offices Appropriation Bill, 1950,* 81st Cong., 1st Sess., S. Rept. 639 (July 8, 1949).

12. This provision, dealing with construction projects costing at least $500,000, required the AEC to get Bureau of the Budget approval and to submit detailed explanations to the Appropriations Committees and the Joint Committee before: (a) starting a project for which no estimate had been included in the budget; (b) starting a project with currently estimated cost exceeding the estimate included in the budget; (c) continuing a community facility project if current estimates exceed the estimate included in the budget.

13. S. 2668, Bill to amend the Independent Offices Appropriation Act, 1950, introduced by Mr. McMahon (October 11, 1949), 81st Cong., 1st Sess.

14. U.S. Congress, Joint Committee on Atomic Energy, *Amending the Independent Offices Appropriations Act for the Fiscal Year 1950,* 81st Cong., 1st Sess., S. Rept. 1201 (October 18, 1949).

15. H.R. 7786, introduced by Mr. Cannon (March 21, 1950), 81st Cong., 2d Sess.

16. U.S. Congress, Senate, *Independent Offices Appropriation Bill, 1951,* Hearings before the Subcommittee of the Committee on Appropriations, 81st Cong., 2d Sess., pp. 337–357.

17. U.S. Congress, *Community Policy,* Hearing before the Joint Committee on Atomic Energy, 81st Cong., 2d Sess., pt. 1.

18. *Congressional Record,* 81st Cong., 2d Sess., Vol. 96 (May 5, 1950), pp. 6505, 6509, 6515, and 6516.

19. U.S. Congress, *Community Policy*, Hearing, etc., pt. 2.

20. U.S. Congress, House of Representatives, *Independent Offices Appropriations, 1952*, Hearing before the Subcommittee of the Committee on Appropriations, 82d Cong., 1st Sess., pt. 1, pp. 834–835.

21. *Congressional Record*, 82d Cong., 2d Sess., Vol. 98 (March 20, 1952), p. 2614.

22. U.S. Congress, House of Representatives, Report to accompany H.R. 7072, *Independent Offices Appropriations Bill, 1953*, 82d Cong., 2d Sess., H. Rept. 1517 (March 14, 1952), p. 6.

23. *Supra*, p. 107.

24. U.S. Congress, House of Representatives, Report to accompany H.R. 8370, *Supplemental Appropriation Bill, 1953*, 82d Cong., 2d Sess., H. Rept. 2316 (June 26, 1952).

25. *Congressional Record*, 82d Cong., 2d Sess., Vol. 98 (June 27, 1952), p. 9564.

26. *Ibid.*, pp. 8348–8353.

27. U.S. Congress, Senate, Report to accompany H.R. 8370, *Supplemental Appropriation Bill, 1953*, 82d Cong., 2d Sess., S. Rept. 2076 (July 2, 1952).

28. *Congressional Record*, 82d Cong., 2d Sess., Vol. 98 (July 5, 1952), pp. 9564 and 9683.

29. S. Res. 28, introduced by Mr. Bricker (February 1, 1951), 82d Cong., 1st Sess.

30. See *Congressional Record*, 83d Cong., 1st Sess., Vol. 99 (Daily Edit., May 19, 1953), pp. 5349–5350.

31. *Supra*, pp. 80–81.

32. U.S. Congress, *Amending the Atomic Energy Act*, Hearings before the Joint Committee on Atomic Energy, 82d Cong., 2d Sess.

33. The statement requested pertained to two new bills, H.R. 4330, introduced by Mr. Durham (June 5, 1951), and its companion, S. 1602, introduced by Mr. McMahon (June 7, 1951), 82d Cong., 1st Sess. The measure provided for specific enabling legislation for all construction projects involving $500,000 or more. The President was to have power to grant authorization in the event Congress failed to pass such enabling legislation within twenty days of the receipt of written request for same.

34. U.S. Congress, *Amending the Atomic Energy Act,* Hearings, etc.

35. *Ibid.,* p. 109.

36. It is not intended to suggest, of course, that nothing of significance occurred in the atomic energy project during this 1952–1953 period. On November 1, 1952, the AEC at Eniwetok tested a device which demonstrated conclusively the feasibility of the so-called hydrogen bomb. In early 1953, two events occurred—the first test of the atomic cannon with an atomic warhead, and announcement of the successful achievement of the breeding process in a reactor at Arco, Idaho. The transitional character of this period pertains only to AEC-Joint Committee relations.

37. For details of the deadlock see "Washington Notes," *Bulletin of the Atomic Scientists,* IX (April, 1953), 83–84, 94; and (May, 1953) 150.

38. The evidence available on other committees is practically nil. The few studies include: Stephen K. Bailey and Howard D. Samuel, *Congress at Work* (New York: Henry Holt, 1952); Eleanor E. Dennison, *The Senate Foreign Relations Committee* (Stanford, Calif.: Stanford University Press, 1942); Ernest S. Griffith, *Congress, Its Contemporary Role* (New York: New York University Press, 1951); E. F. Westphal, *The House Committee on Foreign Affairs* (New York: Columbia University Press, 1942); and Robert A. Dahl, *Congress and Foreign Policy* (New York: Harcourt, Brace and Co., 1950).

39. On such matters as site selection and choice of contractors, for example, there is every indication that the AEC takes full responsibility for the final action. Chairman Dean, describing the Commission's procedure for acquiring a site, states:

"After all the data are in, the final decision as to which of the many sites should be selected is made by the five Commissioners in Washington. Frequently questions arise which entail re-survey and re-evaluation. . . . But the final responsibility rests with the Commission. . . ." *Report on the Atom* (New York: Alfred A. Knopf, 1953), p. 87.

As an indication of the Commission's desire to exercise this final responsibility on its own, a remark made by Representative Price is of interest. At a hearing Mr. Price stated:

"I might say . . . the answer given to a lot of us who were trying to get a plant located somewhere else was that it was going into the Ohio valley because of cheap power." See U.S. Congress, *Atomic Power Development and Private Enterprise,* Hearings before the Joint Committee on Atomic Energy, 83d Cong., 1st Sess., p. 235.

40. One interviewee stated that the Senator's interest was really not so much in atomic energy as in foreign affairs, but that he had to play his role as "Mr. Atom" in order to get the center of the stage.

Chapter VI

1. U.S. Congress, Joint Committee on Atomic Energy, *Atomic Power and Private Enterprise,* Committee Print, 82d Cong., in *ibid.,* pp. 252–254.

2. *Ibid.,* p. 8.

3. "The Utilization of Atomic Energy," a speech before a Science Conference celebrating the Seventy-Fifth Anniversary of Wellesley College, Wellesley, Mass. (March 17, 1949), reprinted in *ibid.,* pp. 252–254.

4. Ralph E. Lapp, *The New Force* (New York: Harper and Bros., 1953), p. 144.

5. *Ibid.,* p. 154.

6. *Atomic Power and Private Enterprise,* Committee Print, p. III.

7. U.S. Congress, House of Representatives, Report to accompany H.R. 5690, *Independent Offices Appropriations Bill, 1954,* 83d Cong., 1st Sess., H. Rept. 550 (June 11, 1953), pt. 1, p. 13.

8. U.S. Congress, House of Representatives, *Independent Offices Appropriations Bill, 1954,* Hearings before the Subcommittee of the Committee on Appropriations, 83d Cong., 1st Sess., pt. 1, p. 375.

9. *Independent Offices Appropriations Bill, 1954,* H. Rept. 550, pt. 1, p. 13.

10. *New York Times,* October 23, 1953.

11. See U.S. Congress, *Atomic Power Development and Private Enterprise,* Hearings before the Joint Committee on Atomic Energy, 83d Cong., 1st Sess.

12. See *ibid.,* p. 571. The AEC noted that the interim report had been prepared and submitted to aid consideration of new legislation. U.S. Atomic Energy Commission, *Fifteenth Semiannual Report of the Atomic Energy Commission* (Washington: Government Printing Office, 1954), p. 20.

13. See *Congressional Record,* 83d Cong., 1st Sess., Vol. 99 (June 1, 1953), pp. 5858–5863 and 83d Cong., 2d Sess., Vol. 100 (Daily Edit., June 22, 1954), pp. 7251–7253.

14. H. J. Res. 317, introduced by Mr. Holifield, and H. J. Res. 318, introduced by Mr. Price (July 29, 1953), 83d Cong., 1st Sess. See also *Congressional Record,* 83d Cong., 1st Sess., Vol. 99 (July 29, 1953), pp. 10427–10428.

15. Representative Holifield's views appear in his statement made a part of the record of the atomic power hearings. U.S. Congress, *Atomic Power Development and Private Enterprise,* Hearings, etc., p. 574.

16. U.S. Congress, Joint Committee on Atomic Energy, *Report of the Subcommittee on Research and Development,* Committee Print, 83d Cong., 2d Sess., p. 6. This contains a statement of the AEC's five-year program.

17. U.S. Congress, House of Representatives, *Message from the President of the United States Transmitting Recommendations Relative to the Atomic Energy Act of 1946,* H. Doc. 328, 83d Cong., 2d Sess.

18. *Congressional Record,* 83d Cong., 2d Sess., Vol. 100 (Daily Edit., July 23, 1954), p. 11021.

19. H.R. 8862, Bill to amend the Atomic Energy Act of 1946, introduced by Mr. Cole (April 15, 1954); its companion bill, S. 3323, introduced by Mr. Hickenlooper (April 19, 1954), 83d Cong., 2d Sess.

20. See U.S. Congress, Joint Committee on Atomic Energy, Report to accompany H.R. 9757, *Amending the Atomic Energy Act of 1946,* 83d Cong., 2d Sess., H. Rept. 2181 (July 12, 1954).

21. *Congressional Record,* 83d Cong., 2d Sess., Vol. 100 (Daily Edit., July 23, 1954), p. 11021.

22. See U.S. Congress, *S. 3323 and H.R. 8862, To Amend the Atomic Energy Act of 1946,* Hearings before the Joint Committee on Atomic Energy, 83d Cong., 2d Sess., pt. II, p. 907.

23. 68 *Stat. at L.* 919–961. (Public Law 703, 83d Cong., 2d Sess., Atomic Energy Act of 1954. Approved August 30, 1954.)

24. *Ibid.*, 923–924 (Secs. 11p and v).

25. *Ibid.*, 924 (Sec. 11s).

26. *Ibid.*, 923 (Sec. 11e).

27. *Ibid.*, 924 (Sec. 11t).

28. Commission opposition on the second score was based on two factors: (1) the Commission already had organizations in existence to perform this function; and (2) the Committee's proposal would interfere with the Commission's flexibility in adapting the inspection function to the particular needs of management. U.S. Congress, *S. 3323 and H.R. 8862, To Amend the Atomic Energy Act of 1946*, Hearings, etc., pt. II, pp. 605–606.

29. The contract takes its name from Mr. E. H. Dixon, President of Middle South Utilities, Inc., and Mr. E. A. Yates, Chairman of the Board, the Southern Company, who made the proposal to the Bureau of the Budget and to the AEC. *Ibid.*, pp. 946–952.

30. 68 *Stat. at L.* 919, 956 (Sec. 202).

31. See U.S. Congress, Joint Committee on Atomic Energy, *A Proposed Act to Amend the Atomic Energy Act of 1946*, Committee Print, 83d Cong., 2d Sess., p. 9.

32. The Commission opposed these provisions on the grounds that they were unnecessary in view of the statutory injunction in Sec. 202 that the Commission must keep the Committee fully and currently informed with respect to all of its activities. U.S. Congress, *S. 3323 and H.R. 8862, To Amend the Atomic Energy Act of 1946*, Hearings, etc., pt. II, p. 603.

33. "The Commission's determination, together with the assent of the President, shall be submitted to the Joint Committee and a period of thirty days shall elapse while Congress is in session (in computing such thirty days, there shall be excluded the days on which either House is not in session because of adjournment for more than three days) before the determination of the Commission may become effective: *Provided, however,* That the Joint Committee, after having received such determination, may by resolution in writing, waive the conditions of all or any portion of such thirty-day period." 68 *Stat. at L.* 919, 929 (Sec. 51) and 932 (Sec. 61). While there was never any official explanation of the Joint Committee's

insistence on these provisions, Mr. Corbin Allardice, Executive Director of the Committee's staff, stated: "The Commission has here, in effect, an extraordinary power of condemnation, and of accepting title or taking title for the government to a whole class of material. It was felt that ordinarily you would have hearings, procedural reviews, and public scrutiny. Perhaps, though, there would be cases where security considerations would be such that full understanding of the problem could not be had publicly." "The Role of the Joint Congressional Committee," *A Forum Report of the Atomic Industrial Forum* (New York: Atomic Industrial Forum, Inc., 1954), p. 113.

34. 68 *Stat. at L.* 919, 942 (Sec. 144).

35. Unlike the thirty-day period for "special nuclear and source materials," the Joint Committee may not waive this period. *Ibid.,* 940 (Sec. 123).

36. For the Commission's opposition, see U.S. Congress, *S. 3323 and H.R. 8862, To Amend the Atomic Energy Act of 1946,* Hearings, etc., pt. II, p. 603. The Department of Defense took much the same view as did the Commission, see *ibid.,* p. 741. The position taken by both the Commission and the Department of Defense was that this was constitutionally a rather unusual sort of provision, although it had occurred to some extent in the past. The Secretary of State agreed but at the same time he thought it was not too objectionable in this particular case. *Ibid.,* p. 699.

37. For the debate which led to this amendment to the Joint Committee's Bill see the discussion in the Senate on the Anderson Amendment (subsequently defeated) and the Ferguson Amendment which was the provision actually adopted, *Congressional Record,* 83d Cong., 2d Sess., Vol. 100 (Daily Edit., July 19, 20 and 21, 1954), pp. 10429–10495, 10584–10629, 10707–10788.

38. Long-term utility contracts entered into by the Commission must be laid before the Joint Committee in a manner similar to that required in the cases of "special nuclear and source material" (see Note 33, *supra*), 68 *Stat. at L.* 919, 951 (Sec. 164).

39. *Ibid.,* 960 (Sec. 261).

40. U.S. Congress, *S. 3323 and H.R. 8862, To Amend the Atomic Energy Act of 1946,* Hearings, etc., pt. II, pp. 605–608.

41. Most of the testimony in the Oppenheimer case is con-

tained in U.S. Atomic Energy Commission, *In the Matter of J. Robert Oppenheimer,* Transcript of Hearing before Personnel Security Board (Washington: Government Printing Office, 1954). The AEC also published the text of principal documents and letters of the Board, the General Manager, and the Commissioners, in a supplementary pamphlet bearing the same title as the transcript of hearings. The transcript of hearings contains the text of the original letter of charges against Dr. Oppenheimer, written by William L. Borden, head of the Joint Committee staff from 1949 until 1953 (pp. 837–838). The Joint Committee made a brief announcement of its policy in the Oppenheimer case on April 13, 1954, pointing out that it was fully informed and would take action if necessary. See *New York Times,* April 14, 1954.

42. *In the Matter of J. Robert Oppenheimer,* Transcript, etc., pp. 94–95.

43. *New York Times,* October 7 and October 20, 1953.

44. *Ibid.,* January 13, 1954.

45. *Ibid.,* December 6, 1953. On the information-sharing already accomplished, see U.S. Congress, *S. 3323 and H.R. 8862, To Amend the Atomic Energy Act of 1946,* Hearings, etc., pt. I, p. 13. Also see *Bulletin of the Atomic Scientists,* X (January, 1954), 32.

46. U.S. Congress, Joint Committee on Atomic Energy, *Report of the Proposed Agreement for Cooperation with NATO for Cooperation Regarding Atomic Information,* 84th Cong., 1st Sess., S. Rept. 267 (May 4, 1955).

47. *New York Times,* December 9, 1953.

48. At the President's press conference on March 31, 1954, Chairman Strauss discussed the March 1 test. See the *New York Times,* April 1, 1954. See also earlier revelations from Congressional sources, reported in the *New York Times,* March 21, 1954.

49. For a summary of UN negotiations in the proposal see *Bulletin of the Atomic Scientists,* IX (January, 1955), 24–27.

50. *New York Times,* November 16, 1954. The United States allocation was later doubled. See the *New York Times,* June 25, 1955.

51. The text of the resolution appears in *Bulletin of the Atomic Scientists,* IX (January, 1955), 27.

52. This was revealed by Chairman Lewis L. Strauss in an address before the Overseas Press Club in New York (AEC Release, June 24, 1955).

53. *New York Times,* June 12, 1955.

54. First public announcement of the plan came on April 25, in an address by the President at a New York meeting of the Associated Press. See *New York Times,* April 26, 1955.

55. U.S. Congress, *Authorizing Legislation,* Hearings before a Subcommittee of the Joint Committee on Atomic Energy, 84th Cong., 1st Sess., pp. 78–92, and 158–170.

56. An address, "Don't Leave Atomic Energy to the Experts," delivered at Marquette University, Milwaukee, Wisconsin. (AEC Release, December 5, 1953).

57. U.S. Congress, House of Representatives, *Message from the President Transmitting Recommendations Relative to the Atomic Energy Act of 1946,* H. Doc. 328, 83d Cong., 2d Sess.

58. U.S. Congress, *S. 3323 and H.R. 8862, To Amend the Atomic Energy Act of 1946,* Hearings, etc., pt. II, pp. 841 ff.

59. "Press Conference of December 17, 1954" as reported in the *New York Times,* December 18, 1954.

60. See U.S. Congress, Joint Committee on Atomic Energy, *Report on the November 13, 1954, Waiver Action by the Joint Committee on Atomic Energy, 83d Congress, 2d Session,* Committee Print, 84th Cong., 1st Sess.

61. Reported in the *New York Times,* January 29, 1955.

62. See U.S. Congress, House of Representatives, Report to accompany H.R. 6766, *Public Works Appropriation Bill, 1956,* 84th Cong., 1st Sess., H. Rept. 747 (June 10, 1955). For the debate in the House see *Congressional Record,* 84th Cong., 1st Sess., Vol. 101 (Daily Edit., June 15 and 16, 1955), pp. 7087–7121, 7134–7203. See also U.S. Congress, Senate, Report to accompany H.R. 6766, *Public Works Appropriation Bill, 1956,* 84th Cong., 1st Sess., S. Rept. 700 (July 1, 1955). The Senate debate on the bill is found in *Congressional Record,* 84th Cong., 1st Sess., Vol. 101 (Daily Edit., July 1, 1955), pp. 8320–8325, and (July 5, 1955) pp. 8440–8467.

63. A number of subsequent developments concerning this contract, though interesting in themselves, do not alter or add to the conclusions here drawn. The President finally ordered cancella-

tion of the contract after the City of Memphis determined to go through with construction of its own power plant, eliminating the need for the Dixon-Yates facility. See the *New York Times,* July 12, 1955.

64. *Congressional Record,* 83d Cong., 2d Sess., Vol. 100 (Daily Edit., February 12, 1954), p. 1600.

65. H.R. 7843, Bill to amend the National Security Act of 1947, introduced by Mr. Cole (February 12, 1954), 83d Cong., 2d Sess. See also *Congressional Record,* 83d Cong., 2d Sess., Vol. 100 (Daily Edit., February 12, 1954), pp. 1600–1601. Note that Mr. Roy Snapp, previously Secretary to the Commission, was appointed on October 1, 1954, to the position of Special Assistant to the Chairman for matters relating to the National Security Council.

66. U.S. Congress, *S. 3323 and H.R. 8862, To Amend the Atomic Energy Act of 1946,* Hearings, etc., pt. II, p. 803.

67. See an article by Cabell Phillips in the *New York Times,* Magazine Section, November 10, 1953. An example of the increased activity of the National Security Council may be seen in the submission of the AEC's power policy statement to an NSC meeting, with the President in attendance, prior to its presentation before the Joint Committee. The statement was basically concerned with the Commission's legislative proposals. U.S. Congress, *Atomic Power Development and Private Enterprise,* Hearings, etc., 83d Cong., 1st Sess., p. 54.

68. *New York Times,* December 5, 1953.

69. See U.S. Congress, *Authorizing Legislation,* Hearings, etc., pp. 158–170.

70. Interview with Gordon Dean, June 25, 1954.

71. *New York Times,* July 16, 1954.

72. "Sec. 21. The Chairman shall be the principal officer of the Commission. . . ." (Provision as originally introduced.) H.R. 8862, A Bill to amend the Atomic Energy Act of 1946, introduced by Mr. Cole (April 15, 1954), 83d Cong., 2d Sess.

73. See U.S. Congress, *S. 3323 and H.R. 8862, To Amend the Atomic Energy Act of 1946,* Hearings, etc., pt. II, pp. 781, 793, 805, 809, and 831.

74. *Amending the Atomic Energy Act of 1946,* H. Rept. 2181, pp. 109–117.

75. The language as incorporated into the law reads:
"Each member of the Commission, including the Chairman, shall have equal responsibility and authority in all decisions and actions of the Commission and shall have one vote. Actions of the Commission shall be determined by a majority of the members present. The Chairman (or acting Chairman in the absence of the Chairman) shall be the official spokesman of the Commission in its relations with Congress, Government agencies, persons, or the public, and as agent of the Commission, shall see to the faithful execution of the policies and decisions of the Commission, and shall report thereon to the Commission from time to time or as the Commission may direct." 68 *Stat. at L.* 919, 924 (Sec. 21).

76. U.S. Congress, *Development, Growth, and State of the Atomic Energy Industry,* Hearings before the Joint Committee on Atomic Energy, 84th Cong., 1st Sess., pt. 1, p. 40.

77. U.S. Congress, *Authorizing Legislation,* Hearings, etc., p. 88.

78. *Ibid.,* p. 146.

79. *New York Times,* June 16, 1954. The Cole-Strauss discussion may be found in U.S. Congress, *S. 3323 and H.R. 8862, To Amend the Atomic Energy Act of 1946,* Hearings, etc., pt. II, pp. 672–673.

80. *Ibid.,* pt. II, pp. 821–822.

81. U.S. Congress, *Development, Growth and State of the Atomic Energy Industry,* Hearings, etc., pt. 1, p. 38.

82. With the beginning of the 84th Congress in January, 1955, the Democrats took control of all committees in House and Senate, and the chairmanship of the Joint Committee passed from the House to the Senate. As a result Senator Clinton P. Anderson of New Mexico became chairman of the Joint Committee at that time.

83. See U.S. Congress, *Authorizing Legislation,* Hearings, etc., p. 165.

84. This and other aspects of the Administration's power policy were the major subjects of floor debate, rather than atomic energy per se. See *Congressional Record,* 83d Cong., 2d Sess., Vol. 100 (Daily Edit., July 16, 1954), pp. 10176–10203, 10207–10208 and 10210–10221; (Daily Edit., July 20, 1954) pp. 10584–10596

and 10601–10629; and (Daily Edit., July 21, 1954) pp. 10707, 10715–10755, and 10758–10788.

85. *Amending the Atomic Energy Act of 1946,* H. Rept. 2181, pp. 25, 71, 99 and 127.

86. For Director Hughes' letter, see Joint Committee on Atomic Energy Release No. 36, July 27, 1955.

87. For debate and passage of the merchant ship bill, see *Congressional Record,* 84th Cong., 1st Sess., Vol. 101 (Daily Edit., July 18, 1955), pp. 9311–9319. In the Senate, a companion bill was cleared by the Interstate and Foreign Commerce Committee and sent to the Joint Committee on Atomic Energy, which reported favorably on this bill as well as on the peace ship bill. See *ibid.* (July 30, 1955), pp. 10677 and 10680.

88. U.S. Congress, *Authorizing Legislation,* Hearings, etc., p. 93.

89. *Washington Post and Times-Herald,* March 31, 1955.

90. The military emphasis may be partially accounted for by the fact that six House members and two Senate members of the Joint Committee in 1955 held committee assignments also on the Armed Services Committees of their respective chambers.

91. U.S. Congress, Joint Committee on Atomic Energy, *Report of the Raw Materials Subcommittee on Its Visit to Australia,* Committee Print, 84th Cong., 1st Sess., especially pp. 1–3. On the sale of heavy water to India, see *New York Times,* February 13, 1955.

92. *New York Times,* August 24, 1955.

93. "New Radioisotopes Policy Announced by AEC," (AEC Release, April 21, 1955).

94. *Congressional Record,* 84th Cong., 1st Sess., Vol. 101 (Daily Edit., June 27 and June 28, 1955), pp. 7943–7947 and 7993–8004.

95. For the text of these and other provisions pertaining to the AEC, see the Independent Offices Appropriations Act, 1955, 68 *Stat. at L.* 272, 275–277.

96. These limitations on substitute projects were as follows: (1) the project must be a substitute for a project authorized in subsections 101(a), 101(d), or 101(f); (2) the Commission must certify that the new project is "essential to the common defense

and security"; (3) the Commission must certify that the new project is "required by changes in weapon characteristics or weapon logistic operations"; and (4) the Commission must certify that it is "unable to enter a contract with any person including a licensee on terms satisfactory to the Commission to furnish from a privately owned plant or facility the product or services to be provided in the new project."

U.S. Congress, Senate, Report to accompany S. 2220, *Authorizing Appropriations for the Atomic Energy Commission,* 84th Cong., 1st Sess., S. Rept. 538 (June 14, 1955), p. 4. Sections 102 through 106 of the authorization bill contained the various language provisions. Not all were restrictive: Section 103, for example, allowed funds to be appropriated for advance planning, construction design, and architectural services, in connection with projects which are not authorized by law. See *ibid.,* p. 10.

97. U.S. Congress, *Development, Growth and State of the Atomic Energy Industry,* Hearings, etc., pp. 539–560.

98. The success of the Joint Committee on Atomic Energy prompted the suggestion from various sources, including the second Hoover Commission, that a similar joint committee be established to exercise Congressional surveillance and control over the Central Intelligence Agency, another highly secret and vitally important organization. (*New York Times,* June 29, 1955.) A bill to implement this recommendation was introduced into the Senate, *Congressional Record,* 84th Cong., 1st Sess., Vol. 101 (Daily Edit., July 22, 1955), p. 9655.

Chapter VIII

1. See Appendix C for a table of the AEC's appropriations in the period from 1947–1954.

1^a. Prior to the passage of the Atomic Energy Act of 1946, appropriations for atomic energy were included in military appropriations. No reference to atomic energy will be found, however, in any appropriation bills before July 16, 1946; on account of the necessary security requirements, funds for the atomic bomb project were concealed in appropriations for other purposes. See U.S. Congress, Joint Committee on Atomic Energy, *The Atomic Energy Act of 1946,* Committee Print, 83d Cong., 1st Sess., pp. 68–70.

2. U.S. Congress, House of Representatives, *Independent Offices Appropriations Bill, 1948,* Hearings before the Subcommittee of the Committee on Appropriations, 80th Cong., 1st Sess., pt. 1, pp. 1484 ff.

3. *Congressional Record,* 81st Cong., 1st Sess., Vol. 95 (April 14, 1949), p. 4647.

4. U.S. Congress, House of Representatives, Report to accompany H.R. 3839, *Independent Offices Appropriations Bill, 1948,* 80th Cong., 1st Sess., H. Rept. 589 (June 13, 1947), pp. 8–9.

5. U.S. Congress, House of Representatives, Report to accompany H.R. 6055, *First Deficiency Appropriations Bill, 1948,* 80th Cong., 2d Sess., H. Rept. 1618 (March 30, 1948), p. 2.

6. U.S. Atomic Energy Commission, *Fifth Semiannual Report of the Atomic Energy Commission* (Washington: Government Printing Office, 1948), p. 131.

7. U.S. Congress, House of Representatives, Report to accompany H.R. 4177, *Independent Offices Appropriations Bill, 1950,* 81st Cong., 1st Sess., H. Rept. 425 (April 11, 1949), p. 9.

8. U.S. Congress, House of Representatives, Report to accompany H.R. 7786, *Independent Offices Appropriations Bill, 1951,* 81st Cong., 2d Sess., H. Rept. 1797 (March 2, 1950), p. 202.

9. U.S. Congress, House of Representatives, Report to accompany H.R. 6829, *Supplemental Independent Offices Appropriations Bill, 1949,* 80th Cong., 2d Sess., H. Rept. 2245 (June 8, 1948), p. 2.

10. U.S. Congress, Senate, *Independent Offices Appropriations Bill, 1948,* Hearings before the Subcommittee of the Committee on Appropriations, 80th Cong., 1st Sess., p. 51.

11. U.S. Congress, House of Representatives, *Independent Offices Appropriations Bill, 1950,* Hearings before the Subcommittee of the Committee on Appropriations, 81st Cong., 1st Sess., pt. 1, p. 1070.

12. U.S. Congress, Senate, *Independent Offices Appropriations Bill, 1950,* Hearings before the Subcommittee of the Committee on Appropriations, 81st Cong., 1st Sess., p. 1207.

13. U.S. Congress, House of Representatives, *Second Supplemental Appropriations Bill, 1951,* Hearings before the Subcom-

mittee of the Committee on Appropriations, 81st Cong., 2d Sess.,
p. 220.

14. *Congressional Record,* 80th Cong., 1st Sess., Vol. 93
(June 17, 1947), p. 7173.

15. *Ibid.* (July 24, 1947), p. 10043.

16. *Supplemental Independent Offices Appropriations Bill,
1949,* H. Rept. 2245, p. 4.

17. *Congressional Record,* 80th Cong., 2d Sess., Vol. 94
(June 18, 1948), p. 8768.

18. For the debates see *Congressional Record,* 80th Cong.,
2d Sess., Vol. 94 (June 10, 1948), pp. 7714–7715 and (June 16,
1948) pp. 8767 and 8768.

19. The Chairman of the Senate Subcommittee of the Committee on Appropriations, Senator O'Mahoney, stated during the
debate that:

"The Atomic Energy Commission sat with us. We consulted
them. . . . I would not say that it [the amendment] has been
formally approved by the Commission; but it [the AEC] does not
and has not objected to me to the amendment in its present form."
Congressional Record, 81st Cong., 1st Sess., Vol. 95 (August 2,
1949), p. 10555.

Chairman McMahon of the Joint Committee on Atomic Energy
added:

". . . we [the Joint Committee] did have a consultation not only
with the Senator from Wyoming [Senator O'Mahoney] who spoke
in behalf of this subcommittee. In that way this language was
worked out." *Ibid.*

20. S. 2668, Bill to amend the Independent Offices Appropriation Act of 1950, introduced by Mr. McMahon (October 11,
1949), 81st Cong., 1st Sess.

21. See General Appropriations Act, 1951, 64 *Stat. at L.*
699, 720 and *Independent Offices Appropriations Bill, 1951,* H.
Rept. 1797, p. 202.

Chapter IX

1. *Supra,* pp. 123-125.

2. U.S. Congress, House of Representatives, *Independent*

Offices Appropriations Bill, 1952, Hearings before the Subcommittee of the Committee on Appropriations, 82d Cong., 1st Sess., p. 828. Here is what Commissioner Pike said in a Joint Committee open hearing:

"What we would like now is to really get a good panel . . . to put some time on it and come up with something we will view as objective and honest and able, rather than try to prejudge what they will come up with—say here is a problem, it is a serious problem, and one thing we can say is that it offers the most serious obstacle right now to getting on with our H-bomb and our expanded program for fissionable material production." (U.S. Congress, *Community Policy,* Hearing before the Joint Committee on Atomic Energy, 81st Cong., 2d Sess., p. 5.)

3. U.S. Congress, House of Representatives, *Independent Offices Appropriations Bill, 1952,* Hearings, etc., p. 828.

4. *Ibid.,* p. 829.

5. U.S. Congress, House of Representatives, *Independent Offices Appropriations Bill, 1950,* Hearings before the Subcommittee of the Committee on Appropriations, 81st Cong., 1st Sess., p. 1213.

6. U.S. Congress, House of Representatives, Report to accompany H.R. 7786, *Independent Offices Appropriations Bill, 1951,* 81st Cong., 2d Sess., H. Rept. 1797 (March 3, 1950), p. 202.

7. *Ibid.*

8. U.S. Congress, House of Representatives, *Independent Offices Appropriations Bill, 1952,* Hearings, etc., pp. 851–853.

9. *Congressional Record,* 82d Cong., 1st Sess., Vol. 97 (May 4, 1951), p. 4885.

10. U.S. Congress, House of Representatives, *Independent Offices Appropriations Bill, 1953,* Hearings before the Subcommittee of the Committee on Appropriations, 82d Cong., 2d Sess., p. 1087.

11. *Ibid.,* p. 1092.

12. *Ibid.,* p. 1087.

13. U.S. Congress, Senate, *Independent Offices Appropriations Bill, 1952,* Hearings before the Subcommittee of the Committee on Appropriations, 82d Cong., 1st Sess., pp. 73–74.

14. U.S. Congress, House of Representatives, *Independent Offices Appropriations Bill, 1953,* Hearings, etc., p. 1094.

15. 63 *Stat. at L.* 634.

16. 65 *Stat. at L.* 269, 271.

17. 66 *Stat. at L.* 395, 396.

18. See U.S. Congress, House of Representatives, Report to accompany H.R. 8370, *Supplemental Appropriations Bill, 1953,* 82d Cong., 2d Sess., H. Rept. 2316 (June 26, 1952), p. 24.

Chapter X

1. For tables showing both original and revised estimates, see U.S. Congress, House of Representatives, *Second Independent Offices Appropriations for 1954,* Hearings before the Subcommittee of the Committee on Appropriations, 83d Cong., 1st Sess., p. 378.

2. Cuts were made primarily in operating expenses; the Commission request for plant and equipment was left intact. The House cut on the operating funds was rejected by the Senate but was accepted by the Conference Committee. See U.S. Congress, House of Representatives, Report to accompany H.R. 5690, *Independent Offices Appropriations Bill, 1954,* 83d Cong., 1st Sess., H. Rept. 550 (June 11, 1953), pt. 1, p. 13 and pt. 2, p. 1; Senate, Report to accompany H.R. 5690, *Independent Offices Appropriations Bill, 1954,* 83d Cong., 1st Sess., S. Rept. 502 (July 8, 1953), pp. 2–4; and House of Representatives, Conference Report to accompany H.R. 5690, *Independent Offices Appropriations Bill, 1954,* 83d Cong., 1st Sess., H. Rept. 882 (July 20, 1953).

3. *Independent Offices Appropriations Bill, 1954,* H. Rept. 550, pt. 1, p. 13.

4. *Independent Offices Appropriations Bill, 1954,* S. Rept. 502, p. 3.

5. *Independent Offices Appropriations Bill, 1954,* H. Rept. 882 (Conference Report).

6. U.S. Congress, House of Representatives, *Independent Offices Appropriations Bill, 1955,* Hearings before the Subcommittee of the Committee on Appropriations, 83d Cong., 2d Sess., pt. 3, p. 2521.

7. U.S. Congress, House of Representatives, Report to accompany H.R. 8583, *Independent Offices Appropriations Bill, 1955,* 83d Cong., 2d Sess., H. Rept. 1428 (March 4, 1954), p. 10.

8. *Ibid.*, p. 7.

9. U.S. Congress, House of Representatives, Conference Report to accompany H.R. 8583, *Independent Offices Appropriations Bill, 1955*, 83d Cong., 2d Sess., H. Rept. 1882 (June 15, 1954).

10. *Independent Offices Appropriations Bill, 1955*, H. Rept. 1428, p. 10.

11. 68 *Stat. at L.* 919, 960 (Sec. 261).

Index

A-bomb: agreement with British on, 39

Accounting, AEC: criticisms and improvements, 196-97

Acheson, Secretary of State Dean: H-bomb role of, 91, 92, 93; work on Acheson-Lilienthal report, 23

Aircraft reactors: stressed by Joint Committee, 180-81

Air Force: and new laboratory, 111, 112

Allardice, Corbin C.: on statutory waiting period, 278, n. 33

Anderson, Senator Clinton P.: constitutes panel on atomic power, 181; gets news leak, 174; investigation of Whitfield ordered by, 179; on thermonuclear power, 181

Appointing power: and AEC, 12

Appropriations: factors affecting, 188; for atomic energy before 1946, 284, n. 1ᵃ; supplemental and deficiency, AEC, 199. See also Expansion program

Appropriations Committees: advice on economy from, 208-9; and new task of AEC budgets, 17; and secrecy, 197-98; comparison of construction riders of, 216-18; complexity of AEC budgets for, 192-93, 195-96; criticism of AEC accounts, 196; factors limiting power, 186; first construction rider, 203-4; forms

of exerting power, 185-86, 187; handling of 1956 budget, characterized, 222-23; method of handling deficiency budgets, 199; provision for commercial power plant, 221; relations to chambers, 187-88; relations to Joint Committee, 1955, 224; rivalry with Joint Committee, foreseen, 20; staff, 185; summary of relation to AEC, 233-34; treatment of first Eisenhower budget, 221; values upheld by, 217. See also House Appropriations Committee; Senate Appropriations Committee

Argonne National Laboratory: condemnation of land for, 53; loss of U-235 at, 64

Armed Services Committees: use of, to control atomic energy, 17-18

Atom pool: U.S. consideration of, 161

Atomic cities: management of, 10

Atomic Energy Act, 1946: choices facing drafters, 4

Atomic Energy Act, 1954: as affected by Dixon-Yates, 155; authorization power granted by, 155-56; Eisenhower proposal on, 149-50; international provisions of, 155; Joint Committee drafting of, 150-51; patent clauses, 177; preference clauses, 176; principal officer clause, 170, 171; Rep. Cole leadership in